TRADE AND TRANSITION
Trade Promotion in Transitional Economies

This study is based on a research project which was prepared in the framework of the ACE-project no. P95-2053-R. Financial support for this project was provided by the EU-Phare ACE program.

TRADE AND TRANSITION
Trade Promotion in Transitional Economies

edited by
ALASDAIR MacBEAN

Economics Department
The Management School
Lancaster University

Routledge
Taylor & Francis Group

LONDON AND NEW YORK

First published in 2000 by
FRANK CASS PUBLISHERS

Published 2023 by Routledge
4 Park Square, Milton Park, Abingdon, Oxon OX14 4RN
605 Third Avenue, New York, NY 10017

Routledge is an imprint of the Taylor & Francis Group,
an informa business

Copyright © 2000 by Taylor & Francis.

British Library Cataloguing in Publication Data

Trade and transition: trade promotion in transitional economies
1. Foreign trade promotion. 2. Foreign trade promotion –
Government policy 3. Foreign trade promotion – Developing
countries 4. Foreign trade promotion – Europe, Eastern
I. MacBean, Alasdair I. (Alasdair Iain), 1933–
382.6′3

Library of Congress Cataloging-in-Publication Data

Trade and transition: trade promotion in transitional economies /
edited by Alasdair MacBean.
     p.   cm.
Includes bibliographical references and index.
ISBN 0-7146-5034-X (cloth). – ISBN 0-7146-8088-5 (paper)
1. Foreign trade promotion – Developing countries. 2. Foreign
trade promotion – Europe, Eastern. I. MacBean, Alasdair I.
HF1413.T693   1999
382′.0947 – dc21   99-38240
                                                        CIP

ISBN 13: 978-0-7146-5034-0 (hbk)
ISBN 13: 978-0-7146-8088-0 (pbk)

Contents

List of Figures

List of Tables

Glossary

ABT	An Bord Trachtala (Irish Trade Board)
ACE	Asesores de Commercio Exterior
AMC	Hungarian Institutional Agricultural Marketing Centre
CEEC	Central and Eastern European Countries
CEFTA	Central European Free Trade Agreement
CETRA	Taiwanese insititutional support for exporting organisation
CFER	Centre for Foreign Economic Relations
CIS	Commonwealth of Independent States
CIT	Confederation of Industry (Czech)
CMEA	Council for Mutual Economic Assistance
CMSA	Constant market share analysis
CSFR	Czechoslovakian Federal Republic
CTT	Coras Trachtala (Old name for Irish trade board, before amalgamation)
CZK	Czech Krona (crowns)
EB	Export Bank (Czech)
EBRD	European Bank for Reconstruction and Development
EC	European Community
ECA	Export Credit Agency
EFTA	European Free Trade Association
EGAP	Export Guarantee and Insurance Corporation (Czech)
EP	Export promotion
EU	European Union
EXPROM	Export Promotion Programme (in Poland)
FDI	Foreign direct investment
FSU	Former Soviet Union
FTO	Foreign Trade Organisations
GATT	General Agreement on Tariffs and Trade
IDA	Industrial Development Agency (Ireland)
IMF	International Monetary Fund
ISI	Import substituting industrialisation
ITC	International Trade Center

ITDH	Investment and Trade Development Public Benefit Company (Hungary)
JETRO	Japan External Trade Organisation
KOTRA	Korea Trade and Investment Promotion Agency
KUKE	Export Credit Insurance Corporation
MEHIB	Magyar Exporthitel-biztosító (Hungarian Export Credit Guarantee Agency)
NESC	National Economic and Social Council (Ireland)
OECD	Organisation for Economic Co-operation and Development
OMFB	Hungarian Technical Development Committee
OPT	Outward processing trade
PTA	Preferential trade agreement
SME	Small and medium sized enteprises
SPE	State owned enterprises
TDI	Trade Development Institute (Ireland)
TPO	Trade promotion organsiation
TRIMs	Trade related investment measures
UN	United Nations
UNCTAD	United Nations Conference on Trade and Development
UR	Uruguay Round
VAT	Value-added tax
WTO	World Trade Organisation

Acknowledgements

The research for this book was funded by the EU-Phare ACE programme within the framework of ACE-project no. P95-2053-R. We are most grateful to the administrators of the programme for funding the travel, research assistance and workshops involved in carrying out the research. Many government officials, officers of export support institutions and managers of companies in the Czech Republic, Hungary and Poland gave generously of their time in answering our questions. We are very glad of this opportunity to thank them all. There are too many to list, and indeed, we promised anonymity to those who filled up our questionnaires and gave us interviews.

Early papers and draft chapters of our research report were presented at workshops held in Warsaw, Prague and Budapest. We thank all the participants for attending and in particular those who commented on our presentations: Pofessor Vlado Benacek, Charles University, Zdenek Drabek, World Trade Organisation, Janos Gacs, IIASA, Vienna, Pal Gaspar, Finance Research Ltd. Budapest, Pofessor Bart Kaminski, University of Maryland and World Bank, Csaba Kovacs, Competition Office, Budapest, Dr Judit Stouracova of Czech Trade, Miklos Szanyi, Institute of Economics of the Hungarian Academy of Sciences. We are particularly grateful for suggestions and criticisms which helped to avoid errors. For the opinions expressed and any errors which remain we are of course solely responsible. But I should like to express here my own gratitude to Mrs Dana Petrbokova who organised the workshop in Prague, arranged interviews, guided and interpreted for me in Prague and Brno. Without her invaluable help the research in the Czech Republic would have been impossible. Magdolna Sass would like to thank Katalin Antalocz for writing a background paper on financing exports, Judit Kiss for a background paper on agricultural exports, and Andrea Elteto for interviewing managers of companies for the chapter on Hungary.

Mary O'Donnell would like to thank participants at a seminar at the Department of Economics in the University of Limerick for helpful comments and suggestions.

Export Promotion in Transitional Economies

ALASDAIR MACBEAN

From the 1980s onwards export promotion (EP), seen as an opposite policy to import substituting industrialisation (ISI), achieved near consensus as the policy advice purveyed by multilateral and most bilateral aid agencies. There was also widespread acceptance among developing countries. Both World Bank and International Monetary Fund conditions for loans under stabilisation and structural adjustment policies usually included the adoption of policies to give more incentives to exporters. Even critics seem to accept that ISI policies must be temporary and that offsetting measures must be taken to reduce their disincentive effects on exporting. Why has EP become the dominant recommendation? Is it just as relevant to the former centrally planned economies of Central and Eastern Europe as for the developing countries of Africa, Asia and Latin America? How do we in this study view export promotion and what is the link with institutional change?

DEFINITIONS

We use the term export promotion to cover the various fiscal, commercial and exchange rate measures which governments can take to ensure at least neutrality between the incentives to produce for the export market and for the domestic market. But we also use it for the more specific measures that can be taken to give direct help to exporters. These include guarantees against political and certain types of commercial risk involved in exporting to some countries and dealing with some trading partners; improving access to, and/or reducing the cost of credit for financing exports; improving access to information about opportunities for foreign sales; assisting firms in making contacts with buyers, in meeting internationally acceptable quality standards and in marketing to foreigners.

Later we shall justify why such measures of support to exporters may be consistent with a quite high degree of faith in markets as guides to resource allocation. But first there remains the question of why increasing exports can be particularly beneficial to an economy, and even more, for an economy in the process of transition.

Answers to this question are not totally self-evident. After all, imports are what are available to a country's citizens to enjoy. Exports require self-denial. They are for the use of foreigners. Exporting is only worthwhile if it enables the citizens of the exporting country to acquire goods and assets, which will enable them to enjoy a higher standard of living than by consuming the exportables themselves. Exports are a roundabout way of gaining higher consumption in the near or longer-term future through exchanging them for goods produced more efficiently abroad. Imports can be used for consumption or for investment, which will raise future consumption. Alternatively, foreign assets can be acquired through current account surpluses and will yield interest or profits and can be liquidated in future to support future consumption, or to repay past debt and so save servicing costs.

These benefits of exporting arise because of better resource allocation. Resources are shifted from making goods or services which a country produces relatively inefficiently into expanding production of goods or services which it can produce efficiently and which can then be exchanged for those produced relatively more efficiently abroad. Access to larger markets also lowers costs in industries where economies of scale are significant. But international exchange does much more.

Open economies, which engage relatively freely in international trade, force their own industries to be competitive through opening them to foreign competition. Competing in international markets brings additional benefits in forcing sellers to recognise the need to maintain acceptable qualities as well as competitive prices. Quality means not only that the goods or services delivered should match international standards in themselves, but that they should be delivered on time and with appropriate back-up in terms of meeting guarantees, providing good servicing and spares. International competition makes new entrants aware of what the opposition can do. They learn of new technologies and innovations in both products and production methods. For countries which have experienced long eras of withdrawal from open competition, as the centrally planned socialist economies did, the experiences of competing with foreigners may be painful but also bring many such useful lessons. Benefits from these tend to spill over into production for the domestic market too. There they are driven partly by the need to compete with imports, but facilitated by the knowledge acquired from meeting and competing with foreign firms in their own and in third markets.

International trade destroys jobs in uncompetitive industries, but creates more productive jobs in exports. Wage levels in export industries, reflecting higher productivity in exporting, generally are higher than in industries producing for the home market. In transitional economies the need to create new jobs is vital. Their old, inefficient, polluting, large-scale, state-owned industries, burdened with far more workers than needed and with all the high social costs associated with employees of state owned industries in transitional economies, cannot survive long term. Many have been propped up by subsidies or loans from state directed, or heavily influenced, banks to prevent their collapse into bankruptcy. Such policies cannot be supported long term because of their high budgetary costs or the risk of destruction of the banking systems. When the traditional industries shrink and shed labour the need to create new jobs will become paramount. Increased exports represent one way in which jobs could be created. This and the need to pay off past debt form powerful reasons why the Transitional Economies must do everything that they legitimately can to foster increases in their exports.

EXPORT PROMOTION

Why need governments go beyond freeing markets to create neutral incentives as between foreign and domestic markets? Can it be left simply to market forces to allocate resources among production of tradables for export or import replacement, and non-tradables for purely domestic use? If all prices reflected benefits and costs to society, all parties, both local and foreign, had equal access to information, and futures markets to handle risk, governments would have little reason to intervene save to meet the society's distribution objectives. They would, of course still have the immense tasks of providing public goods such as law, order, national defence, basic education and health. But most nations' governments actually do much more. Certainly in the sphere of foreign trade all governments do intervene to a greater or lesser degree. Of particular concern to our study is the propensity of governments to provide various types of support for exports. Are they in principle justified? And, even if justified in principle, are they justified in practice, and to what extent?

Even the most neo-classical of economists recognise that market failures exist in all real economies. Free markets do not solve all economic problems. The price of chemicals does not cover the costs of pollution from their production and disposal. Economies of agglomeration do not necessarily bring sufficient gains to induce the first firms to invest in a region. Only when a sufficient number of firms are operating in the region do the economies of agglomeration kick in. The training costs of producing skilled labour may not be adequately recovered when workers are free to move to other firms. Access to information, and adequate markets for insuring against risks may not be available, especially for small and medium-sized firms. These all represent examples of types of market failure, which might justify government intervention to offset them. But it can be argued that in many cases governments are incapable of improving the situation by actions to correct or offset the market failure without inducing side effects which cause more damage to the economy than the original market failures. Knowledge that a government is willing to give subsidies or protection stimulates businesses to activities designed to gain such assistance through campaigning, lobbying, and even corrupt practices. Once obtained, firms devote resources to keeping these privileges. Planning controls and regulations lead to evasion and corruption. The costs to the economy of such 'rent seeking' or 'directly unproductive practices' can be high [*Bhagwati, 1980; Krueger, 1974; Lal and Rajapatirana, 1987*]. They come on top of costs from temporary or long-term miss-allocation of resources in supporting currently uncompetitive firms due to the time taken for the industry to repay the costs of the assistance, or to government errors in selection of activities to get support.

It is not easy to acquire the special expertise needed to identify and measure market failures and design the best interventions to correct for them. As put by the late Professor Harry Johnson, a distinguished international economist:

> Determination of the conditions under which a second-best policy actually leads to an improvement in social welfare requires detailed theoretical and empirical investigation by a first-best economist. ... it is therefore very unlikely that a second-best welfare optimum will result based on second-best arguments [*1970: 101*] quoted in Krueger [*1997*].

Even first-best economists may also lack the expertise and the relevant information to select workable remedies. For every success story of picking winners in, say South Korea, there are a great many examples of infant industries, or technological wonders, in Latin America, Asia and Africa that have become dinosaurs, draining the public purse and diverting resources from more productive uses. The inefficiencies in the industrialisation policies of many developing countries have been amply illustrated in studies by Balassa [*1971*]; Bhagwati [*1978*]; Krueger [*1974, 1978*]; Little, Scitovsky and Scott [*1970*]. Arguments such as these make one hesitant, even on general principles, to advocate a great deal of government expenditure to support exporting. Still more worrying is the lack of compelling empirical evidence to demonstrate the gains in terms of increases in exports from the various ways in which governments have aided exporters (see McAleese and O'Donnell, Chapter 2, below for a summary of studies on export supports).

Of course it is inherently difficult to link an increase in exports to any one factor, particularly if the expenditures on export support are relatively small.

4

Many factors are at work: exchange rate changes, wages and productivity, changes in quality and reputation, swings in fashion to name but a few. These are all possible explanations for a rise or fall in the sales of a particular export. Most empirical evidence on export support programmes deals with such issues as whether it reached the right people, whether they found it of any real help, whether they attributed any of their sales to specific support received and so on. The doubts and agnosticism expressed by students of such programmes can often be attributed to poor design and implementation of the programmes. And the developing countries which have figured in some studies were often still operating general economic policies: high protection, overvalued exchange rates and high inflation, which militated strongly against their exports and would swamp any effects from export support. But none of this means that well-designed programmes of export support cannot help exporters and bring significant net benefits to the economy.

Highly successful exporting economies devote substantial resources, both official and through private sector organisations such as chambers of commerce, and consultancy firms, to providing many types of help to exporters. This is true of Britain, Germany, Italy, Japan and South Korea, Singapore and Hong Kong among many others (see ACE, Task 4, Appendix, 1996 for data on Britain, Germany, Italy, Ireland and Spain). Export credit guarantees, help with standards, marketing information, and marketing services are all part of their assistance. Trade missions, strong commercial sections at embassies, and government help with trade fairs are also common. As these are all quite sophisticated societies it is unlikely that their use of such policies is misguided.

For transitional economies the magnitude and frequency of market failures will greatly exceed their prevalence in developed market economies. Transition has been from situations where markets hardly existed, where most managers had no opportunity to experience the specific problems of selling and buying in free markets. Most trade was within the CMEA among planned economies, usually at arranged prices and volumes, so that even the managers of the specialised state foreign trading organisations had little experience of the cut and thrust of competition. Managers of manufacturing companies were almost all cut off from foreign markets as foreign trade was the monopoly of the state trading companies. Foreign travel was difficult for many. For producers there was no foreign business travel though some travelled privately for leisure. But few could become fluent in foreign languages or knowledgeable about the market institutions and culture of foreign countries. Risk-taking and independent decision-making were discouraged. This lack of important experience and skills represents a type of market failure that time may remedy. But in the short run it means that many such managers will fail to spot market opportunities or will be unable to exploit them because of lack of experience or lack of institutions to take care of risk, credit, and information.

In Chapters 2 and 3 of this study an attempt has been made to assess whether government policies have indeed succeeded in increasing exports. A technique used there attempts to see how much of the behaviour of exports can be explained by the commodity composition and market orientation of each country's exports. If a country happens to be specialised in products which have enjoyed rapid growth world-wide, and the country's main markets have also grown rapidly, most of its export growth could be explained by this fortunate combination. But if its exports have grown fast while the general fortunes of the types of goods it exports have been dismal, and its markets slow growing then other factors must have been responsible for its export success. This does not prove that the government's policies were the main explanation, but it suggests that they may have been important and warrant a search for further evidence. Clearly, for Ireland, the decision to join the European Community was a major factor. But the package of policies designed to attract export oriented foreign investment probably was a significant factor, and other export supporting policies may at least have made a small contribution to Ireland's outstanding successes over the last twenty years. In Japan and South Korea serious efforts were devoted to increasing export earnings and in both countries rapidly rising exports were a prominent feature of their economic development. In neither of these cases, nor indeed in any of the East Asian 'Miracle Economies' did commodity composition or market orientation provide any explanation for most of the period of their rapid growth (see Chapter 3). Most commentators accept that their export promotion policies including much official direct support and encouragement to exporters were highly significant in explaining their export successes.

JUSTIFICATION FOR STATE SUPPORT FOR EXPORTING

A market failure justification for government interventions to promote exports can be particularly strong in the case of economies in transition from situations of state planning, where enterprises were state controlled and trade was handled exclusively by a few huge specialised trading companies. It can draw on arguments that are specific to transitional economies in addition to those of general relevance. The way foreign trade was handled meant that enterprises faced few, if any, of the standard problems of international trade such as gaining adequate information about foreign markets, learning how to market products in countries with different institutions, culture and tastes, assessing risks in foreign trade. In developed market economies managers have long experience in dealing with such matters and various institutions have developed to supply information, handle marketing, and hedge risks. These experiences and the facilities and institutions which have emerged to help

6

managers to cope with them were lacking in pre-reform countries. They take time to develop and while that is happening firms in transitional economies are handicapped compared with their counterparts in industrially developed countries. Government intervention to correct these market failures is justified. But what types of interventions are likely to do more good than harm?

GOVERNMENT SUPPORT FOR EXPORTING

This section assumes, quite reasonably, that the countries of Central and Eastern Europe such as the Visegrad Countries have already largely adopted WTO conforming import and export regimes, that is, their trade is largely free of self-imposed barriers. In fact for the Czech Republic, Hungary and Poland imports are as free as most OECD countries [*EBRD, 1997*]. But for much of the period the real exchange rate (the nominal rate adjusted for relative inflation) was not kept low enough to help exporting, particularly in Poland, but also in Hungary. In both of them the exchange rate was held high to dampen inflation. But that policy deterred exporters while encouraging imports.

In the Czech Republic the exchange rate was devalued drastically in the early stages of reform. The real exchange rate was held down from 1990 to 1993 by controlling inflation through stringent monetary, fiscal and wage policies, but for various reasons it was allowed to become overvalued in the mid-1990s. The normal policy of rebating to exporters import duties on imported inputs and value added taxes on other inputs is common in these countries, though different methods are used. But what policies of direct support for exporting could be adopted and what are their likely direct and indirect costs?

Official institutions to provide export credit guarantees against political and commercial risks are common to most countries. Disputes centre on the permissible degree of subsidy implied by the charges to exporters who use the services. The same is true of export credits. They are acceptable to organisations such as the WTO and the OECD so long as they are not at interest rates much below the rates charged by commercial banks or are at least above the government's own borrowing rate. The CEEC countries have all set up such organisations.

There are risks here of policy capture. Large or well-connected firms may succeed in attracting credit guarantees and subsidised credit. This may harm the prospects of smaller but potentially more successful exporters. Smaller and newer firms often lack the staff who can fill up the complex forms and they cannot afford the delays involved in meeting the requirements of such institutions unless special arrangements are made to accommodate them. There is evidence from the surveys reported in subsequent chapters that indeed the main beneficiaries of credit and tax concessions for exports have been large, often very large, formerly state owned companies. Small and medium sized companies have felt excluded, but the reasons for this seem often to lie in the complexities of meeting the standards of the institutions rather than deliberate policy. Large companies can afford expert staff to fill the forms and design the applications. Small and medium sized firms find the bureaucracy and delays involved a serious barrier to use of such services. They complain that they cannot keep customers waiting while they negotiate with official institutions.

Given such a bias, however, the system of export credit guarantees and credits could have institutional effects. It could support the growth of monopolies in the export sector, or cushion old firms against the need to restructure, and slow the growth of smaller firms and new entrants to exporting. In practice, the impact of these measures has up to now been quite small. Only between one and four percent of exports actually received credit guarantees in these countries during the period studied. Normally without a credit guarantee they would be unable to obtain official export credit.

Several institutions in CEEC countries have been created or adapted to provide marketing and other information needs, help with attendance at trade fairs or taking part in trade missions, and technical help in such matters as meeting foreign countries' customs and other regulations. These range from sections of Ministries to Chambers of Commerce. The main risk is that if only their services are subsidised, their activities may kill off the growth of private sector institutions such as trading companies and consultancy firms, which might, for various reasons do the job better.

Technical assistance in helping firms to satisfy internationally accepted quality standards, and for training export managers are other ways of helping exporters. Lack of experience may lead potential exporters to fail to appreciate the need for such help and may justify government provision or subsidies to private providers. Such services seem unlikely to have bad side effects.

All-in-all, provided the level of subsidies is kept within bounds, the access to them is kept open and objective, and entry and exit from the provision of export support services is open it seems unlikely that there would be significant external costs. There will of course, be direct budgetary costs. But in relation to most government activities these are likely to be small. It may be true that the contribution of direct support to exporting is small compared to the effects of general macroeconomic policies and policies which increase competitiveness such as privatisation, good governance, efficient banking, and free competition in most markets. But as long as the properly discounted benefit to cost ratio is positive the investment in export support policies is justified.

WHAT HAVE BEEN THE PRACTICES, SUCCESSES AND FAILURES?

By most measures the Czech Republic, Hungary and Poland lead progress in transition among the countries of Central and Eastern Europe (CEEC), and the former Soviet Union [*EBRD, 1997: Table 2.1*]. Their recovery from the collapse of income and trade brought about by the rouble crisis and sharp fall in trade among the former Communist countries has been remarkable. Their trade has been successfully restructured both in terms of market orientation and commodity composition (see chapters 4, 5 and 6 below). The timing and rates of progress have differed among them partly due to pre-reform conditions and partly due to the strategies and sequencing of policies adopted. Some of the results in their foreign trade sectors are compared in Table 1.1.

TABLE 1.1
EXTERNAL SECTOR IN THE CZECH, HUNGARIAN AND POLISH ECONOMIES

	1990	1991	1992	1993	1994	1995	1996	1997
Exports: Annual % change								
Czech Republic	–	–	6.7	7.5	0.4	16.1	5.4	10.2
Hungary	–5.3	–13.9	2.1	–9.1	13.7	13.4	7.4	26.4
Poland	15.1	–1.7	10.8	3.2	13.1	23.6	12.5	9.9
Current-Account Balance in $bil.								
Czech Republic	–1.1	0.3	–0.3	0.1	0.0	–1.4	–4.3	–3.2
Hungary	0.1	0.3	0.3	–3.5	–3.9	–2.5	–1.7	–1.0
Poland	0.6	–2.0	0.9	–0.6	2.3	5.5	–1.3	–4.3
Foreign-Direct Investment $bil. Net								
Czech Republic	–	–	1.0	0.6	0.7	2.5*	1.3	1.0
Hungary	0.3	1.5	1.5	2.3	1.1	4.5	2.0	2.1
Poland	0.0	0.1	0.3	0.6	0.5	1.1	2.8	3.0
External Debt/ exports %.								
Czech Republic	–	80.8	83.8	65.4	76.3	77.1	96.1	94.8
Hungary	–	245	214	303	375	247	194	121
Poland	–	375	340	347	248	192	166	140

Source: EBRD [*1998*].

Notes: (1) The Czech Republic was separated from the Slovak Republic in 1993. Pre-1993 data have been adjusted for the Czech economy to be compatible with the later period where possible.

(2) Poland's population at 38.5 million makes it between three and four times larger than Hungary or the Czech Republic, each with about 10.5 million.

* 1995 was an exceptional year caused by the privatisation of Czech Telecommunications

– Not comparable or omitted.

Czechoslovakia had the handicap of being the most centrally and bureaucratically controlled of the three countries while the others had experimented for many years with various attempts at market direction. But the Czechoslovak economy had a much lower burden of debt (Table 1.1), and relatively low inflation.

The three countries chose different methods and rates of privatisation and industrial restructuring. These affected foreign investment in their countries and foreign trade. Clearly, the Central and Eastern European Economies were by no means, a homogenous group. As a result there were many transformation strategies. Even though the measures adopted were similar there was a different hierarchy of measures; timing and even the aims of each measure could be different in one economy from another.

Research on the three countries briefly reported here was based in part on surveys conducted in each. Each interview schedule and questionnaire sent was based on a common set of questions for ministries, agencies and institutions which framed export policies or provided export support. Other sets of questions were used for manufacturers and trading companies which were the users or potential users of export support services. The questions are set out in the Appendix at the end of this book.

EXPORT PROMOTION IN POLAND

Opening up the economy was important in all, but export promotion policy had a different ranking in each. Certainly in Poland it was very different from either the Czech Republic or Hungary. This stemmed largely from a macroeconomic situation that in Poland was much worse than in either of the others. Poland had a dire combination of deficits, high foreign debt and runaway inflation. Obtaining relative stability involved high 'costs'. So for Poland macroeconomic stabilisation occupied the central position in its transformation strategy. That is why in Poland the exchange rate was held high and used as 'an anchor' to help stabilise the economy and fight inflation rather than allowed to depreciate to support exports.

During the transition Poland's foreign trade sector was subject to major institutional change. Its development was strongly affected by the export activity of newcomers. These were firms that switched sales from the domestic to the foreign market or which were created to produce or trade in exports. New entrants to the export sector brought about changes in the organisation of exports and in the share of particular groups of exporters in the structure of Polish exports. The share in the value of Polish exports of the largest exporters, including the foreign trade organisations that had previously monopolised exports during socialism, declined progressively. At the same time the small and medium sized exporters' share in the value of exports rose.

Although the entry rates of small and medium-sized enterprises (SMEs) were higher than their penetration rate in exports, SMEs quite evidently became among the most active agents of Polish exporting. The other key group of exporters was companies with foreign participation. That was also the case in Hungary where they accounted for 80 per cent of exports (Chapter 5). And in the Czech Republic it has recently emerged that about sixty per cent of exports are from foreign-owned companies.

During transition, despite the obstacle of the high exchange rate, the major source of export growth in Poland came from the general transformation strategies: liberalisation of prices, entry by new firms into formerly controlled markets and foreign trade, and macroeconomic policy to control inflation. Stabilisation and liberalisation offset most of the institutional and market imperfections, which previously hampered exports.

This conclusion stems from our, and other studies, of the Polish government's attempts to promote exports through direct incentives and institutional support. In Chapter 6 it is reported that few Polish firms were able to take advantage of such aids as credit insurance and subsidised export finance. They either did not need such help because of their foreign partnerships, or if they were SMEs, they often found it more profitable to operate in the 'Grey Economy'. There they could avoid taxes and the high social costs of employing workers officially. This was more profitable than to reveal the true extent of their activities in order to benefit from government support for exporting. Export insurance, for example benefited only about one per cent of Polish exports. The duty drawback schemes could only be used effectively by large exporters who used imported inputs for export-oriented production. Indeed, Poland's export promotion policy has been, and still is, mainly oriented towards supporting the exports of large and specialised exporters. Only they can benefit from the system of financial support (especially tax incentives).

An evident drawback of this policy was its neglect of the infrastructure in the foreign trade sector. The development of good infrastructure to provide support for newcomers is crucial. These newcomers were of key importance for the development of Polish exports. But, the demonopolisation of the export infrastructure through breaking up the state trading companies and privatising the commercial banks was not accompanied by government support for the development of a new export infrastructure.

Export promotion policy in Poland requires improvements if it is to be successful. The export infrastructure is underdeveloped. Poland's experience confirms that policies to encourage exports are not really those that are simply specific to the export sector. The general policies of stabilisation, liberalisation and privatisation had much more to do with export success than the rather fainthearted direct support policies for exporting introduced

11

belatedly by the Polish Government. But could better policies, more aggressively pursued have achieved more? In our view they could. Policies aimed more at the small to medium-sized firms would have been and still could be more relevant. More encouragement to a wider and more competitive set of institutions would give a greater chance of success. Probably the more the actual provision of services to exporters can be through private rather than public institutions the more likely the services will be provided effectively under the spur of competition.

EXPORT PROMOTION IN THE CZECH REPUBLIC

In Czechoslovakia after the Velvet Revolution of 1989 the new democratic government's economic policies were aimed at attaining macroeconomic stability and freeing the economy of its bureaucratic controls. It moved rapidly on privatisation of most industries. But it neglected the problems of corporate governance and the regulation of banking and investment funds that are required to avoid corruption and to stimulate efficiency. Towards exports its policies were largely a matter of leaving it to market forces and managements to decide whether to orient production towards export markets, and which markets and products to develop. The main stimulus to exports came from the massive devaluation of the Czechoslovak currency in the early days of the reforms. The Czech Republic's tariffs are low and there are few restrictions on imports or exports. Trade treaties with the EU and Nafta, other trading associations and membership of the WTO make most Czech foreign trade relatively free of artificial barriers.

After the initial drop in exports due to the currency chaos and collapse of CMEA trade, exports and the trade balance proved to be relatively buoyant until 1995. But from then on the trade balance went deep into the red. Policies to expand exports became a clear option for paying off debt, meeting requirements for consumers and producers, capital goods, and jobs. The response was a revival of interest in ways to promote exports by expanding the provision of support for exporters. An Export Guarantee and Insurance Company (EGAP) was created and urged to expand export credit guarantees. The Czech Export Bank was also urged to expand credits to exporters and reforms of institutions designed to provide support through market information, quality assurance, marketing, and public relations were instituted.

Several studies, including our own, of the institutional support for exporting in the Czech Republic have been carried out between 1994 and 1997. They have found serious problems in relations between exporters and the institutions. Managers were confused about where to go for help, dissatisfied with the credit risk and financial assistance provided, and with the help from the commercial sections of the embassies and local organisations.

Only about three per cent of Czech exports in 1996 received guarantees against territorial or commercial risks. Almost all export credit guarantees and export credits went to large firms, often involved in turnkey projects or other large export orders. Small and medium-sized firms were generally unable to satisfy the conditions or could not afford to wait while the bureaucratic processes were completed. Embassy commercial sections have been understaffed and the officials relatively inexperienced in commercial work. Few of the special institutions intended to assist exporters have attained a high profile or provided help recognised by exporters as significant (see Chapter 4 for detail).

In 1997 the Czech Government decided to rationalise the provision of institutional support for exporting. Proposals include 'One stop shop' centres within the district offices of the Economic Chambers. These are intended to be the first point of contact for most companies seeking information. They are linked to Infocentrum in Czech Trade (formerly the Centre for Foreign Economic Relations) so that inquiries which need research or are more specialised than can be handled by the district centres can be passed to Infocentrum. Firms are intended also to be able to access data banks and web-sites at Czech Trade for information relevant to exporting. Firms can commission marketing or other studies to be carried out by Infocentrum. They will have to pay for all the services, including participation in trade fairs, but many will, at least for a time be subsidised from a Phare export support fund. The centres are expected to be self-financing from fees and contributions from clients.

Worries remain concerning the small amount of resources being provided and the ability to find staff with adequate training and experience to fill the posts in Infocentrum and in the one stop shops given the competition from commerce for people with foreign language and marketing skills. It might also provide a greater stimulus to efficiency in these institutions if companies could seek export information and consultancy services from a broader range of providers. At present it is only payments to official bodies such as the Centres and Infocentrum for support services that can be refunded in part by the Support Fund. If companies could choose freely from private sector organisations, domestic and foreign consultancy firms, and claim subsidies of the same order as those for using the official providers this could meet the needs of many companies better. The market discipline would force inefficient providers of services out of business and expand those that were effective.

EXPORT PROMOTION IN HUNGARY

Hungary was different in having embarked on sustained economic reforms much earlier than the other two countries. Reforms started in 1968 and gradually decentralised the system of foreign trade, at least for trade with industrially developed, non-CMEA, countries. Some companies gained direct trading rights. The earlier start brought both advantages and disadvantages for a country embarking on thoroughgoing reforms in the 1990s.

Pre-1989 trade within the CMEA still accounted for more than half Hungary's foreign trade. In this trade, company staff had no direct contact with buyers, finance was state bank supplied and there was no need for insurance. There were none of the normal market incentives. But in trade with the developed market economies, prices, exchange rates, insurance, credits and overall profitability had a greater role. Staff therefore did have some relevant experience for operating in a fully market directed environment. There was, however, also a complex system of subsidies, which varied according to product and market. In agriculture, for example, direct export subsidies were used extensively. They were higher on trade to the rouble area because of the low, controlled, prices for food in the Soviet Bloc.

Export promotion was organised by the Foreign Trade Ministry. There were trade representatives in the most important markets to help Hungarian exporters. Foreign trade companies, specialised by sector, handled all trade apart from that of companies with the special right to trade internationally. But all this played a small role in stimulating exports in the planned economy. The real incentives were the exchange rate and the system of subsidies. The effective export promoter was the Ministry of Finance through these instruments. But, at least compared with the Czech businessmen Hungarians had more experience relevant to competing in world markets.

The disadvantages of the early, partial reform beginnings were that the open inflation present in semi-reformed Hungary set up inflationary expectations which made control of inflation in the post-reform era much more difficult. Also it allowed the build-up of foreign debt, and encouraged illegal black market activities which have increased the difficulty of increasing the revenues from taxation. Currently the black economy is estimated at some 30 per cent of Hungary's GDP.

Up to 1991 the dominant characteristics of Hungary's external sector were the state monopoly over trade and the restrictions on foreign currency holdings. Foreign trade remained under the control of the Finance Ministry and the Hungarian National Bank. Control was operated through the use of multiple exchange rates and the implicit subsidies attached to them, and the use of differential credits. The Foreign Trade Ministry also played a role through diplomacy, institutional support and regulations. Finally, the Hungarian State Insurance Company had influence through the provision of credit insurance. Basically, at the start of the proper transition process in the late 1980s, Hungary had a 'reformed' planned system of foreign trade. Distortions persisted, but compared to other planned economies the share of foreign trade with market economies was greater and more managers had direct experience of trading in a market environment. In trade with the CMEA, however, the old system survived until the start of the transition process.

In this process, the reform of the foreign trade system had two main aims: liberalisation of trade and the creation of an organisational infrastructure along market economy lines. After the first of January 1991 the dual trade policy, split between CMEA and market economies, ended. By 1997 almost all non-tariff barriers had gone and tariffs had been cut from 50 per cent to 8 per cent. Hungary's foreign trade is probably at least as liberal now as that of most OECD countries. The institutional structure has also changed dramatically. The old specialised trade companies have gone, either bankrupted or broken up and privatised. By 1997 there were over 100,000 companies engaged in foreign trade (many of them tiny).

The old system of foreign trade representatives continued up to 1997 but was then divided between the embassies and the Investment and Trade Development and Benefit Company (ITD), 100 per cent owned by the Ministry of Trade and Industry in 1998 but soon to be privatised. Various other institutions were created to provide credit guarantees, export credits, help with marketing and so on.

External relations, especially membership of the WTO and agreements with the EU, soon restricted subsidies as a form of support. In particular this forced severe reductions in subsidies to agricultural exports. The system of rebates of VAT on inputs for exporting was introduced and this works swiftly and effectively for Hungarian exporters.

Since about 1994 Hungary's exports have performed relatively well. But our analysis of the existing system of institutional support for exporting suggests that it has had little influence on that success. It has had little impact upon small and medium sized firms. Many companies have had no need of the agencies because their activities were largely outward processing or they were subsidiaries or joint ventures with foreign companies who provided all the necessary facilities for selling their products abroad. The most outstanding characteristic of Hungary's exports is that about 80 per cent are from foreign-invested firms. These probably have little need of export support services. The environment for exporting has been supportive because of the general reform measures adopted that have sought to create stability, and market incentives through liberalisation of prices, privatisation, and restructuring industry and services. These factors, especially the suppression of domestic demand between 1995 and 1998, plus the success in attracting foreign direct investment have been the driving forces behind Hungary's exports. Hungary has attracted more foreign direct investment (FDI) per head since reforms than any of the other transitional economies. This seems to be the result of its early start to the reform process and the confidence that this created among foreign investors.

CONCLUSIONS

The broad conclusions which emerge from this study are that general export promotion, in terms of getting macroeconomic stability, allowing market forces to determine prices, developing an open and liberal economy which is attractive to foreign investors, does work. These were the factors that drove exports in most of the countries studied. This seems particularly true of Ireland and the three CEECs studied in depth. But in the present international trading climate, the interventionist policies of South Korea and Taiwan in subsidising exports and protecting 'key' domestic industries would be inadmissible in any case, whether or not they worked for them in the 1960s and 1970s.

The specific institutional support policies which most countries provide such as credit guarantees, export credits, and quality and market information services probably have only marginal effects in aiding exports. When they are provided in the rather half-hearted and underfunded way that has been characteristic of the CEEC then it is hardly surprising that they have been relatively ineffective. But this does not mean that properly funded and well-directed institutional support for exporting would not help. The arguments for such help in the context of the particular weaknesses and market failures characteristic of transitional economies are strong. They do not need to have a dramatic effect on exports to be justified. All that is required is that they have a sufficiently high benefit to cost ratio. This seems to be likely given the very real needs for better credit guarantees and more accessible credit for both pre-production and export of goods from firms handicapped by lack of good commercial facilities, and for help to meet quality and marketing standards in world markets. In relation to the main items of government expenditure the costs are relatively low, under $4 per head in most OECD countries. Some are self-financing. It requires only a small increase in the value of exports to justify an investment in support services.

It is crucial to identify the appropriate targets for help. From our surveys these are mainly small and medium-sized enterprises, particularly those without foreign connections. Because of the weaknesses of the existing institutions it is probably not sensible to give them exclusive access to the subsidised provision of export support services. It is likely to be more productive in the long run to use the market as the main medium to select which providers are the most effective. This can be achieved by subsidising the purchase of the service rather than the provider. Firms that wish to buy market information or assistance with developing a product for a specific market should be able to choose the provider from a wide range of completely private as well as official and semi-official sources. As the buyers would be putting up most of the money themselves they would have a strong interest in getting the best service for the money paid. Dissatisfaction would result in loss of custom to the provider and would force reform or bankruptcy fairly soon. Measures to prevent false billing and other forms of fraud or corruption would be required, but should not be impossible to devise.

REFERENCES

ACE (Asesores de Commercio Exterior S.L.), 1996, 'Design of Czech Export Programme', mimeo, Prague.

Balassa, B., 1971, *The Structure of Protection in Developing Countries*, Baltimore: Johns Hopkins University Press.

Bhagwati, J., 1978, *Foreign Trade Regimes and Economic Development: Anatomy and Consequences of Exchange Control Regimes*, Cambridge, MA: Ballinger.

Bhagwati, J., 1980, 'Lobbying and Welfare', *Journal of Public Economics*, Vol.14, No.3.

EBRD (European Bank for Reconstruction and Development), 1997, *Transition Report*.

Johnson, H.J., 1970, 'The Efficiency and Welfare Implications of the International Corporation' in I.A. McDougall and R.H. Snape (eds.), *Studies in International Economics*, Amsterdam: North-Holland.

Krueger, A., 1974, 'The Political Economy of the Rent Seeking Society', *American Economic Review*, June.

Krueger, A., 1978 *Foreign Trade Regimes and Economic Development*, Cambridge MA: Ballinger.

Krueger, A., 1997, 'Trade Policy and Economic Development: How We Learn', *American Economic Review*, Vol.87, No.1, March.

Lal, D. and S. Rajapatirana, 1987, 'Foreign Trade Regimes and Economic Development', *World Bank Research Observer*, Vol.2, No.2.

Little, I., Scitovsky, T. and M. Scott, 1970, *Industry and Trade in Some Developing Countries: A Comparative Study*, London: Oxford University Press.

2

Institutional Support for Exporting: Issues and Evidence

DERMOT McALEESE and MARY O'DONNELL

An export promotion (EP) strategy can encompass a wide range of policies and instruments. They range from macroeconomic measures which deal with the exchange rate, tax and financial incentives, to those which are designed to provide institutional support services for exporting, such as the technical assistance and information activities of trade promotion organisations. While there is a substantial body of literature on the experience of various economies in implementing EP strategies (see, for example, World Bank [*1993*]; Pyong-Nak [*1994*]; Amsden [*1989*]), that on institutional support for exporting is less extensive.[1] This chapter presents some of the existing evidence on institutional support for exporting, highlighting areas of consensus and dispute on how these services should be organised, whether they should be private or public and what types of services should be offered. The purpose is to summarise the main elements so that lessons can be drawn for transitional economies, or any other economies which may be interested in establishing effective institutional support services for exporters.

INSTITUTIONAL SUPPORT SERVICES DEFINED

In many countries the mechanism for providing institutional support services to the exporting community is commonly known as a trade promotion organisation (TPO). One way of setting out a transparent definition of institutional support services is by reviewing the types of services provided by a typical TPO. The existing evidence tends to focus on the activities of a TPO in either a developing or a developed country. TPOs in developing countries are typically found to provide assistance to exporters by selecting promising export markets and products, assisting companies in adapting supply requirements, marketing export products, identifying constraints to exporting, satisfying exporters' and buyers' information needs and so on [*Keesing and Singer, 1991a*]. Furthermore, providing training and manpower development, advising on design and packaging, organising trade fairs and missions, offering transport and shipping advice, are other activities which a TPO in a developing country might provide [*Hogan, 1991*]. The categorisation by the International Trade Center (ITC), one of the main agencies involved in providing assistance in establishing export support services in developing countries, provides a useful classification of these and other activities which might be provided by a TPO and are set out in Table 2.1.

TABLE 2.1
SELECTED ACTIVITIES OF A TPO (TRADE PROMOTION ORGANISATION)

Product and Market Identification and Development

identification of foreign market opportunities
preparation of company profiles
preparation of product profiles
Trade Information Service
establishment of a trade information service
Technical Assistance Services
legal matters
export financing
export procedures
quality control
export packaging
transportation
Promoting Activities Abroad
participation in trade fairs
invitation to foreign buyers
commercial representation offices abroad
Provision of Support to Other Institutions
training of the export community
export credit insurance
investment promotion
establishment of free zones

Source: adapted from Jaramillo [*1992a*].

The available evidence indicates that the types of institutional support services provided by TPOs in developed and developing countries appear broadly similar [*Crick and Czinkota, 1995; Seringhaus and Rosson, 1990*] and accord with the classification above by the ITC. But, the precise activities which a TPO emphasises in practice will depend on the circumstances prevailing in the country, including the requirements of the export community and the available human and financial resources. Differences are likely to exist among countries in terms of the coverage of services provided. Further-more, while there is agreement regarding the general nature of institutional support services, there is some debate surrounding the activities which an 'ideal' or 'successful' TPO might engage in as well as whether these services should be provided by public or private sector institutions. These issues will be considered later in this chapter.

EVALUATION OF INSTITUTIONAL SUPPORT SERVICES

Assessing the effectiveness of the support services provided to exporters is difficult; nevertheless, some efforts have been made. Interestingly, the results are overwhelmingly negative, reflecting the view that institutional support for exporters has rarely been effective. There is some agreement regarding the factors which are believed to have rendered institutional support services in developing countries ineffective. These include poor positioning and weakness in design and process, where TPOs are set up under the auspices of ministries of trade with an absence of consensus on their objectives. The lack of qualified personnel to staff TPOs and general inadequate human resources are also blamed for ineffective institutional support services. There is also criticism regarding the lack of sustained intervention in the sense that donor agencies have been ambivalent towards the outcome of projects with a lack of monitoring of projects they have assisted in, or provided funding for [*Keesing and Singer, 1991a*].

Another reason for the failure of support services in the past is that policies have rarely been directed at supply aspects of exporting such as adjusting supply to the requirements of a target market or of attaining international standards. This has been exacerbated by a frequent division in responsibilities between export marketing and production which has not been helpful in expanding exports [*Keesing and Singer, 1991a*]. While this appears to be a valid reason why support services are ineffective, it is unclear how this division has arisen or why such aspects have been neglected given that the International Trade Center (ITC), one of the main providers of institutional support services in developing countries emphasises 'in-depth' market studies as serving 'as a basis for initiating product adaptation and marketing activities' [*Jaramillo, 1992b: 2*]. Keesing and Singer's criticism could possibly be explained by ITC assistance in this area being recent rather than being provided to TPOs in the past.

There is debate on the role of the legacy of import substitution (IS) as a cause of the ineffectiveness of institutional support services. Keesing and Singer [*1991a*] identify the controls and regulations associated with an IS regime as often resulting in a slower response by businesses in terms of production, which can be critical to exporting success, as well as resulting in a lack of knowledge and experience regarding production, packaging, and so on, for exporting. The legacy of import substitution, by affecting the wider environment in which TPOs operate, can also contribute to the ineffectiveness of support services in those countries which have pursued an IS strategy [*Hogan, 1991*].

Another disputed issue is whether the choice of providers of institutional support services has contributed to their ineffectiveness. That is, support and assistance to exporters is usually provided via a public supplier. This is viewed by some commentators as an ineffective delivery mechanism due to the inflexibility of government procedures, the unsuitability of government employees and the neglect of commercial services by such organisations. These organisations tended to be viewed as the panacea for improved export performance and thus frequently diverted attention from the crucial need for overall policy reform [*Keesing and Singer, 1991a*]. To be effective, these organisations require the support of the business community, adequate funding, qualified staff, and a level of independence from government. However, the ITC note that when private sector TPOs have the full support of government and the exporting community, together with freedom in relation to absence of public administration procedures, and constraints with regard to human and financial resources, they are 'the ideal type of institution, in many situations' [*Jaramillo, 1992b: 3*]. Thus, many of the factors critical to the success of public sector TPOs are also necessary for private sector TPOs to function effectively. Hence, the criticism of public sector TPOs purely because of their public nature appears unwarranted. But, while there are common elements for the successful operation of a TPO, it is possible that a private sector organisation is more likely than one in the public sector to have the highly qualified staff, sufficient funding, and independence from government. As a further criticism of public sector TPOs, Keesing and Singer [ibid.] question the existence of TPOs altogether. However, Hogan [ibid.] argues that the problems can be corrected and that there is no need to abandon the mechanism altogether; he also believes that Keesing and Singer have discounted available evidence on successful TPOs from some OECD countries.

The evidence from developed countries is similarly negative on the effectiveness of institutional support services. Export support programmes for US exporters provided by the US Foreign and Commercial Service in the International Trade Administration are examined by Luke [*1993*]. He finds that support services have generally been 'weak and ineffective in fulfilling the critical information provider role ... in disarray, unfocused, inefficient, inaccurate and out of date' [*Luke, 1993: 77*] due to the nature of the structure, organisation and culture of support services and activities. Essentially, he sees a clash between the approach of the providers of the services (federal bureaucracy) and the requirements of the users of the services (small and medium sized businesses). Some empirical evidence on institutional support services in developed countries is provided by Crick and Czinkota [*1995*]. Their findings showed little correspondence between customers and exporters on the relative importance of different attributes of products and different support services. This result indicates one of four things.

First, firms are already satisfying customer needs and are capable of doing so without seeking outside assistance. Secondly, firms are ignoring customer needs; if it is the case that firms are not making use of services which cater for and satisfy customer needs (that is, if support services are not effective), this could potentially be damaging to exports. Thirdly, the problem of exporters not seeking assistance which satisfies customers' needs may be due to a lack of awareness of the services provided by TPOs. Fourthly, this result could be indicative of firms not using particular services because they are wary of governments getting involved in these particular aspects of exporting. For example, results showed that managers were 'uneasy about any outside assistance in case it brought about a loss of control ... and product-related activities were judged to be the total responsibility of the firm' [*Crick and Czinkota, 1995: 70*]. This analysis indicates that even if assistance on supply-related aspects of exporting were available, firms in developed market economies would be extremely wary about using them. Again, while this may be true of firms in developed economies, firms in developing or transitional economies should seek assistance on these aspects of exporting given their lack of contact with western markets.

Several common themes recur in the literature explaining the ineffectiveness of support services. First, supply related assistance to exporters may either not have been available in practice or else have been ineffective in operation, perhaps because of a lack of appropriate information. Firms themselves can also be responsible for the ineffectiveness of support services in this regard due to their ambivalence in using or finding out about available services, or being wary about getting 'outsiders' involved in activities that the firms see as their own concern. Second, the lack of sustained intervention and leverage by donors, has contributed to the ineffectiveness of publicly provided support services. Third, many factors identified as due to the role of government, such as inadequate financial and human resources, lack of an integrated approach, bad advice and so on, are not unique to the public sector; they also constrain the effective functioning of private sector TPOs. Thus, criticism of public service TPOs purely on the grounds of their public nature may not be entirely warranted, although it is acknowledged that such factors contributing to the lack of successful TPOs may be more prevalent in public than private sector TPOs.

It should be noted that the evidence presented relates to both developed and developing countries; while there are common elements regarding the reasons for the ineffectiveness of institutional support services, the extent to which these factors prevail in rendering services ineffective will vary from country to country since different countries have different priorities in terms of the types of services offered to exporters.

POLICY IMPLICATIONS FOR TRANSITIONAL ECONOMIES

Although various views have been put forward to explain why support services have been ineffective in the past, it is possible to formulate some policy recommendations to enable export assistance to be more effective. These focus on the activities which export support institutions should undertake, to whom these services should be made available, whether they should be provided free of charge, and the issue of whether the provider should be a public or private sector body.

First, in terms of the services which should be provided by a TPO, the importance of concentrating primarily on supply-related matters to enable developing countries to update and improve their supply practices is stressed by Keesing and Singer [*1991b*]. As already outlined, empirical evidence from the UK and the US economies indicates that firms can be wary of seeking assistance from outside agencies in these matters [*Crick and Czinkota, 1995*], in addition to which, the extent to which all firms in all countries would require assistance with supply-related matters is likely to vary; firms in the majority of developing or transitional economies would be in greater need of such assistance than firms in developed economies. There is little disagreement however that exporters [and buyers] should have access to top quality services in relation to marketing advice and information as well as insurance, warehousing, quality, testing and management consultants. As Hogan [*1991*] states, there should be relevant services keyed to real needs. In order to establish what services are required by firms, it may be necessary to consult with existing and potential exporters.

Keesing and Singer [*1991b*] argue that these services should come initially from abroad, from well-developed versions of the industries and exports that are beginning to emerge. As exports become more successful, this should foster development of support services within the country. One important service that is likely to be required is relevant information for buyers and exporters. The contribution of this to increasing the effectiveness of support services lies not merely in making such information available, but in many cases, in improving the quality of existing information and data collection procedures. Indeed Luke recommends that great emphasis should be accorded to the provision of accurate, timely and opportunity-specific marketing and sales data, rather than general consulting and planning services [*Luke, 1993*].

The mere provision of these services will not make institutional support services effective; these services need to be accompanied by a strong promotional package. That is, firms should be made aware of the benefits and advantages of exports, with a view to increasing the ranks of 'active' exporters [*Keesing and Singer, 1991b*]. But some of the characteristics which they suggest 'active' exporting firms should possess, are somewhat unrealistic for developing economies where resources may be limited and stretched as it is. For example, they suggest that 'in all active exporting firms, a board director spends several months each year overseas' [*Keesing and Singer, 1991b: 28*].

In terms of the availability of services, they should be narrowly focused in terms of catering for specific sectors, markets or even companies. Commentators also believe that these services are likely to be particularly effective when targeted at firms with strong export potential [*Keesing and Singer, 1991b*]. It appears to make sense to target specific firms and an ideal TPO should recognise that not every company is a potential exporter and that it is 'a waste of resources to offer services to any and all, willing, unwilling, or indifferent companies' [*ACE, 1996: 32*]. In practice however, it can be difficult to 'pick winners'. Aside from the issue regarding the firms in specific sectors having access to institutional support services, there is also an issue regarding the size and nationality. Keesing and Singer [*1991b*] are of the opinion that local firms should be accorded priority in this regard. They see foreign investment as 'likely to prove a good way to get started only in exceptional export industries ... and in most industries, foreign owned firms have no lasting advantage' [*Keesing and Singer, 1991b: 20*]. While it is reasonable to target these services at small local firms with little experience of exporting rather than large foreign firms which tend to have better access to such resources, Keesing and Singer's view that foreign firms do not contribute much to exporting disregards the experience of countries such as Ireland, Singapore and Mauritius where attracting foreign firms has been a central part of the EP strategies of these countries.

On the issue of who should pay for the services, it is generally recognised that these services should not be provided free of charge to exporters. One suggestion is for services to be provided through the use of cost sharing grants; this has the advantage of preventing the development of a grant culture as well as a means of improving the responsiveness and resource allocation within TPOs [*Keesing and Singer, 1991b*]. If services were subsidised [in a way that is GATT-compatible] for a limited period, firms could use services which they might not otherwise have used had they not been subsidised; because they have a financial stake in the services, they will be motivated to get more out of the services and get value for money, and the entire process would alert firms to the benefits of exporting. Making exporters pay for these services can also lead to benefits in terms of increased efficiency and financial accountability [*Hogan, 1991*]. It is of course possible that if firms must pay for their services, they may not use them at all. One way of overcoming this problem, is to offer services free for a limited time so that firms may experience the benefits of exporting for themselves. Support services may be easier to sell on this basis to firms with no first hand knowledge of exporting, who are unaware of the potential benefits which may accrue to them, rather than any form of costs being imposed on the firms, at least initially. Once the firm becomes aware of the benefits of exporting, costs could then be imposed as it is agreed that there must be something at stake for the exporter in order for them to be interested in using these services to their full potential (see also ACE [*1996*]).

Regarding the actual operation of an ideal TPO, if it is public sector in nature, autonomy in operations is also considered to be important. This relates to its position in the national hierarchical structure as well as its objectives and function [*Seringhaus and Rosson, 1990*]. That is, if it is accorded a low position and lacks authority, then its influence on exporters will be severely curtailed; this will also be a reflection of the government's commitment to export development and is likely to affect the level of confidence which a TPO enjoys from both government and exporters. The position of a TPO will also affect the human resources and finance aspects of the organisation; having staff that are experienced and trained for the job, and sufficient finance to do the job well will be important aspects of any ideal TPO, public or private [*Hogan, 1991*].

On a broader level, beside the specific aspects of a TPO outlined here, it is reasonable to assume that the effectiveness of any TPO and institutional support services is likely to be determined by the general policy environment in which such an organisation is operating. That is, institutional support is unlikely to be effective in a policy environment which is not conducive to exporting, no matter how good the services which that TPO may be offering [*Keesing and Singer, 1991b; Hogan, 1991*]. There is some debate about the stage at which institutional support should be provided. Keesing and Singer [*1991b*] are of the view that it is wasteful of resources and futile to set up and operate a TPO in an inappropriate policy framework when benefits from it, in terms of increased exports, will not be fully realised. While this seems reasonable, it is unlikely that such an ideal policy environment will ever exist in any country. Thus, where some effort has been made toward attaining satisfactory policies towards manufactured exports and where there is a real and credible commitment towards further improvement, it is likely that the provision of institutional support services can contribute to improving export performance.

Should export services be provided by public sector bodies or by the private sector? There is no consensus in the literature one way or the other. Arguments in favour of private sector providers highlight the bureaucracy associated with public service which makes staffing with experienced, entrepreneurial business persons, unlikely, a problem which is unlikely to be resolved by increased funding [*Luke, 1993*]. Of course government can still play a role in providing institutional support by subsidising private based business organisations. Given that Luke's justification for privatising support services is because of staffing quality and attitudes, then it is possible that institutional support service could be provided by a public sector body if it was the case that human resources were seconded or hired from the private sector. Thus rectifying the human resource problem, rather than the mechanism would achieve the same aim, but, levels of remuneration are likely to be crucial.

Private sector provision of support has also been advocated on the grounds that private sector bodies in developed economies, such as local and regional chambers of commerce, are more accessible for exporters. Given that they also are in close contact with their members, this would render support services provided by such bodies more effective as they would have a better idea of the types of services required by members. Obviously where such organisations do not in exist it might be considered an option to establish them along with institutional support services. However, it is recognised that a successful private sector TPO in practice may be difficult, if not impossible to achieve 'in an economy ... where private enterprise does not play a predominant role' [*Keesing and Singer, 1991b: 24*]. Seringhaus and Rosson [*1990*] also note that where private sector provision of EP support services is lacking, governments may have to assume a more critical role in the provision of these services.

SUMMARY AND CONCLUSIONS

This chapter assessed some of the published evidence on institutional support for exporting. It examined issues such as how these services should be organised, whether they should be provided by private or public sector bodies and what types of services should be offered. The purpose of this exercise was to enable lessons to be drawn for transitional economies on how to provide effective institutional support services for exporters.

The term institutional support for exporting was clarified. While the existing evidence relates to both public and private sector TPOs, as well as TPOs in developed and developing economies, there is general agreement with regard to what types of services should be provided to exporters. These include technical assistance on exporting procedures and product-related matters, providing information and advice to exporters on foreign market requirements and opportunities, as well as to foreign buyers on firm capabilities, and organising trade fairs, trade missions and export credit insurance and guarantees.

A review of the evidence on the effectiveness of support services provided to exporters in developed and developing economies revealed that, with few exceptions, they have been largely ineffective. Among the possible reasons for this, one was that supply related assistance to exporters may not have been provided. Another reason was that the assistance was ineffective in operation, often because of a lack of appropriate information. In addition, in developing countries the lack of sustained intervention and leverage by donors has influenced the effectiveness of publicly provided support services. Inadequate financial and human resources, lack of an integrated approach, bad advice, and so on, have also constrained the effectiveness of institutional support services in both the public and private sector. Firms themselves can also be responsible for the ineffectiveness of support services due to their ambivalence in using or finding out about available services, or being wary about getting 'outsiders' involved in activities seen as the firms' sole concern. Of course the extent to which these factors prevail in rendering services ineffective will vary from country to country since different countries have different priorities and emphases in terms of the types of services required by exporters.

There is substantial agreement on what factors are crucial in determining the effectiveness of the functioning and operation of TPOs in both developing and developed countries. First, exporters should have easy access to top quality, relevant services. Second, these services should be accompanied by a strong promotional package to alert existing and potential exporters to the benefits and advantages of exporting. Third, the services provided by TPOs should be focused on specific sectors/markets/companies, although it can be difficult to identify these in practice. Fourth, these services should not be provided free of charge; by having to pay for the services, firms are likely to be motivated to get more out of the services and get value for money. Fifth, the human resource element of the TPO is crucial. Well qualified personnel who are experienced and trained for the job are essential. The level of remuneration is likely to be important in attracting suitable staff and so having adequate funding of TPOs will also be important in ensuring that institutional support services are effective. Sixth, there is some agreement that these factors are more likely to be present in a private rather than a public sector TPO. But, in practice an adequate institutional framework may be lacking. Consequently, trade promotion services may have to be provided by a government or a public sector agency. It is not clear from the literature whether there should be more than one organisation or whether competition should be encouraged among a variety of providers of export support. In recommending private over public sector providers, this would seem to indicate that there should be some degree of competition among the providers. Seventh, even if all these recommendations are followed, if it is the case that the TPO has to function in an inappropriate policy framework this is likely to make services ineffective; thus an important element of successful and effective institutional support is a policy framework which is consistent with improving export performance.

The business environment can vary enormously across countries. Ultimately, a country or region's own circumstances, as well as the requirements of exporters, will influence the extent to which our recommendations are relevant for improving the effectiveness of TPOs. While there may be common elements, a system which has been successful in one setting may not be successful in another setting; these recommendations may help, but cannot guarantee success.

NOTE

1. Unfortunately, there is a relative dearth of literature on this topic, with the articles reviewed here the few which focus on institutional support for exporting. All of these authors are in agreement on the ineffectiveness of support services which have been provided to date. This conclusion is based more on impressions and theory rather than empirical evidence, with Crick and Czinkota's article the only empirically based assessment of export support services.

REFERENCES

Amsden, A.H., 1989, *Asia's Next Giant: South Korea and Late Industrialization*, Oxford: Oxford University Press.

ACE (Asesores de Commercio Exterior S.L.), 1996, *Task 4: Czech Export Support Policy*, Madrid: ACE.

Crick, C. and M. Czinkota, 1995, 'Export Assistance - Another Look at Whether We are Supporting the Best Programmes', *International Marketing Review*, Vol. 12 No.3, pp.61–72.

Hogan, P., 1991, 'Some Institutional Aspects of Export Promotion in Developing Countries', in *The Role of Support Services in Expanding Manufactured Exports in Developing Countries*, EDI Seminar Series, Washington, DC:World Bank.

Hogan, P., Keesing, D. and A. Singer, 1991, *The Role of Support Services in Expanding Manufacturing Exports in Developing Countries*, EDI Seminar Series, Washington, DC: World Bank.

Jaramillo, C., 1992a, *The Basic Functions of National Trade Promotion Organizations*, Geneva: International Trade Center.

Jaramillo, C., 1992b, *Trade Promotion Organizations: A Variety of Approaches*, Geneva: International Trade Center.

Keesing, D. and A. Singer, 1991a, 'Development Assistance Gone Wrong: Failures in Services to Promote and Support Manufactured Exports', in Hogan, Keesing and Singer [*1991*].

Keesing, D., and A. Singer, 1991b, 'Assisting Manufactured Exports Through Services: New Methods and Improved Policies', in Hogan, Keesing and Singer [*1991*].

Luke, J., 1993, 'Domestic Institutional Barriers to Increased U.S. Exports', in M.E. Kreinin (ed.), *International Commercial Policy: Issues for the 1990s*, Washington, DC: Taylor & Francis.

Pyong-Nak, S., 1994, *The Rise of the Korean Economy*, Oxford: Oxford University Press.

Seringhaus, F. and P. Rosson, 1990, *Government Export Promotion – A Global Perspective*, New York: Routledge.

World Bank, 1993, *The East Asian Miracle: Economic Growth and Public Policy*, New York: Oxford University Press for the World Bank.

3

A Comparative Analysis of Export Growth in Selected Asian and European Economies

MARY O'DONNELL

One possible way for the central and eastern European countries (CEECs) to improve their export through an export promotion (EP) strategy is to see what lessons can be taken from the experience of other countries. This chapter firstly examines the EP policies, measures and strategies pursued by three of the South-East Asian 'Tigers'. While this is likely to be of interest to the CEECs, the experiences of countries within the European Union (EU) are also increasingly relevant in the lead up to their accession to the EU. For this reason the experience of export promotion policy in Ireland is also covered. The second focus of this chapter is on how the types of EP policies pursued have affected overall export growth. This is examined through a constant market share analysis of export growth. This technique is used to see how export performance in these countries has been influenced by changes in the commodity composition and market destination pattern of exports. By controlling for these factors we seek to assess the extent to which other factors, such as institutional support for exporting, technological improvements, and other price and non-price factors, have affected export performance.

EXPORT PROMOTION STRATEGIES AND POLICIES

This section sets out the salient features of the EP policies pursued by three of the Tigers and Ireland. The motive for going beyond the experience of the Tigers is that the CEEC countries are constrained by membership of the World Trade Organization (WTO) and future accession to the EU. Many of the measures employed by the south east Asian Tigers could not now be used by other nations wishing to emulate their success.[1] Nevertheless there are still valuable lessons to be learned from the experience of the south east Asian countries. In looking to the experience of countries within the EU that adopted EP, Ireland is an obvious choice. Its successful performance, both in terms of exports and the wider economy have earned it the name 'Celtic' or 'Emerald' Tiger.[2]

The purpose of examining EP policies and strategies is to identify what, if any, EP bodies were established, what mechanisms for credit and other assistance were provided and what types of incentives and support were given to exporters. We also focus on how differences in the policies used resulted in different effects on the market sector and through that on export performance and growth in the wider economy. At the end of this section, we draw some conclusions on the lessons from the Asian and Irish experiences.

SOUTH KOREA

One of the main differences between the path pursued by Korea and that chosen by other East Asian nations is the extent to which natural resources were part of the industrialisation process. Essentially, Korea being largely devoid of natural resources, did not have the option to develop a resources-based strategy, for example, like Malaysia. Thus, manufacturing had to be developed in order to enable the economy to grow. 'Trade oriented industrialisation has been the basic strategy of Korea since the early 1960s making foreign trade inseparable from industrialisation' [*Song, 1994: 82*].

Two main features of Korea's approach to improving export performance can be identified, along with the strong degree of government intervention that characterised policy for over three decades. First, there was extensive use of subsidies and other incentives as a means of promoting exports and second, the use of tariff and non-tariff barriers to control imports. The Korean EP strategy has been described as one of 'protection and correction' whereby the bias in favour of the domestic market (which resulted from import protection) was corrected by providing incentives to firms to sell abroad [*The Economist, 1990: 18*]. These features can be seen clearly in trade and industrial policy in the 1960s and later in the sequence of five year plans (FYPs) that were implemented in Korea.

Korea's export performance in the 1950s was less than impressive. During President Rhee's term (1948–61), Korea had no clear-cut trade strategy and growth was based primarily on an import-substitution regime. Problems hampering firms at that time included old plants and equipment, weak marketing channels, exchange rate problems and import restrictions in export markets. This was especially so in one of Korea's oldest industries, the textile/cotton industry. Despite efforts to improve export performance, polices such as devaluing the won and a variety of export incentives were unsuccessful in overcoming impediments to exporting. After President Park took power in 1961, the policy emphasis changed markedly to one where exports were seen as the key to economic development. Park's favourite maxim was '*suchul ipguk*' (nation-building through exports). Some commentators have noted how Park's regime 'increasingly made exports a compulsion rather than a choice for the private sector' [*Amsden, 1989: 70*] and a strong element of coercion underlay firms' export performance.

During the first FYP between 1961 and 1965 there was an 'export incentives boom' [*Koteva, 1992: 36*] in which incentives were granted to all exporters indiscriminately. While trade policy in the first FYP was undoubtedly biased in favour of exports, it was neutral with regard to the actual composition of exports. Incentives offered to exporters included tariff and tax exemptions which were important in providing exporters with cheap imported inputs.

Other incentives provided included wastage allowances and loans at preferential interest rates, where export performance was increasingly used as a measure of credit worthiness. Given the low level of internal savings, businesses were obliged to rely on bank loans to finance the expansion of their firms and this created a dependency between businesses and government [*Amsden, 1989*]. The lack of liberalisation of capital markets enabled the government to exercise a large degree of discretion over capital flows. All exporters could borrow at preferential rates. For long-term capital loans, the government exercised discretion over who could have access to these loans, with firms in shipbuilding, steel, machinery and cement being favoured over firms from other industrial sectors. The Korean Development Bank had responsibility for the allocation of credit on behalf of the government. Amsden *et al.* note how 'government policy was to emphasise the importance of public development banks and downplay the importance of private commercial banks' [*Amsden et al., 1994: 120*].

The second FYP, 1966–72, contained highly discretionary instruments such as multiple exchange rates, direct cash payments, permission to retain foreign exchange earnings to import restricted commodities and permission to borrow in foreign currencies [*World Bank, 1993*]. Even when the government exercised less discretion, the continuing importance of exemptions from import controls for exporters was stressed. The textile industry was particularly effective at taking advantage of the range of incentives offered by the government due to strong business organisations [*Amsden, 1989*].

It was also during this plan that the government made efforts to establish export industrial estates and in 1969 a law was enacted which was aimed at developing at least one regional industrial estate in every regional capital. Within these estates firms could access cheap water, electricity and other services.

The third FYP 1973–79, was different from the previous ones in the sense that the government was more aggressive in targeting specific industry sectors to improve export performance and at the same time influence the industrial structure. Again, support was in the form of tax incentives and preferential financing. One example of this targeting is the establishment of the Heavy Chemical Industry Promotion Committee. In terms of the effect on the industrial structure, there was an increase in the degree of industrial concentration [*Song, 1994*]. In addition to this, changes in the industrial structure impacted on the composition of exports. During the 1960s exports were predominantly primary commodities, whereas by the late 1970s manufactured exports had not only increased but also changed from being labour-intensive to capital- and technology-intensive.

One, oft-cited, feature of Korea's industrialisation is the importance of general trading companies in the whole industrialisation process. In 1975 the legal framework for the creation of the general trading companies (GTCs) was established. GTCs were established with the aim of speeding up export expansion. Not just any firm could become a GTC – certain criteria had to be fulfilled in terms of export growth, number of overseas branches and so on. Even when firms managed to earn the status of a GTC there was considerable work involved in maintaining it as the government frequently increased the minimum export value required to be designated as a GTC. The incentive for firms to become GTCs was that there were many cash subsidies for GTCs. It is widely recognised that Korean GTCs are the worlds most successful adaptation of what was originally a Japanese system [*Song, 1994*].

The fourth and fifth FYPs covered the decade 1980–90. These plans reduced the emphasis on many of the incentives provided for exporting firms, including the generous credit policies and cash subsidies (such as those given to GTCs), and increased the emphasis on indirect tax and tariff exemptions. Interestingly, there was also a switch away from targeting specific firms in these FYPs, which was a complete reversal of the strategy pursued for most of the previous two decades. This change of policy was accompanied by a switch also away from government intervention and towards market forces and promoting competition, with extensive financial and import liberalisation programmes implemented. As part of this, the Tariff Reform Committee was set up. These liberalisation programmes were a feature also of the 1990s when continued financial market liberalisation was required to establish a less dependent financial sector after the effects of years of extensive government intervention and the consequent lack of competition.

For most of the plan periods, in addition to incentives, the government also provided administrative support to exporters. Monthly EP conferences were held and these were attended by the President as well as a number of high ranking officials. These conferences were seen as a means of exchanging information, revising and extending institutional support. In addition to this, it was at these meetings that medals and citations were awarded, based on successful export performance. Song notes how this type of 'moral persuasion

32

based on loyalty has been a very powerful supplement to monetary incentives in Korea ... and appears to be one of the most important policy instruments in Korea and other East Asian countries' [*Song, 1994: 101*]. It has also been noted that 'the Chinese heritage – either ethnic or cultural – plays an important role [in the four Tigers]' [*Chow and Kellman, 1994: 113*]. However, there are limitations to the extent to which such an institutional support measure could be replicated by other countries. Non-monetary rewards such as these could be viewed with less enthusiasm in other countries where such cultural factors are not present.

One of the more notable features of Korea's export strategy is the extent to which foreign direct investment played such a minor role. Essentially all industrial sectors were closed to foreign direct investment (FDI) [*Luedde-Neurath, 1986*]. Even though the government tried in the late 1970s to encourage FDI, particularly in high-tech industries, FDI as a proportion of GNP in Korea was lower in 1985 than it had been in 1965 [*Amsden, 1989*]. This route to industrialisation is in marked contrast, for instance, to the industrialisation strategy followed by Ireland and Singapore over the same period, where vigorous efforts were made to attract foreign direct investment as a means to promote exports.

A distinct feature of Korea's industrialisation and export experience was the effect which policies had on the size of firms in the economy. In essence, the policies pursued resulted in a small number of very large firms or *chaebol*. Again, this is one of the differences in the industrial structure in Korea and its fellow tigers. Several explanations have been put forward to explain these differences.

One of these focuses on the fact that Korea was not limited by a small domestic market, as was the case in either Singapore or Taiwan.[3] This meant that it could use the domestic market to develop industries which took advantage of scale economies which would naturally result in larger firms. A limited domestic market precluded this in the other cases. Another explanation claims the extent of government intervention in the economy was a factor contributing to the large size of firms. Basically, the Korean government preferred dealing with a small number of large firms, rather than a large number of small firms, as this was easier from an administrative point of view.

The link between credit policy and the resulting industrial structure has also been highlighted. This explanation goes as follows 'when a government keeps interest rates below the market-clearing rate, it usually does so in the vague belief that this will help the little guy. It does the opposite. Cheap money helps borrowers, mostly big firms. It also encourages more capital-intensive methods of production ... and larger firms' [*The Economist, 1990: 18*]. The credit policy pursued in Korea would have been along these lines and thus contributed to the large firm size.

Until the 1980s there were a small number of large firms in Korea and little increase in the number of firms. After that, there was a change in policy which as well as assisting existing firms, also emphasised promoting small manufacturing industries. This was reinforced by a law enacted in 1986 to support the creation of small firms.

Thus overall, Korea's strategy to promote exports was characterised by strong direct export incentives, combined with protection against imports and strong government intervention between 1960 and 1980. While there was still an emphasis on EP in the 1980–90 decade, the means through which this was achieved was markedly different than previously, as the emphasis on special incentives decreased and extensive liberalisation programmes were the order of the day.

TAIWAN

Several elements of South Korea's strategy were shared in Taiwan's, in particular the combination of EP with import protection together with a degree of government intervention. But there are also contrasts.

At around the same time that South Korea, under Park's leadership, began to promote exports in a concerted manner, Taiwan too embarked on a programme which aimed at raising export growth. This move towards EP was precipitated by the anticipated end of US aid and the consequent need to obtain an alternative source of foreign exchange [*World Bank, 1993*]. Thus the beginning of the 1960s saw trade reform which included strengthening existing incentives to exporters. Barriers to importing in place at this time included tariff, non-tariff barriers and foreign exchange budgeting. The latter involved the government stipulating quotas for foreign exchange for various commodity classifications and was an important method of import control until its abolition in 1961. The remaining tariffs and NTBs were subsequently the main instruments at the government's disposal.

During the 1960s and 1970s tariff levels increased and it was not until 1979 that tariff levels fell significantly. The increase in imports during this period was not because NTBs fell, but was due mainly to an increase in demand for imported inputs (for exports) as exports grew, as well as an improvement in the terms of trade. Even though tariffs and NTBs were significant between 1960 and 1980, exporters were not affected adversely owing to the favourable treatment they received on tariffs. They were permitted to seek tariff rebates not only on tariffs but on all taxes on materials used for export goods. Tariffs were likewise rebated for certain types of capital and machines in iron, steel and other industries that Taiwan wanted to expand. The incentive scheme was designed to encourage exporters to buy imports from domestic rather than foreign suppliers by refunding a higher proportion of the actual duty paid.

As well as the more familiar NTBs such as health regulations, quality standards and quantitative restrictions, Taiwan also made use of an 'import list'. This comprised a catalogue of items which it was 'permissible' to import. There was some effort to try to reduce the level of NTBs between 1970 and 1974 and additional items were added to the import list. This, however, was quite superficial on the face of it, as in practice, not all permissibles were freely importable (due to rules of origin for example). Even when restrictions were met, this did not automatically mean the goods could be imported [*Wade, 1990*]. The object of the import list was to ensure that there would be strong domestic demand for products seen as important by planners as enabling firms in those industries to take advantage of economies of scale.

Despite these quite stringent import licensing restrictions on imports, exporters were by and large able to purchase inputs at close to world prices. There was little progress on reducing or removing NTBs and up until the mid-1980s, substantial impediments to imports remained; in 1984 over half of Taiwan's total imports faced restrictions. Interestingly, the view of the World Bank on the import liberalisation programme differs from other commentators. While the World Bank's view is that tariffs and import controls were gradually reduced between 1958 and 1972, this characterisation is strongly disputed by among others, Wade [*1990*] and Amsden, [*1989*], who note that it was only post-1979 that a large fall in tariffs took place; in the mid-1960s–1970s the trend was an increase in tariff levels. It has been remarked that 'evidence only appears to be, but is not a sufficient argument for the eventual conclusion, that there was definitely a substantial import liberalisation in Korea during the 1960s' [*Koteva, 1992: 28*]. This at least in part assists in explaining the differing viewpoints of Wade and the World Bank on this point.

As well as rebates on imports and exemptions from import controls, exporters could also avail themselves of other tax incentives such as preferential treatment for revenues from exports. In some cases firms were given five year tax holidays where exports accounted for more than 50 per cent of total output, and some small firms' export earnings were exempt from tax.

Other measures to promote exports included the establishment of export processing zones and bonded factories. Both initiatives were established in 1965 and although not the most important incentives, together they accounted for about 20–25 per cent of total exports from Taiwan through the 1970s and 1980s [*Wade, 1990*].

Export credit was another incentive offered to exporters in Taiwan, but on a much less favourable basis than in Korea. While the government in Taiwan also exercised a large degree of discretion in allocating credit on the basis of both past and projected export earnings [*Kwon, 1998*], by 1981 the government had curtailed its activities in this area. In practice most export credit came from non-bank sources such as Japanese trading companies and upstream firms. Thus, a crucial difference between Korea and Taiwan is in respect of the degree of government intervention in the provision of loans and credit to exporters. This is reflected in the levels of development and independence of the financial sectors in both economies. The lack of credit from bank sources in Taiwan also serves to highlight the importance of institutions other than banks in providing export credit.

Non-price incentives were also offered to exporters. For example, Taiwan established an export award scheme, but this was less successful and not as highly regarded as the equivalent Korean scheme. An export quality inspection scheme was designed to improve the quality of Taiwanese exports. Exporters producing certain goods were required to have a quality control system in place; this was then inspected and graded prior to goods being exported. If the grade was below a certain level, the goods could not be exported. Since the fee for this service was inversely related to the grade received, the incentive was clearly for firms to improve the quality of goods exported. While this scheme was quite extensive during the 1970s, it has been scaled down. Since the mid-1980s only about 20 per cent of total exports came under the scheme. Rather than signalling a decline in the importance attached to the quality of exports, this is still important, but the emphasis has shifted to quality control associations.

The government also provided institutional support to exporters under the auspices of CETRA, the Taiwanese trade promotion organisation which was established in 1970. The staff of CETRA comprised ex-government officials as well as members of industrial and exporting associations. In Taiwan the functions of trade promotion and trade administration were separate, although they were considered to be 'two wings of the same bird'. CETRA's main functions were to provide information and advice to exporters, organise participation in trade fairs, provide results from and undertake market research. It maintained an extensive data bank of details on foreign buyers and domestic suppliers, details of foreign markets and so on. Its main aim was to diversify Taiwan's trading partners and expand into the most promising market and product areas. In return for the use of CETRA's data bank exporters were required to pay a small fee, but the bulk of its revenue was from a small levy on exports. In terms of its clientele, CETRA aimed to assist small firms of less than about 300 employees.

One important facet of export promotion which was utilised by the Taiwanese government but avoided by Korea, was the attraction of FDI. But, the access of FDI was still strongly restricted and controlled. Proposals were evaluated in terms of how they would assist Taiwan in accessing new markets, the transfer of technology and so on. To be allowed to operate in Taiwan, many foreign firms had to have a certain level of technology and some firms were even required to upgrade the capabilities of local firms. The government protected certain sectors from FDI in order to protect firms supplying to the domestic market, but this was not a major issue as most FDI production was export-oriented rather than for the domestic market. Indeed the World Bank notes that during the 1958–72 period in particular, FDI played a catalytic role in the development of Taiwan's export performance [*World Bank, 1993*]. Of course, low inflation and macroeconomic stability during this period and subsequent years were crucial.

In essence, the EP strategy pursued by Taiwan can be summarised as one with government intervention, but on a smaller scale than in Korea (as reflected in credit policy), combined with a liberal import regime for export inputs and subsidies for exporters, including tax incentives and institutional measures to encourage exporting.

SINGAPORE

Various elements were common to the EP paths of Taiwan and Korea. What is interesting about Singapore is the extent to which it is similar to the other Tigers in pursuing an EP strategy, but different in the means.

One major difference relates to the extent and use of barriers to imports. In the former two Tigers these were combined with EP incentives, as the Economist noted, 'correction and protection'. In Singapore the emphasis of policy has been heavily on EP rather than on a combination of IS and EP. Another notable difference is the extent to which FDI has played a pivotal role in the Tigers; Singapore was more dependent on FDI than Hong Kong, Taiwan or Korea.

The strong link between FDI and the export-oriented strategy pursued by Singapore can be explained by a number of factors. First, the small size of the domestic market meant that an import-substitution regime could not be pursued for any prolonged period and in fact, 'except for a brief period of import substitution in the early 1960s, the government has never sought to impose quota restrictions on imports; protective tariffs have been few' [*Murray and Perrera, 1996: 97*]. Amsden noted the large size of the Korean market and Murray *et al.* also contend that neither Taiwan nor Korea were constrained by a small domestic market as was the case in Singapore. Given then that EP seemed the only option and the fact that Singapore was 'anxious to leap into international markets' [*Murray and Perrera, 1996: 96*], how did this result in the emphasis on FDI to promote exports? The official perception in the early 1960s was that indigenous firms were seen as ill-equipped to become successful exporters and that successful export manufacturing could be more readily achieved through direct foreign investment [*Lim et al., 1988*]. This resulted in FDI being the focus of the EP strategy pursued by Singapore. The importance of FDI to Singapore is reflected in the fact that foreign firms and foreign-owned joint ventures, as well as moving into sectors which are heavily export-oriented [*Lim and Pang, 1991*], have accounted for 80–90 per cent of direct exports from Singapore's manufacturing sector since 1970 [*Murray and Perrera, 1996*]. This is of a similar magnitude to Ireland where multinational companies (MNCs) contributed substantially to industrial growth and in the late 1990s accounted for about 70 per cent of manufactured exports [*Arrow, 1997*].

In order to attract FDI this necessarily resulted in investment policy which was more liberal than many of its South East Asian neighbours and various tax and non-tax incentives were given by the government. This differs from the approach of other countries, such as Korea, where indigenous firms were pushed or encouraged by various incentives to undertake and improve export performance. In examining the incentives provided to promote exports this requires taking a broader perspective than was the case in either Taiwan or Korea. That is, we do not focus exclusively on the export incentives offered by the government but also include general incentives which may not have been aimed at EP but that may effectively have ended up boosting exports. For example, general industrial incentives may have been important in attracting MNCs which eventually went into export-oriented activities. This is a feature of Singapore's EP strategy which is common to Ireland's industrial policy.

The first moves to promote export-oriented industrialisation through the use of incentives can be traced back at least to 1959 when tax incentives were first introduced. Since that time the coverage of these incentives has been extended. For example, in 1979, tax incentives to promote investment in research and development were introduced. An important aspect of the EP strategy of Singapore was the extent to which the emphasis of policy was not confined exclusively to manufacturing but incentives were also aimed at encouraging the development of trading, technical and consultancy services [*Murray and Perrera, 1996*].[4]

Incentives which were aimed directly at exporting, these can be divided into tax and non-tax incentives. Tax incentives included an exemption on 90 per cent of increased export profits (from a fixed base) for certain products and services. Some enterprises could claim exemption for five to 15 years on increased export profits depending on certain conditions being satisfied. To encourage (a) international trading houses to set up regional offices in Singapore and (b) energy trading activities, lower taxes were imposed on income earned from certain aspects of these activities. Any firm engaged in counter trade and certain international consultancy firms were exempt from tax on profits for five years. To encourage firms to seek and develop new markets, 50 per cent of income from sales of certain goods abroad was exempt from tax. Non-tax incentives which the government offered included an extensive export credit insurance scheme to cover commercial and non-commercial risks and to provide letters of assignment and pre-shipment credit guarantees.

As already mentioned, other incentives which were aimed at general industry and not specifically at exporting activity may, in effect, have improved export performance by attracting MNCs to the country. Most of these incentives are administered by the Economic Development Board and include a capital assistance scheme to provide long term fixed rate finance to manufacturing and services. Tax holidays were given to companies which manufactured products and provided services with 'favourable' prospects. Even after this tax holiday ended, concessionary tax rates were applied. Other tax incentives were aimed at encouraging investment in new productive equipment by giving tax relief on income generated by the equipment. To encourage firms to locate research and development activities in Singapore any research and development related expenses were deemed tax deductible (which was not usually the case).

In an attempt to assist small and medium sized enterprises or indigenous firms in upgrading and expanding their operations, local enterprise finance and technical assistance schemes were established. The market development assistance scheme was designed to assist SMEs in developing opportunities, especially in international markets with incentives such as grants to set up overseas marketing offices, improve product design and packaging.

Singapore's approach to EP was one where free-trade prevailed to a much greater degree than in either Taiwan or Korea. Of all the east Asian examples, Singapore may thus have the most to offer the CEEC in terms of taking lessons from the strategy which they pursued.

IRELAND

Ireland's growth experience is relevant to the CEECs in several respects. The Irish authorities saw membership of the EU as providing an avenue to higher living standards. Like the CEECs it was a relatively poor country at the time of accession, but with the ambition of attaining average EU living standards through judicious use of the opportunities of access to the EU market.[5] In this chapter we discuss possible reasons for, what is considered by international standards to be, Ireland's remarkable success [cf. *OECD, 1997; The Economist, 1997; Financial Times, 1996*]. Many commentators have noted the important role of FDI in this success. Exports from the FDI firms played a key role in Irish development. For instance, some commentators believe that 'it is probably not an exaggeration to say that the growth in foreign investment is at the heart of an understanding of the Irish economic miracle' [*Gray, 1997: xviii*]. The OECD, also comments that Ireland's outstanding performance has been associated with 'sustained foreign investment' [*OECD, 1997: xx*]. To explain why FDI has played such a critical role in Ireland's export success, we briefly review the main elements of Ireland's industrial policy. As was the case with Singapore, where FDI has also been crucial, Ireland's export success cannot be tied merely to export incentives but on balance owes more to its industrial strategy and accompanying incentives.

The lack of natural resources and the consequent need to use manufacturing as a means of industrialisation is one element of the export strategy which is common to both Ireland and Korea. Initially an import-substitution regime was pursued but this era of protectionist industrial growth came to an end in the late 1950s. After this the focus of policy changed to promoting exports. The main elements of the strategy were '(i) substantial capital grants and tax concessions to encourage export-oriented manufacturing, (ii) the attraction of foreign manufacturing enterprise, again aimed at exports, and (iii) the dismantling of protection in return for greater access to markets abroad' [*Kennedy et al., 1988:116; also O'Malley, 1992*].

In attracting FDI incentives can be classified according to whether they are quantitative or qualitative in nature. The former includes tax incentives while the latter refers to factors which will affect long-run performance such as the skill level of the workforce, infrastructure, and availability of high quality sub-supply. Ireland's strategy has been 'to attract investment by maximising as far as possible the attractiveness of its quantitative factors while implementing a long-term strategy to develop the qualitative factors' [*NESC, 1997: 333*]. The first type of quantitative incentive offered to firms was an 'Export Profit Tax Relief' (EPTR) whereby tax remissions were given on the increment of profits over the previous year. This was increased from 50 per cent to 100 per cent in 1958 and in 1960 the period of relief was also extended from 10 to 15 years. However, this net-export bias 'was in ... breach of the Treaty of Rome because the implicit export subsidies interfere with competition in foreign markets in the same way as protection does in domestic markets' [*Ruane, 1991: 347*]. Thus, in 1981 the EPTR was abolished and replaced by a corporation tax rate of ten per cent for manufacturing industry. This incentive has been crucial for the manufacturing sector, given that it is now the lowest corporate tax rate in Europe (see Figure 3.1). In comparing the importance of tax incentives as against other factors in attracting FDI (or in terms of qualitative versus quantitative factors), NESC [*1997*] argue that 'although the ten per cent corporation tax probably remains the most important factor in attracting FDI to Ireland, it would seem that the qualitative factors are becoming increasingly important'[*NESC, 1997: 333*].

Following the Industrial Development Act of 1958 restrictions on foreign

FIGURE 3.1
CORPORATION TAX RATES (PER CENT) IN MANUFACTURING AND
QUALIFYING SERVICES

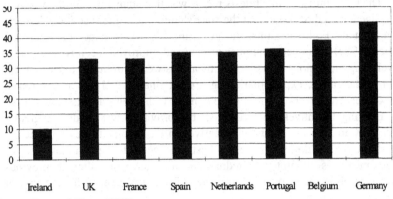

Source: Ernst and Young [1997].

ownership and control and restraints on repatriation of profits were abolished. This has been a long-standing incentive for attracting FDI to Ireland and remains in place today.

The third focus of policy, that is, 'the dismantling of protection in return for greater access to markets abroad' related to Ireland's entry into a free trade agreement with the UK in the mid-1960s, its main trading partner at that time, and subsequent entry into the European Community in 1973. This meant that protection against imports was gradually dismantled and Ireland adopted the Common External Tariff in trading with the rest of the world [Ruane, 1991]. It has been suggested that this factor has been important and that 'perhaps one reason for Ireland's success where others have failed, even pursuing similar strategies, is that while many of them sought to attract foreign firms ... not many have gone as far as Ireland in entering into full free trade agreements with major advanced industrial countries' [O'Malley, 1992: 107].

Ireland's industrial policy remained largely unchanged from the 1960s until the mid-1980s. Despite the importance of foreign-owned firms to Ireland's export performance and its overall economic prosperity, there were several criticisms of policy in the early 1980s. There was concern that Ireland had come to be over-reliant, on FDI and MNCs. This was first highlighted by the Telesis Consultancy Group (1982). The policy focused excessively on large foreign firms. As Ruane states 'during the 1970s and in the early 1980s industrial development policy in Ireland could be said to have been driven by a primary concern with establishing overseas plants, rather than with developing indigenous companies' [Ruane, 1991: 361]. There were no specific measures in place to assist small firms which were 'rather like

Cinderella before the ball: very active but totally ignored by those in any position of power' [*Ruane, 1991:363*].

The main thrust of the Telesis report was that state aid should be shifted to indigenous industry and that the state should play a more active role in its development. Following this, the government's White Paper on Industrial Policy [*1984*] contained a number of new and improved incentives aimed at developing indigenous firms. Policy measures were introduced to assist them with management, export marketing, export finance and export insurance, market research, market entry, development technology acquisition, and so on. Existing incentives were retained, but provision was made for greater selectivity in the case of these incentives in an attempt to develop sectors which would be likely to have the best prospects of international success. These measures attempted to redress the imbalance of policy in previous years whereby support provided to foreign firms was given at the expense of indigenous industry.

Two specific programmes announced in the White Paper were the Company Development Programme (CDP) and the National Linkage Programme (NLP), both were implemented in 1985. The CDP involved offering support to promising companies on the basis of their requirements and objectives. This was found by companies to be 'very worthwhile' [*Review of Industrial Performance, 1990: 54*].

Irish policy towards FDI has been criticised for its failure to create significant linkages between MNCs and the rest of the economy. One explanation for the poor linkages in the past was that Irish firms apparently had difficulty in meeting the quality standards required by MNCs. Another explanation is that MNCs lack information on locally available supplies. Yet another is the claim that the tax system encourages transfer pricing. But that requires imported inputs to enable the transfer of profits overseas. If common it would discourage local sourcing [*Ruane, 1991*]. In an attempt to improve this situation the NLP was introduced. Its purpose was to 'develop a strong competitive sub-supply based in Ireland that will maximise local purchases of Irish materials, components and services by overseas firms based' [*Review of Industrial Performance, 1990: 54*].

In terms of the linkages between MNCs and the economy, the Irish experience in the 1970s and 1980s contrasts with that of Singapore where FDI has developed extensive linkages with the local economy and has 'stimulated and often nurtured the creation of local suppliers who have increased their range and improved their quality, competitiveness and price ... so much so that they have eventually been able to export directly on their own account' [*Murray and Perrera, 1996: 98*]. However, the situation in Ireland has changed, even in the past eight years or so. Expenditure by MNCs on wages, raw materials and services in Ireland has grown at about eight per cent per year between 1989 and 1995 [*Forfas, 1997*]. In addition to this, IDA, the state development authority, is now actively promoting the quality of locally available supplies of raw materials and services. Their web page states that 'Ireland is one of the most attractive locations for investment by electronics companies because of its sub-supply base ...' [*IDA, 1998*].

One of the main changes in the 1980s to the incentives offered to firms was their extension to exported services, including financial services. Overall these changes resulted in the level of incentives given to overseas firms in the 1980s being less generous than that which prevailed in the 1970s [*Ruane, 1991*]. In addition to this, 'there was a reduction of grants in real terms per job to industry [between 1987 and 1997]' [*Sweeney, 1998: 101*]. There were further changes to policy in 1992 on the recommendation of the Culliton Report [*1992*] when the IDA was split up into Forbairt, which focused on indigenous industry, the IDA name was kept for foreign-owned industry, and Forfas, which was the policy-making body.

Companies automatically benefit from Ireland's low corporate tax rate, a mere ten per cent. Other incentives on offer over time, but which companies do not automatically qualify for, include financial assistance from the IDA for fixed asset investment[6] – cash grants, rent and interest subsidies, management training, research and development expenditures and marketing activities (administered in co-operation with the Irish Trade Board and only available to indigenous firms). The IDA's criteria for assisting MNCs relate to, among other things, whether it is a stand-alone activity, the number and quality of jobs, and the level of technological sophistication of the project. As in Singapore the conditions on which assistance is provided also include the extent to which the project is likely to contribute increased value-added in the Irish economy.

Firms can also avail themselves of the deductibility of interest payments on debt-financed capital and accelerated depreciation allowances on fixed-asset capital investment against corporate income tax. Ireland has also made use of incentives which result in the costs of finance being below the market rate. As Ruane notes, 'The Irish corporate tax system also lends itself to attractive options in tax-based financing, such as asset leasing, so that the cost of finance is well below the apparent market rate. In addition, the Business Expansion Scheme ... has also reduced the cost of finance by allowing funds invested in manufacturing enterprises which satisfy certain conditions to be offset against Irish income tax' [*Ruane, 1991: 358*]. There are elements of the Irish EP strategy which have much in common with that pursued by Singapore. But while the policies pursued by Singapore and Korea are deemed to be quite different, Ireland has elements in common to both (credit policy with Korea and FDI as pursued in Singapore). In addition to this, the effect of the credit policy pursued by Korea, has also had the same effect on the industrial structure in

Ireland resulting in large firms. While this may not be the only reason for the presence of large MNCs in Ireland it probably partly explains it.

Other assistance to exporters in the past was provided by the export credit insurance scheme. But, recently the government has decided that no further cover will be issued since 'the risk which such insurance currently imposes on the Exchequer is disproportionate to any benefit it may give to exporters' [*Department of Enterprise and Employment, 1998*].

As well as tax incentives and grants offered, an important part of Ireland's EP strategy has been the institutional support offered to firms. Various measures have been employed over time. In 1985 the Market Entry Development Scheme was established to provide assistance to firms to develop new markets via provision of repayable loans. There was, however, a very poor uptake of the scheme which suggests that it was not the lack of financing which was preventing them from entering export markets, but the risk of not succeeding [*Ruane, 1991*]. This programme was subsequently replaced by the Marketing Consultancy Programme in 1990. The aim was to provide non-repayable grants of up to 75 per cent of cost of marketing consultancy services to draw up marketing strategy. If the strategy was approved by the trade board, firms would be entitled to a grant for one third of the cost (up to a limit of £0.25million) together with a performance related loan up to one third of the cost. However, the performance related loan was repayable and repayment had to start within two years of commencement of the project. The repayment was made through a levy on new export sales. Other initiatives offered include the Special Trading House Scheme introduced in 1987 which enabled special marketing companies to be eligible for ten per cent corporate tax rate as well as BES status.

The emphasis of the marketing policy of the trade board shifted in the mid to late 1980s from marketing promotion (for example, trade fairs) to marketing development. It was around this time also that the trade board was required to become self-financing by way of a levy on new export sales achieved from projects assisted [*Review of Industrial Performance, 1990: 87*]. Increased emphasis was placed on providing assistance to indigenous small and medium sized firms in developing export markets in 1991 when ABT was founded (by amalgamating CTT, the old trade body and the Irish Goods Council). The remit of ABT is described by the Department of Enterprise and Employment as follows: 'The nature of assistance consists mainly of tailored market intelligence coupled with direct grant support and on-the-ground assistance through its overseas offices or through Irish embassies. Such assistance is aimed at addressing a number of continuing structural weaknesses in the indigenous exporting sector which are masked by global export performance *figures*' [*Department of Enterprise and Employment, 1998*].

The state development authority, the Industrial Development Authority, has stressed several factors to explain the inflow of FDI to Ireland. These include the availability of skilled labour, low tax and *generous* (our emphasis) incentives towards start-up costs including capital investment, training and employment costs, as well as towards investment in research and development projects [*IDA, 1998*]. In relation to the availability of skilled labour, Ireland's success on this front was reflected in the results of the *World Competitiveness Yearbook* (1997) illustrated in Figure 3.2. Ireland scored second only to Germany in terms of 'exceptional ability of skilled people' and achieved the best country score for having 'the most relevant educational system in Europe for a competitive economy'.

The IDA also emphasises that profits 'can be freely repatriated and are not subject to withholding taxes' [*IDA, 1998*]. In addition, to encourage firms to locate their research and development activities in an Irish subsidiary, patent royalty income on products developed in Ireland is tax free. This is an attempt to offset to some degree the disincentive to firms to locate research and development activities here due to the low rate of corporation tax; it is more beneficial to write these costs off in a high tax area [*Ruane, 1991*]. Another factor emphasised by the IDA is the low cost environment especially regarding labour and telecommunications costs. In relation to the latter they cite how these 'are increasingly a key consideration for international investors ... Ireland enjoys one of the lowest tariffs in Europe' [*IDA, 1998*].

Before leaving the topic of Irish industrial policy it is worth examining briefly some of the changes in the industrial structure which have resulted from Ireland's EP and industrialisation strategy, in particular, in terms of employment changes in the foreign (export) sectors versus indigenous sectors. Important structural change occurred in the industrial sector between the mid-1960s and the mid-1980s. Traditional industries such as textiles, clothing and footwear declined and chemicals and electronics increased in importance as foreign firms concentrated in these sectors. Between 1973 and 1983 employment in foreign-owned firms increased by 37 per cent while employment in indigenous manufacturing firms fell by 11 per cent [*Fitzpatrick and Kelly, 1985*]. These changes were paralleled by similar changes in output where the rate of growth of output in foreign-dominated sectors was consistently greater than that in indigenous sectors [*Ruane, 1991: 351*]. Even where output in traditional sectors did grow, this was not accompanied by increases in employment in these sectors. This gap between output growth and employment growth can in part be attributed to the adjustment to free trade as well as a shift away from labour-intensive to more capital-intensive industries. Some of these changes are illustrated in Table 3.1

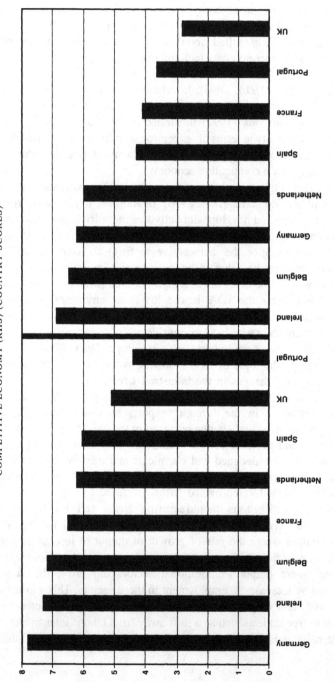

FIGURE 3.2

EXCEPTIONAL AVAILABILITY OF SKILLED PEOPLE (LHS) AND THE MOST RELEVANT EDUCATION SYSTEM IN EUROPE FOR A COMPETITIVE ECONOMY (RHS) (COUNTRY SCORES)

Source: IIMD, World Competitiveness Yearbook, 1996.

TABLE 3.1
INDUSTRIAL EMPLOYMENT BY SECTOR: CHANGES AND PERCENT SHARES
1973–90

Sector	1973–90			Share of Total (per cent)	
	Job Gain	Job Loss	Net Change	1973	1990
Non-Metallic Minerals	15578	18447	–2869	6.9	6.0
Chemicals	18927	14871	+4056	4.9	7.4
Metals and Engineering	121844	101106	+20738	21.3	33.4
Food	54705	65225	–10520	22.3	18.8
Drink and Tobacco	5140	9270	–4130	5.2	3.6
Textiles	18962	28488	–9526	9.4	5.3
Timber and Furniture	19838	21032	–1194	4.8	4.6
Clothing, Footwear, Leather	34413	48614	–14201	13.0	7.0
Paper and Printing	14091	15527	–1436	7.1	7.0
Miscellaneous	20980	17285	+3695	4.0	6.2
Mining, Quarrying & Turf	2331	3333	–1002	1.1	0.7
Total	326809	343198	–16389	100.0	100.0

Source: IDA Employment Survey Files.

While industrial output grew strongly over the 1970s and 1980s employment actually fell between 1973 and 1990. As is evident from Table 3.1, while there was little change in overall numbers employed, there was considerable change within sectors. The main decline in employment was in the traditional sectors of food, clothing and textiles. These falls were in part offset by increases in employment in chemicals and metal engineering. The decline in employment in traditional sectors, certainly in the 1980s was influenced by grants given automatically to new firms starting up, as it is likely to have given rise to some non-viable plants which subsequently closed. These figures illustrate the contrasting experience of foreign dominated sectors and indigenous sectors which has resulted in a dualistic industrial structure both in terms of output and employment.

Regarding the changes in the export sector, industrial and EP policy have given rise to three distinct changes in Ireland's export performance over the last quarter of a century or so. These are a shift away from reliance on the UK market and diversification towards the rest of the EU, a move out of agricultural exports and into 'high-tech' exports, and the increasing dominance of foreign MNCs in total Irish exports [*O'Donnell, 1997*]. The third feature has arisen, due to IDA policy to try and 'pick winners' and the consequent flow of FDI into particular sectors. This policy is still advocated today and the IDA's web page states that 'Ireland welcomes investment in manufacturing and internationally traded services in the following priority sectors: electronics, engineering, healthcare, consumer products, financial services, international services' [*IDA, 1998*]. The first two changes in the composition and market orientation of exports can be seen as a consequence of the increased presence of FDI. That is, during the 1950s and 1960s, FDI was concentrated in labour-intensive sectors such as clothing, footwear and textiles, but towards the end of the 1960s FDI began to move into more technologically advanced sectors such as electrical and electronic machinery and equipment, pharmaceuticals and so on, a trend which has increased to the present.

One feature of the dualistic industrial structure is the contrast in firms' size. By and large the indigenous sector comprises many small firms, whereas foreign owned firms are much larger. This was not always the case. At one stage there were large firms in the indigenous sector but as protection was removed these firms were unable to survive the increasing level of competition. Today, 'Irish industry is relatively lacking in large-scale enterprises and there is ... relatively little indigenous activity in those sectors in which economies of scale are most important' [*O'Malley, 1992: 109*]. The relatively poor performance of indigenous industry can be explained by the barriers to entry which these firms face in trying to get into these sectors, including difficulties relating to lack of marketing and technological strength which competitors have amassed. This in part explains why sectors dominated by MNCs do not have a strong indigenous presence. The view has been put forward that 'it is surprising that indigenous industry seemed unable to respond to the many incentives which were attracting foreign industry' [*Sweeney, 1998: 38*]. Given the barriers faced by indigenous industry identified by O'Malley, it does not appear so surprising. Since foreign MNCs have been able to operate here successfully suggests that explanations for the poor performance of indigenous industry which focus on the problems relating to the labour force or labour costs, tax system, and infrastructure, are not entirely convincing.

In looking at the industrial structure there is no debate regarding how these differences have evolved. It is due to EP policy which has resulted in large inflows of FDI into the Irish economy. But there is considerable debate about what factors, exactly, have been responsible for attracting the huge volume of FDI to Ireland. It is in the answer to this question that there is a critical role for Ireland's EP policy, but only as part of the explanation. Here, we attempt to give a very short summary of some of the views which have emerged recently on causes of Ireland's economic success.

Ireland's close proximity to European markets has undoubtedly contributed, along with the tax incentives offered. Membership of the EU has provided tariff-free access to its large market for the exports of Irish and foreign firms.[7] This is encouraging for the CEEC countries given their

FIGURE 3.3
RATE OF RETURN ON US INVESTMENT IN SERVICES IN EUROPE 1984–93
(PER CENT)

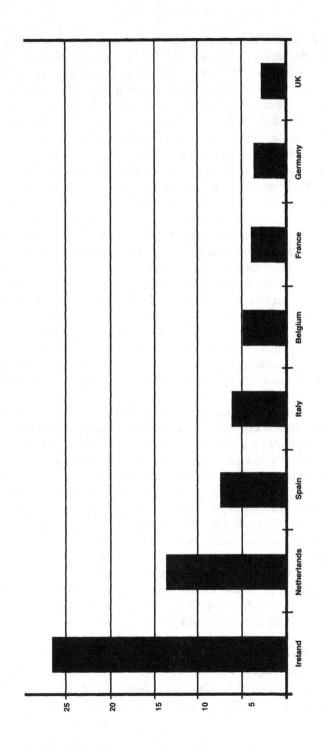

Source: US Department of Commerce.

proximity to the EU. Krugman [*1997*] cites changes in economic geography, such as the decreasing importance of transport costs, which have increased Ireland's attractiveness. While macroeconomic factors have played a role, changes in the business climate and the world economy in which firms operate and in particular the changing character of international trade, have also contributed. But, this does not explain why it is that other peripheral locations, where labour costs are low, have not performed as well as Ireland, for example, Portugal or Spain. This may be because Ireland has managed to develop a critical mass of firms in certain sectors where scale economies are important [*Krugman, 1997*] and this encouraged other firms to locate here, thereby reinforcing these advantages through demonstration and cascade effects. Interestingly, Krugman cites the CEEC as a possible threat to Ireland's current success. They can compete with Ireland on the basis of highly trained workers and relatively lower wages. But, in a comment which underscores the importance of other factors in Ireland's success in attracting FDI, he notes that 'at the moment lack of infrastructure and political uncertainty hold back exploitation of that resource; but this could change and could pose a threat to Ireland's special advantages' [*Krugman, 1997: 52*].

The profit rates which FDI have been able to enjoy here may also act as a spur both for other American companies and non-US companies. US Department of Commerce figures show that Ireland has offered a higher rate of return than other major European economies over the 1984–93 period (see Figure 3.3).

In explaining Ireland's success, Sachs [*1997*] focuses on the relationship between government expenditure (and so taxation) and FDI. His thesis is that in the early days, FDI policy with its generous grants and corporate taxes operated together with high levels of government expenditure. Following the fiscal spree of the late 1970s and early 1980s there was a dramatic cutback in government expenditure in the late 1980s. The result of this Sachs argues: 'Ireland's rapid growth was put on course ... and supported a surge in export-led growth' [*Sachs, 1997: 59*]. The importance of fiscal discipline has also been noted by de la Fuente and Vives [*1997*]. Coinciding with the turnaround in fiscal policy, the success of attracting FDI in recent years was also helped by 'the renewed interest of American and other international firms in gaining a foothold in Europe ... which came with the ... accession of new members in 1986 and the formulation of clear plans for the completion of the Single Market in 1992' [*de la Fuente and Vives, 1997: 126*].

Specific institutional and structural factors have also been identified as favouring the rapid growth of Ireland's exports and GDP. The Global Competitiveness Report [*World Economic Forum, 1997*] identifies four factors where Ireland has had favourable policies relative to most other EU countries; labour markets, corporate taxation, exchange rate policy and technology transfer via foreign direct investment. While it concentrates on the last five years or so, it nevertheless gives an indication of factors which have been important in the turnaround of the Irish economy. Overall, in terms of the most competitive countries, Ireland has risen from 22nd to 15th between 1996 and 1997.

Clearly, in Ireland's EP strategy it can be said that FDI was of overriding importance. It was attracted by the range of incentives offered by the state development authority, as well as by a well-educated highly-skilled workforce in a relatively low cost and stable macroeconomic environment. In more recent times Ireland's success is due to developments not confined to internal policies. Indeed its attractiveness as a location for FDI has been enhanced by changes in economic geography and moves for further integration by the European Union. But the policies pursued for the best part of three decades gave rise to a dualistic industrial structure where indigenous industries were poorly catered for and so were not major players in terms of Ireland's export success. While policy changed somewhat during the mid-1980s, the contribution of indigenous industry to Ireland's overall export performance lags significantly behind the contribution of foreign-owned companies.

LESSONS OF EXPERIENCE

What are the broader lessons which the CEEC can take from these examples? We summarise briefly the main points from our analysis of export policy in these four instances by classifying these 'lessons' by the degree of government intervention, followed by the type and extent of import controls and export incentives.

There are many difficulties in taking lessons from other countries' experiences and trying to apply them to the CEEC. For example, 'East Asian infant exports were concentrated in far fewer products than Eastern Europe; this simplified EP in terms of investment allocation and commercial diplomacy' [*Amsden et al., 1994: 106*]. This difference may require greater efforts on the part of governments to ensure the success and effectiveness of an EP strategy. Starting from different levels of development necessarily complicates the situation. Second, 'world conditions are less favourable to emerging exporters in the 1990s and east Asia was not in a severe depression such as that faced by Eastern Europe in the 1990s' [*Amsden et al., 1994: 99*]. Again, this would indicate that more effort is required if EP is to be effective in the environment facing the CEECs today than for the south east Asian nations faced in the past.

An EP strategy encompasses direct and indirect means of promoting exports. Firms are aware that it is not just export subsidies, for example, which comprise an EP strategy but many more measures besides. There

51

should be no misconceptions regarding what EP is together with an understanding of what can be expected from such policies. This awareness by firms is an important element of the success, not only of institutional support services provided for exporters, but of an overall EP strategy. In addition to this, it is recognised that governments in the CEECs may face additional barriers in trying to pursue an EP strategy in terms of lack of support from firms and hostility to the government providing help. It is crucial that efforts are made to overcome such barriers.

The general lessons indicated by the experiences of the countries which we have reviewed here are set out below. Much of the debate surrounding the success of the south east Asian economies has centred on the role of government. On the one hand there is the view that market forces and market friendly policies lay behind much of the success, while on the other, there is the view that the state and government are integral to any explanation of the determinants of the unprecedented growth in these economies [*Kwon, 1998; Rasiah, 1998; Cheng et al., 1996; Panchamurkhi, 1996*]. More recently, it has been acknowledged that the role of the state in the development of these economies 'has gone beyond what would have been achieved by the exclusive reliance on market forces and private sector initiatives' [*Jomo, 1996: 13*]. As outlined here in the review of the EP strategies pursued by Korea and Taiwan, government intervention was pervasive and was, by and large, effective; yet this does not mean that is a panacea for all [*Wade, 1990*]. As Koteva notes 'incompetent government intervention is worse than no intervention' [*Koteva, 1992: 28*]. A case in point here is Portugal where there was massive government intervention but this resulted in ineffective state assistance due mainly to excessive bureaucracy. In addition to this, the Korean experience has illustrated that the huge extent of government intervention in credit-rationing during the 1970s resulted in, among other things, a severely underdeveloped financial sector which is still in need of major reform. The drive to promote investment in specific sectors, notably during the heavy chemical industrialisation drive in the 1970s, resulted in a large number of failures. The lessons from the experiences of these countries indicate that the type, nature and degree of government intervention must be motivated not by the state's desire to intervene but due to specific failures in the market-place [*Jomo, 1996;* see also Chapter 1]. Where these failures exist, the state 'must remain a large and active participant in the economic system' with quality and commitment being important elements of success together with detailed analysis of the market failures in order to formulate effective policy prescriptions [*Killick and Stevens, 1991: 689*]. Furthermore, government support should be dynamic in adjusting to new circumstances and the changing international environment [*Jomo, 1996*].

From the experience of these countries, we summarise here some guidelines regarding the use of import controls and export incentives as part of an EP strategy. The lessons from export incentives rather than import controls are emphasised given that there is likely to be more scope for the CEECs to use the former measures than the latter.

There are a great variety of import controls to choose from including quotas, import licensing, import taxes or surcharges. The experience of Ireland and Singapore contrasts sharply here with that of Korea and Taiwan; free trade prevailed to a much greater extent in the former than in the latter cases, where extensive import controls were used. The lessons from import controls used in other countries can be summarised as follows. First, 'East Asian evidence suggest that protection can also be used in combination with other measures to foster the creation of internationally competitive industries' [*Wade, 1990: 361*]. However it is likely that any country who pursued a strategy today similar to that taken by Korea in the past, would risk countervailing actions and retaliations by trading partners in today's somewhat more liberalised world trading environment. Second, import controls can be executed by some less visible measures than quantitative restrictions, for example, an approval mechanism. Third, import controls should be selective, the aim of which is to enhance strategic inputs for exporting industries tied to export performance criteria. Fourth, the trend should be towards a reduction in tariffs to a uniform rate, or at least towards lessening the dispersion of tariff rates to avoid unintended incentives to particular industries.

The use of export incentives is designed to eliminate an anti-export bias or to create a pro-export bias. Instruments used to achieve this include export subsidies, export credit, and tax incentives. The main lessons to be taken from the use of export incentives are as follows. First, export incentives, although not an indispensable part of an EP strategy, are apt to form part of an overall strategy to promote exports. For example, while Chile did not employ export incentives, export growth was still achieved but would have been even higher had export incentives been used [*Papageorgiou et al., 1991: 282*]. When export incentives are used, evidence suggests that exports are likely to be of a higher quality and technological level where incentives are given for certain sectors. Again we encounter the problems of which industries to select and precisely what export incentives to recommend. While obviously 'various export incentives have their pluses and minuses and it is difficult to give a universally valid recipe of which are best and what the combination should be' [*Koteva, 1992: 40*], there are some general conclusions indicated by the experiences of each of the countries here.

First, Ireland's experience indicates that indirect incentives can be as important if not more important than direct incentives. Indirect incentives, such as preferential rates of profit on taxes have also been important elements of the EP strategies pursued by Korea, Taiwan and Singapore. Second, where effective tariffs are high and there is no risk of countervailing measures from other countries, preferential access to imported inputs for exporters is an effective means of promoting exports. Third, when export incentives are provided, they should be strong enough to offset the anti-export bias from any import controls which might exist. Some commentators (notably Amsden,[*1989*]) believe that the reason that Korea has experienced success where others have encountered failures is due to the fact that the anti-export bias due to import barriers was offset by export subsidies; however, the export incentives offered in countries such as Brazil and Mexico which attempted to pursue the same path, were insufficient to offset their high import barriers.

The experience of the South East Asian countries and Ireland cannot offer universal prescriptions for other countries wishing to emulate their success. What we have set out here are some guidelines for other countries to take into account in developing and formulating an EP strategy. We now turn our attention to investigating the extent to which the commodity composition and market destination of exports can explain the export performance of certain countries, or whether other factors may explain export performance better and so offer options for improving export performance.

A COMPARISON OF EXPORT GROWTH IN SELECTED ASIAN AND EUROPEAN ECONOMIES

The previous section set out the main elements of policy pursued by some of the Asian Tigers and Ireland. It reviewed changes in the industrial structure of these countries which have resulted from these policies. In this section we aim to take the analysis one step further by establishing the extent to which two particular changes in export structure have affected overall export growth. That is, we examine how export performance in these countries has been influenced by changes in the commodity structure and market destination pattern of their exports. In addition to this, we try to assess the extent to which other factors such as institutional support for exporting, technological improvements, and other price and non-price factors have affected their export performance. The layout of this section is as follows. We first detail the methodology and data used to assess the influence of these factors on export performance. We then discuss the results and draw some conclusions.

METHODOLOGY AND DATA

Constant market share (CMS) analysis, developed by Leamer and Stern [*1970*] has been extensively used in assessing how a country's export performance is affected by the commodity composition and geographical destination of its exports [cf. *Gehlhar and Volrath, 1997; Feldman, 1994; Dumble, 1994; Chow and Kellman, 1993; Thirlwall and Gibson, 1992; OECD, 1989; MacBean and Nguyen, 1987; Panoutsopoulos, 1981; Kennedy and Dowling, 1975; Little et al., 1970*]. This method is a variant of shift-share analysis which is widely applied in analysing unemployment and regional policy [e.g., *Barry and Hannan, 1996; Moore et al., 1986; Tyler, 1980*]. Since the novelty here is in the application of this methodology to Irish data, readers are referred to Leamer and Stern [*1970*] for a detailed derivation of the methodology. The essence of CMS analysis is that changes in a country's export market share can be attributed to a number of distinct effects; the average change in a country's exports, associated with the general rise in world export growth; the commodity effect, reflecting patterns of commodity specialisation; import demand in the specific markets which a country exports to, and a residual associated with neither of these effects.[8]

Thus, a country's export growth above or below the world trend can be explained by the commodity composition, market destination of exports and a residual. If a country is experiencing rapid growth in exports relative to world export growth, it will have above trend growth in exports. This indicates that a country increases its share of world export markets. If exports are growing slowly relative to world export growth then the country's share of total world exports declines. The commodity composition effect, indicates to what extent a country's exports are concentrated in products which grow faster or slower than the world average for all exports. The commodity composition effect will be positive if a country's exports are concentrated in commodities for which import demand is growing faster than total world exports and this term will be negative if a country's exports are concentrated in commodities for which import demand is growing slower than growth in total world exports.

The market effect, captures the influence of import demand growth in the markets for which exports are destined. This term will be positive if import demand in export markets is growing faster than the world average and negative if demand is growing slower than the world average.

The residual is the proportion of export growth which is not explained by either the commodity or market effects. This term captures the influence of many different factors on a country's export share and is sometimes labelled as a 'competitiveness' effect [e.g., *Dumble,1994; Chow and Kellman, 1993; Thirlwall and Gibson, 1992, Leamer and Stern, 1970*]. Some studies interpret the residual as capturing the influence of internal forces on a country's export market share. For example, Little *et al.* [*1970: 248*] take the residual as prima facie evidence that 'countries have some control over their level of export earnings' [also *Chow and Kellman, 1993*]. Dumble [*1994: 225*] notes that the value of the residual 'could be the result of any factor which increases the demand for and supply of ... [a country's] ... products ... which are not directly related to the regional or commodity composition of exports'. An important supply factor of relevance for Ireland which Dumble notes, is that the influence of FDI may be captured in the residual via increasing the supply of tradable goods. The residual term also captures factors, such as, efficiency in marketing, increased reliability, efficiency in order filling. [*Leamer and Stern, 1970*] price and quality competitiveness, other supply side effects [*OECD, 1989*] and whether a country has a good export organisation [*Lamfalussy, 1963*]. Thirlwall and Gibson [*1992: 310–11*] note that the residual reflects the change in export shares due to 'non-price factors, supply constraints ... and a host of factors connected with competitiveness and the characteristics of the products exported'. Fagerberg [*1988: 356*] finds that regression results for 15 OECD countries during 1961–83 show factors related to 'technology and capacity are...very important for medium and long-run differences in growth of [export] market shares ... while cost competitiveness plays a more limited role than commonly assumed'. Thus, this term can reflect any number of factors which influence the supply of and demand for a country's exports and can be positive or negative.

The EU countries in this analysis are Ireland, Greece, Portugal, the United Kingdom (UK) and Germany. It was felt that these countries represented varying degrees of success in terms of their export performance. For these countries, all data were from the OECD, are 1-digit SITC and are expressed in current values (US$million). With regard to the SEA countries, we do not calculate the CMSA results here but draw the results from an existing study by Chow and Kellman [*1993*]. Thus, the time period for this analysis was dictated by the existing results for the SEA countries, namely 1970, 1975, 1980, 1985 and 1990.[9]

RESULTS

We begin by discussing the overall export growth of the European economies over the period 1970–90 in Table 3.2. The figures in this table illustrate the extent to which each economy has experienced export growth greater or less than the world average. All figures are expressed as a percentage of the value of exports in the base period.

These results show that the experience of these countries has not been uniform over time. Ireland appears to have fared better than any of the other economies, with exports growing faster than the world average in every sub-period between 1970 and 1990. While Greece experienced above trend growth in the 1970–80 period, it experienced relatively slow export growth subsequent to this. Although not noted for its successful export performance, Portugal's export growth has been faster than the world rate in every sub-

TABLE 3.2
EXPORT GROWTH – THE EUROPEAN ECONOMIES*

	Ireland	Greece	Portugal	UK	Germany
1970–75	55.7	89.7	–59.1	–36.8	–2.8
1975–80	51.3	8.3	20.6	45.2	–3.4
1980–85	19.4	–13.4	22.3	–13.0	–6.1
1985–90	39.2	–18.7	97.5	–7.2	27.0

Source: own calculations from OECD data.
Note: *(per cent) growth greater (+) or less (–) than the world average

period since 1975. This may in part reflect the fact that Portuguese exports started from a relatively low base. The UK and Germany have the least impressive export growth of all countries, below trend in three out of four of the sub-periods. Thus, a comparison of the export growth rate of each country with the growth rate of world exports, illustrates that some of these countries have clearly been more successful than others. The question is to what extent this export growth is a function of the particular products these countries exported and the particular markets they exported to? To answer this question, the commodity and market effects are examined in Tables 3.3 and 3.4 below.

The value of the commodity effect shows the impact of a country's commodity structure on its export growth. The results for the commodity effect for Ireland reveal that on the whole, the above trend growth of Irish exports was not due to the commodities exported. Even though Irish exports were concentrated in commodities which grew faster than the world average between 1970 and 1975 and 1980 and 1985, the size of the commodity effect is small relative to the above trend growth. Portugal's export growth was slightly better than for Greece but still relatively poor for half the 1970–90 period. The same is true of the UK (albeit for different sub-periods). For Germany, with the fastest export growth, the commodity effect is rather small, but at least positive in three out of four periods.

TABLE 3.3
THE COMMODITY EFFECT (PER CENT) – THE EUROPEAN ECONOMIES

	Ireland	Greece	Portugal	UK	Germany
1970–75	14.6	–10.6	–10.8	–2.9	0.5
1975–80	–7.5	4.2	0.7	0.3	–0.9
1980–85	–5.6	–6.8	–4.3	2.0	2.3
1985–90	4.9	–9.9	3.7	11.0	7.3

Source: own calculations from OECD data.

Several observations may be of use to the CEEC countries. First, the commodity effect for the countries in this analysis has been negative in most periods. This underscores the importance for them in the future of expanding exports in commodities which can impact positively on export growth: commodities for which import demand is growing faster, rather than slower, than the world average. Ireland's policy of attracting high-tech companies is one possible method of achieving such an objective. At first glance these results may not bode well in terms of the impact of a country's commodity structure on exports, but as Ireland's example shows this situation can be altered. Second, the commodity composition of exports, in general, does not appear to be significant in explaining the above trend export growth of these countries. It only explains a small proportion of export growth in each country, with the exception of Germany. There the magnitude of the commodity effect and overall export growth are relatively similar. Thus, even if a country does not have a commodity structure weighted towards ones which are experiencing faster than average world, the negative effect on the country's export growth is usually small. But, it may not always be the case: for the UK between 1985 and 1990 and Greece between 1980 and 1990, the commodity effect contributed substantially to the trend in export growth. For the CEEC countries, this would seem to indicate that a 'wrong' commodity structure can sometimes be costly in terms of export growth.

How do the results for the market effect compare for the different countries? That is, can we establish the extent to which import demand in a country's export markets affects their export growth? Overall, the destination pattern of exports has impacted more favourably on export performance than the commodity effect; with the exception of Portugal and Ireland, the market effect is positive in three out of four sub-periods. Thus, the targeting of buoyant export markets would appear to represent an option for countries wishing to improve their export performance. It may also be easier to influence the market destination of exports than to alter their commodity structure. The former would require industrial policy measures and initiatives, while the latter could be achieved via institutional support for exporting. Also, it could be applied to existing exporters without needing to attract new firms to specific product areas. The large negative value for the market effect for Ireland for 1970–75 stems from the relatively slow growth in Irish export markets for agricultural products. This result is surprising given that it was during this period that Ireland joined the European Community. The explanation may be relatively slow growth in the UK, the main market for Irish agricultural exports then.

Two qualifications need to be added at this juncture. First, the CEEC countries may be able to improve export performance by switching to more buoyant markets but note that the sign of the market effect is the same for all

TABLE 3.4
THE MARKET EFFECT (PER CENT) – THE EUROPEAN ECONOMIES

	Ireland	Greece	Portugal	UK	Germany
1970–75	–123.8	24.8	–28.4	1.1	0.03
1975–80	2.8	5.8	5.7	4.6	5.3
1980–85	–3.3	–3.7	–5.7	–3.7	–5.5
1985–90	14.5	6.1	18.7	3.1	16.1

Source: own calculations from OECD data.

countries across all sub-periods (apart from Portugal and Ireland in 1970–75). This means that countries may find it hard to buck the trends in import demand. All economies seemed to have been subject to the same trend in import demand in the 1980–85 period (negative) and also in the 1985–90 period (positive). But it could be that their exports have similar destinations. Second, while the market effect is predominantly positive, it is not always as large as the commodity effect. In Ireland, for example, the negative commodity effect generally outweighed the market effect. Also, for Greece, the same applies between 1980 and 1990 and in two out of four periods for the UK. Better choice of markets may raise exports, but, perhaps, not much.

TABLE 3.5
THE RESIDUAL/COMPETITIVENESS EFFECT (PER CENT) – THE EUROPEAN
ECONOMIES

	Ireland	Greece	Portugal	UK	Germany
1970–75	165.0	75.5	–19.8	–35.1	–3.5
1975–80	56.0	–1.7	14.2	40.3	–7.8
1980–85	28.3	–2.9	32.3	–11.3	–2.9
1985–90	19.9	–14.9	75.2	0.7	3.6

Source: own calculations from OECD data.

The influence of factors captured in the residual has varied both over time and across countries. Ireland is the only country for which the residual is positive in all sub-periods, and also the largest of all the influences on export growth. It is also the only country which experienced above trend growth in all sub-periods. Thus the relatively strong growth in Irish exports between 1970 and 1990 cannot be explained entirely by relatively rapid growth in the particular commodities Ireland has exported or the particular markets Ireland has exported to; Irish exports have increased by more than that 'predicted' by the constant market share analysis. Unfortunately, one of the limitations of this analysis is that it does not specify which factors precisely have contributed to the growth in exports which is captured in the residual.

Is the residual of similar importance in other countries? The simple answer to this question is no. In none of the other countries has the residual been as large and positive as in Ireland. Thus, for Greece, the residual is negative in three out of four sub-periods. At different times (1970–75, 1985–90) the residual has been the dominant influence on Greek export growth, but at other times the market effect (1975–80) and the commodity effect (1980–85) have been more important. For Germany, too, the residual was negative in three out of four sub-periods. The dominant influence on German export growth was the residual/competitiveness effect between 1970–80, and the market effect between 1980–90. While the importance of other factors in the UK and Portuguese economies can be seen by the dominance of the residual/competitiveness effect in three out of four of the sub-periods. These policies did not meet with similar success in both economies. For the UK, the effect was negative between 1970 and 1975 and 1980 and 1985, while in Portugal, it was positive in all periods (1975–90).

There appears to be no clear pattern here between the magnitude and sign of the residual/competitiveness effect and the overall level of export growth above or below trend. However, these results seem to show that for the most successful European country in terms of export performance, Ireland, such a clear link does exist. What differentiates the experience of Ireland from those of the other European economies in this analysis is the clear role which can be accorded to the residual.

TABLE 3.6
EXPORT GROWTH – THE ASIAN ECONOMIES*

	South Korea	*Hong Kong*	*Taiwan*	*Singapore*
1970–75	387.4	37.8	246.0	711.8
1975–80	128.9	104.8	208.8	191.1
1980–85	55.9	15.9	80.8	56.6
1985–90	52.5	−21.8	0.6	128.2

*(per cent) growth greater (+) or less (−) than the world average
Source: Chow and Kellman [*1993: 39*].

Table 3.6 clearly illustrates how it came about that these South East Asian nations were nicknamed the 'Tigers'. Not only did they experience export growth faster than the world average in almost all sub-periods, but the actual strength of that export growth was quite phenomenal, although not as strong on the whole in the 1980s as for the 1970s. The experience of the Tigers differs quite substantially from that of the majority of the European countries in our analysis, both with regard to the sign as well as the magnitude of the overall level of export growth. Ireland is the one exception to this. Whereas the European economies experienced a mixture of above/below trend growth between 1970 and 1990, Ireland, despite quite poor commodity export structure for most of the period, was the only European country which experienced above trend growth for the entire period. Purely on the basis of these results it is perhaps easy to see why Ireland has been called the Celtic or Emerald Tiger. Having established that there are major differences in terms of the overall level of export growth in the two sets of countries, can we detect similar differences in the roles played by the commodity, market and competitiveness effects?

TABLE 3.7
THE COMMODITY EFFECT (PER CENT) – THE ASIAN ECONOMIES

	South Korea	Hong Kong	Taiwan	Singapore
1970–75	8.2	11.5	10.9	8.3
1975–80	−1.7	−0.1	0.2	1.1
1980–85	1.1	7.0	5.1	11.2
1985–90	1.4	4.9	2.2	4.4

Source: Chow and Kellman [1993: 39].

The most striking result for the commodity effect for the Tigers is that it has been positive for all countries in almost all periods. Even in the two instances where the commodity effect is negative (for Hong Kong and South Korea in the 1975–80 period), it was small, especially when compared to their overall export growth. This pattern contrasts sharply with the European Economies, where the commodity structure exerted a mixed influence on exports over time. Also, while the commodity effect differed across the European countries, the values for the commodity effect for the Tigers are fairly uniform in each sub-period. This may be due to the relative stability of the commodity structure of exports across the Tigers. For both groups of countries the size of the commodity effect is small relative to the above/below trend export growth. Herein lies one of the lessons for the CEEC countries from the export experience of the Tigers. The experience of the European countries indicated that getting the commodity structure of exports 'wrong' proved costly. But the experience of the Tigers illustrates that even if the commodity structure is 'right', this may only be of limited benefit in improving export growth. But, if the commodity structure of the Tigers cannot fully explain their export success, what role did the market destination pattern of exports and the 'competitiveness' effect play?

The results for the Asian Tigers for the market effect are less encouraging than for the commodity effect. Whereas the commodity effect was positive in almost all sub-periods for all countries, for all the Tigers for both the 1970–75

61

and also the 1985–90 period, the market effect was negative. During these sub-periods, import demand for products which the Tigers concentrated on exporting actually grew more slowly than world import demand for those products. Between these times, however, the market effect for all Tigers was positive. All Tigers seem to export to similarly behaved markets. This is supported by data in Chow and Kellman [*1993*] which shows that roughly the same proportion of exports was destined for the EC, Japan and the US markets. The differences in the actual magnitude of these effects are probably due to differences in the particular commodities exported by each Tiger to each market.

TABLE 3.8
THE MARKET EFFECT (PER CENT) – THE ASIAN ECONOMIES

	South Korea	Hong Kong	Taiwan	Singapore
1970–75	–16.0	–11.2	–15.6	–9.9
1975–80	2.2	2.3	3.1	4.3
1980–85	19.4	11.7	27.0	15.0
1985–90	–15.1	–17.0	–22.8	–15.6

Source: Chow and Kellman [*1993: 39*].

These results indicate first, that the negative market effect across countries in the same sub-periods may reflect similarity in terms of the destinations of exports and that even the Tigers were not immune to dips in world import demand. Second, even the Tigers when successful in targeting relatively fast growing export markets, this may only be of limited help in increasing export growth and improving export performance.

TABLE 3.9
THE RESIDUAL/COMPETITIVENESS EFFECT (PER CENT) – THE ASIAN
ECONOMIES

	South Korea	Hong Kong	Taiwan	Singapore
1970–75	395.2	37.5	250.7	713.4
1975–80	128.4	102.6	205.5	185.7
1980–85	35.4	–2.8	48.7	30.4
1985–90	66.2	–9.7	21.2	139.4

Source: Chow and Kellman [*1993: 39*].

Given that the commodity and market effects only explain a small proportion of the overall growth above trend for the Tigers, this can only mean that the most significant role in export growth must be accorded to the residual/competitiveness effect. The results in Table 3.9 show clearly that this indeed is that case; for all countries, the residual/competitiveness effect accounts for most of the above trend growth in exports. The exception is Hong Kong between 1980 and 1990, where the residual was actually negative. Although the role played by factors captured in the residual is significant the size of the residual has diminished over time. The experience of the Asian Tigers is different from the European Economies (with the exception of Ireland). But for CEEC countries the scope for policies to expand the residual positively is limited by the rules governing international trade.

IRELAND – INSIGHT INTO THE RESIDUAL

Competitiveness is a multi-dimensional concept which captures both price and non-price factors. The residual in constant market share analysis can be interpreted as an indicator of external competitiveness. This section supplements the CMSA with several more conventional measures of price competitiveness. There is considerable debate in the literature regarding the concept, definition and measurement of competitiveness. Much of the debate centres around trying to arrive at a single measure or set of measures deemed to represent competitiveness. Notwithstanding this lack of consensus, one of the most widely used indicators of price competitiveness is movement in real exchange rate indices. These indices can be based on various cost or price measures but of particular importance in international comparisons are real exchange rate indices based on unit labour costs in manufacturing, unit labour costs in the total economy, deflators of total expenditure and consumer prices [*Deutsche Bundesbank, 1994*]. These indices provide useful indications of competitiveness, but any single measure cannot adequately reflect all the facets of competitiveness given the difficulty with quantifying non-price factors such as quality, reliability and so on. As the Deutsche Bundesbank outlines 'it must always be remembered that ... these yardsticks can never reproduce the entire competition scenario in all its complexity; they address only one aspect - albeit a particularly important one – namely, competitiveness in terms of costs and prices' [*Deutsche Bundesbank, 1994: 46*]. We begin by presenting and discussing some real exchange rate indices based on the manufacturing sector and then proceed to review indices of more broad based measures.[10]

Real exchange rate indices for the manufacturing sector are frequently based on unit labour costs (RULC). These indices by and large are interpreted as a good indication of a country's competitiveness 'because manufactured products generally make up by far the greatest share of the goods traded internationally by industrial countries' [*Deutsche Bundesbank, 1994: 50*]. Ireland is no exception and in 1995 manufactured goods were 87 per cent of merchandise exports. This index is plotted in Figure 3.4 alongside relative normalised unit labour costs (RNULC) in manufacturing. The purpose of normalising the RULC index is 'to remove distortions arising from cyclical

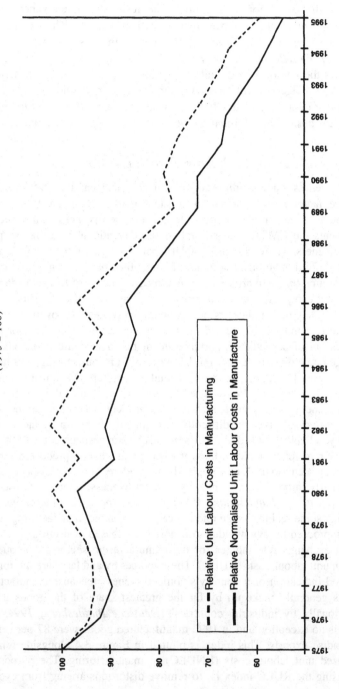

FIGURE 3.4
REAL EFFECTIVE EXCHANGE RATES FOR MANUFACTURING IN IRELAND
(1975 = 100)

- - - - Relative Unit Labour Costs in Manufacturing

——— Relative Normalised Unit Labour Costs in Manufacture

Source: IMF International Financial Statistics.

FIGURE 3.5
REAL EFFECTIVE EXCHANGE RATE INDICES FOR MANUFACTURING AND BROADER-BASED INDICES IN IRELAND
(1975=100)

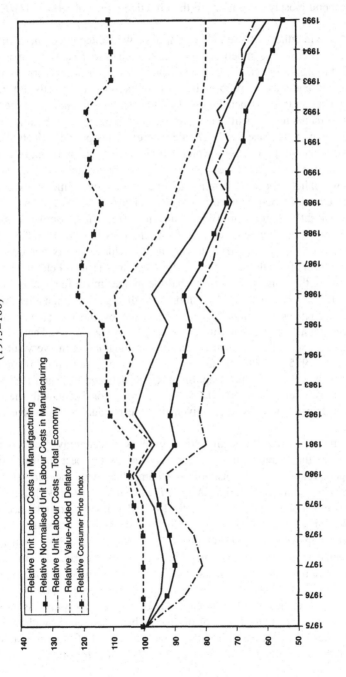

Source: IMF International Financial Statistics and European Economy.

movements which occur largely because changes in hours worked do not correspond closely to changes in the effective inputs of labour' [*IMF, 1997: 891*].

A rise in either of these indices implies a worsening in competitiveness as the ratio of costs to competitors rises (either due to Irish costs rising or others' costs falling). Conversely, a fall in the index implies an improvement in competitiveness as the ratio of Irish to competitors' costs falls. Interpreting the indices in this manner, Figure 3.4 indicates that Ireland has experienced improvements in competitiveness, as the underlying trend in both indices has been downwards since 1981. The decline over this period reflects the rapid growth in labour productivity which has not been offset by rising labour costs in the manufacturing sector or an upward movement of the real exchange rate. The two indices appear to be reasonably consistent over time. RULC actually indicated a deterioration in competitiveness between 1975 and 1981, with the index slightly higher in 1981 than in 1975. This compares with an improvement in competitiveness, albeit slight, as indicated by the RNULC index over the same period. Note that the behaviour of the two indices in this regard differs from the same indices for Germany. That is, Feldman [*1994*] in examining the same indices finds that the indices move fairly close together up until the early to mid-1980s, but begin to diverge somewhat after this time.

The changes in competitiveness indicated by the movements in these indices are also consistent with the results from the CMSA. That is, CMSA results indicated that there was a positive residual effect in every sub-period between 1975 and 1990 and both indices indicate improvements in competitiveness (with the exception of RULC between 1975 and 1980). Thus, for this sub-period, the RNULC index is more consistent with the CMSA results than the RULC index, given that the residual was positive for this period.

It has been recognised that for a small open economy such as Ireland, RULC in the manufacturing sector may not be the best indicator of cost competitiveness and the use of this competitiveness measure should be approached with due caution [*McGettigan and Nugent, 1995*]. Among the drawbacks associated with this indicator is that it does not take account of changes in the capital/labour ratio. In Ireland, there was a shift away from labour-intensive into capital-intensive industries in the 1980s which was not paralleled in its trading partners. Thus, the RULC during this time would exaggerate improvement in Ireland's competitive position. In addition to this, the RULC index may also overstate improvements in competitiveness as it does not take account of increases in the price of capital (as labour is substituted for capital). Many of these drawbacks associated with the RULC are borne out by the empirical tests conducted by McGettigan and Nugent. Given these and other problems [e.g., *Lipschitz and McDonald, 1991; Turner and Van't dack, 1993; Wickham, 1993; Marsh and Tokarick, 1994*] associated with RULC for the manufacturing sector, RULC for the whole economy, while still not perfect, may represent a better indicator of competitiveness. Figure 3.5. below shows the behaviour of RULC for the whole economy over the period 1975-95. This figure also contains real exchange rate indices based on the consumer price index and the value-added deflator. The latter index can be interpreted as a measure of costs per unit of output 'but in this case it covers total costs which include the prices of all factors of production and therefore supplement and extend the information based on unit labour costs' [*Feldman, 1994: 6*].

There are a number of interesting points indicated by Figure 3.5. First, the movement of the real exchange rate based on RULC in the total economy points to greater improvements in productivity in the total economy than in the manufacturing sector alone (at least up until 1989 where the RULC index for the total economy fell faster than the RULC for manufacturing). Secondly, the correlation of RULC in the total economy with that in manufacturing suggests that growth of RULC in manufacturing has not differed greatly from the growth of RULC for the economy as a whole. Manufacturing has been very important to the growth of the Irish economy; as its share has increased over time, the indices have tended to converge. Thirdly, what is also striking is that the levels of the broader based indices suggest a much smaller depreciation (even appreciation) of the Irish pound since the early 1980s than those based on unit labour costs alone. Considering that both indices are above the unit labour cost indices, this is consistent with the contention that RULC in manufacturing alone may overstate improvements in competitiveness in Ireland in the 1980s [*McGettigan and Nugent, 1995*]. Certainly *prior* to 1986, the broader based indices were increasing while the other indices fell between 1975 and 1986. However, despite the fact that there are different indications of competitiveness given by the indices based on ULC and the broader based indices at different times, all indices are lower in 1995 than in 1986 indicating unambiguously that Ireland's competitiveness improved over that period even if there is debate regarding the extent of this improvement.

In comparing the indices with the results from the CMSA, it has been noted that those based on RULC are consistent with the result that for the sub-period 1975-80, Ireland's competitiveness improved; likewise for these indices for the sub-periods 1980–85 and 1985–90. However, neither the CPI nor the value-added deflator indices indicate improvements in competitiveness between 1975–80 or 1980–85. While it might thus appear that these indices are completely at odds with the results for the CMSA for these sub-periods, Abeysinghe and Yeok [*1998*] note that an increase in the real exchange rate index could in fact be associated with increased export volume if the import content of exports is large.

In comparing what the real exchange rates indicate as to changes in the direction of Ireland's competitiveness over the period, we conclude that Ireland did indeed experience improvements in competitiveness relative to its competitors, as suggested by the CMSA results, and that this is likely to have continued post-1990. As to changes in the magnitude of that competitiveness, those indicated by the broader-based value-added deflator may be more accurate than the changes suggested by unit labour costs in manufacturing alone. But, while there may be debate regarding the magnitude of the improvements in competitiveness, there is little doubt regarding their direction over time.

CONCLUSIONS

This chapter began by reviewing the export promotion policies, measures and strategies pursued by the south east Asian Tigers and Ireland. The general lessons indicated by the experiences of the countries were outlined; these included recommendations regarding the type, nature and degree of government intervention. This should be motivated by specific failures in the market place and be dynamic in adjusting to the changing international environment. Guidelines were also given regarding the use of import controls and export incentives as part of an EP strategy. Extensive use of import controls in today's somewhat more liberalised world trading environment means that countries are at greater risk of countervailing actions and retaliations by trading partners than was the case in the past. Where they are permitted, they should be selective and enhance strategic inputs for exporting industries. Export incentives, although not an indispensable part of an EP strategy, are apt to form part of an overall strategy to promote exports. Again, they are likely to be most effective when selective. Ireland's experience indicates that indirect incentives, such as preferential rates of profit on taxes, can be as important if not more important than direct incentives. These incentives should also be strong enough to offset any anti-export bias from import controls.

The second part of this chapter set out to compare export performance of certain European countries, with the South East Asian Tigers. Four main conclusions emerge. First, as one might have expected a priori, export growth in the Tiger economies was generally faster than in the European economies, with Ireland's export growth exceeding that of the other European economies.

Second, the commodity structure of exports in the European economies affected export growth negatively more often than not; the size of this effect also tended to be larger than for the Tigers. Yet, in both groups, the commodity effect generally only explained a small proportion of export growth. This is encouraging for the CEEC countries; a country's commodity structure is only one of several factors which affect export growth.

Third, for both groups, the direction of the market effect tended to be the same across countries for particular sub-periods (although not the same for the two sets of countries at the same time). This may reflect the fact that an individual country or exporting firm may only have limited discretion over determining their export markets or in using market diversification as a means of securing faster export growth. But, like the commodity effect, the market effect could only explain a small proportion of export growth. Again, this is encouraging for the CEEC countries as 'bad', or relatively slow growing export markets may only have a relatively small impact on export growth. It also means however, that institutional support for exporting which assists exporters in targeting new markets may bring only small improvements for total exports.

Finally, for all the countries in all but one instance, when the residual was negative, the overall level of export growth was less than the world average. Competitiveness, or whatever else is contained in the residual effect, seems generally to be more important to exporting success than commodity or market selection; where countries experience relatively rapid export growth, only a small proportion of this can be explained by faster than average growth in the particular commodities they have exported, or the particular markets they have exported to. This is perhaps the most important conclusion for the governments of the transitional economies. However, an important qualification to this conclusion concerns the level of aggregation involved in these analyses; the use of single digit SITC data may be driving some of these results. This means that the possible gains from specialising in particular commodity or service exports cannot be ruled out; few could deny that the demand for mobile phones in the last few years has grown much faster than for electrical products in general. Fortunate is the nation whose exports contain a large proportion of such products at the right time. Good policies can help that to happen as Ireland's success in exporting, which stems largely from its industrial policies and attraction to FDI, demonstrates. This means that at least some of the responsibility for successful export performance in the CEEC lies in the hands of policy-makers.

NOTES

1. See Panchamukhi [*1996*] for a discussion of the policy options permitted under the WTO.
2   We have picked these countries for a number of reasons. First, given the space constraints here it would not have been possible to document evidence from every country's experience in any great depth or detail. Second, there is a large amount of published information on each of these cases and very little on the less successful experiences, such as Portugal and Greece, for example.
3. Although the World Bank disagree on this point. They argue that Korea did not have

sufficiently large domestic population to consider a strategy other than export-led development.

4. Interestingly, Ireland also offered incentives to attract various service activities, including financial services, but these were offered much later than in Singapore.

5. Of course in addition to the issue of market access, membership has brought additional gains to the Irish economy in the form of structural funds, and the agricultural sector has also benefited from the common agricultural policy of the EU (see Leddin and Walsh [*1996*] for a fuller discussion of these issues).

6. This was the most important of the incentives, accounting for 60 per cent on average of total grant aid given to indigenous and 70 per cent of grant aid given to foreign companies [*Ruane, 1991*].

7. Sachs [*1997*].

8. It should be borne in mind when reading the results that OECD total export data detail exports from OECD countries only; thus, world import demand here refers to world imports from OECD countries.

9. All data are derived from IMF International Financial Statistics, with the exception of RULC for the total economy which is taken from European Economy. While it would have been preferable to examine changes in the indices over the same time period for which the CMSA was conducted this was not possible due to data constraints. That is, most of the real exchange rate indices were only available from 1975 onwards, and some of them were only available from 1982 onwards.

10. Since data for both the CPI index and the value-added deflator were only available from 1978 and 1979 respectively, these indices show no movement between 1975 and these dates.

REFERENCES

Abeysinghe, T. and T. L. Yeok, 1998, 'Exchange Rate Appreciation and Export Competitiveness: The Case of Singapore', *Applied Economics*, Vol. 30, pp.51–5.

Amsden, A.H., Kochanowicz, J. and L. Taylor, 1994, *The Market Meets Its Match: Restructuring the Economies of Eastern Europe*, Cambridge, MA: Harvard University Press.

Amsden, A.H., 1989, *Asia's Next Giant: South Korea and Late Industrialization*, New York: Oxford University Press.

Arrow, K.J., 1997, 'Economic Growth Policy for a Small Country', in Gray [*1997*].

Barry, F. and A. Hannan, 1996, 'Education, Industrial Change and Unemployment in Ireland,' Centre for Economic Research Working Paper No.WP96/18, Dublin: University College.

Cheng, T.J., Haggard, S. and D. Kang, 1996, 'Institutions, Economic Policy, and Growth in the Republic of Korea and Taiwan Province of China', Study No.6 of Project on East Asian Development, Geneva: UNCTAD.

Chow, P.C.Y. and M.H. Kellman, 1993, *Trade: The Engine of Growth in East Asia*, Oxford: Oxford University Press.

Collins, S.M. and D. Rodrik, 1991, *Eastern Europe and the Soviet Union in the World Economy*, Washington, DC: Institute for International Economics.

Culliton, J., 1992, *A Time for Change: Industrial Policy for the 1990s: Report of the Industrial Policy Review Group* [The Culliton Report], Dublin: Stationery Office.

De la Fuente, A. and X. Vives, 1997, 'The Sources of Irish Growth', in .Gray [*1997*].

Department of Enterprise and Employment, 1998, *Trade Policy – The Key Success Factors,* at www.irl.gov.ie/entemp/success.htm.

Deutsche Bundesbank, 1994, 'Real Exchange Rates as an Indicator of International Competitiveness', in *Deutsche Bundesbank Monthly Report*, May, 1994.

Dumble, A., 1994, 'UK Trade – long Term Trends and Recent Developments.' *Bank of England Quarterly Bulletin*, Aug. 1994.

The Economist, 1990, 'Taiwan and Korea', *The Economist*, 14 July.

The Economist, 1997, 'Europe's Shining Light', *The Economist*, 17 May.

Ernst and Young, 1997, *World Tax Guide*, Ernst & Young.

Fagerberg, J., 1988, 'International Competitiveness', *Economic Journal*, Vol. 98, pp.355–74.

Feldman, R.A., 1994, 'Measures of External Competitiveness for Germany', IMF Working Paper WP/94/113, Washington, DC: IMF.

Financial Times, 1996, 'Mission for Miracle Workers', *Financial Times*, 25 Oct.

Fitzpatrick, J. and J. Kelly, 1985, 'Industry in Ireland: Policies, Performance and Problems', in J. Fitzpatrick and J. Kelly (eds.), *Perspectives on Irish Industry*, Dublin: Irish Management Institute.

Forfas, 1997, *Annual Survey of Irish Economy Expenditures – Results for 1995*, Dublin: Forfas.

Gehlhar, M.J. and Volrath, T.L., 1997, 'US Export Performance in Agricultural Markets', *Economic Research Service Technical Bulletin No. 1854*, US Department of Agriculture.

Gray, A.W. (ed.), 1997, *International Perspectives on the Irish Economy*, Dublin: Indecon Economic Consultants.

IDA, 1998, 'Ireland – The Competitive Location in Europe', at www.ida.ie/consec.htm.

IDA, *Employment Survey: Review of Employment Trends in Manufacturing and Internationally Traded Services Sectors*, Dublin: IDA/Forfas, various issues.

IMF, *International Financial Statistics*, Washington, DC: IMF, various issues.

Jomo, K.S., 1996, 'Lessons from Growth and Structural Change in the Second Tier South-East Asian Newly Industrialising Countries', Study No.4 of Project on East Asian Development, Geneva: UNCTAD.

Kennedy, K. and B. Dowling, 1975, *Economic Growth in Ireland: The Experience since 1947*, Dublin: Gill & Macmillan.

Kennedy, K., Giblin, T. and D. McHugh, 1988, *The Economic Development of Ireland in the Twentieth Century*, London: Routledge.

Killick, T. and C. Stevens, 1991, 'Eastern Europe: Lessons on Economic Adjustment from the Third World', *International Affairs*, Vol.67, No.4.

Koteva, M., 1992, 'The Experience of Developing Countries with Trade Policy Reform with Special Reference to Bulgaria', Discussion Paper No. DP310, University of Sussex: Institute of Development Studies.

Kwon, J., 1998, 'The East Asian Model: An Exploration of Rapid Economic Growth in the Republic of Korea and Taiwan Province of China', UNCTAD Discussion Paper No.140, Geneva: UNCTAD.

Krugman, P., 1997, 'Good News for Ireland: A Geographical Perspective', in Gray [*1997*].

Lamfalussy, A., 1963, *The United Kingdom and the Six: An Essay on Economic Growth in Western Europe*, London: Macmillan.

Leamer, E.E. and R.M. Stern, 1970, *Quantitative International Economics* Chicago, IL: Aldine Publishing Company.

Leddin, A. and B. Walsh, 1996, 'Economic Stabilisation, Recovery, and Growth: Ireland 1979–1996', Centre for Economic Research Working Paper No.WP97/8, Dublin: University College.

Lim, C.Y. *et al.*, 1988, *Policy Options for the Singapore Economy*, Singapore: National University of Singapore and McGraw-Hill.

Lim, C.Y. and E.F. Pang, 1991, *Foreign Direct Investment and Industrialization in Malaysia, Singapore, Taiwan and Thailand*, Development Centre of the OECD, Paris: OECD.

Lipschitz, L. and D. McDonald, 1991, 'Real Exchange Rates and Competitiveness: A Clarification of Concepts, and Some Measurements for Europe', *IMF Working Paper, WP/91/25*, Washington, DC: IMF.

Little, I., Scitovsky, T. and M. Scott, 1970, *Industry and Trade in Some Developing Economies*, London: Oxford University Press.

Luedde-Neurath, R., 1986, *Import Controls and Export-Oriented Development: A Reassessment of the South Korean Case*, Boulder, CO: Westview.

MacBean, A.I. and D.T. Nguyen, 1987, *Commodity Prices: Problems and Prospects*, London: Croom Helm.

McGettigan, D. and J. Nugent, 1995, *Competitiveness Measures for Ireland: An Assessment*, Technical Paper 6/RT/95, Dublin: Central Bank of Ireland.

Marsh, P. and S. Tokarick, 1994, 'Competitiveness Indicators: A Theoretical and Empirical Assessment', *IMF Working Paper WP/94/29*, Washington, DC: IMF.

Moore, B.C., Rhodes, J. and P. Tyler, 1986, *The Effects of Government Regional Policy*, London:

HM Stationery Office.

Murray, G. and Perrera, A., 1996, *Singapore: The Global City-State*, Folkstone: China Library.

NESC, 1997 *European Union: Integration and Enlargement*, Dublin: National Economic and Social Council.

OECD, *Commodity Statistics Volume I: Exports*, Paris: OECD, various years.

OECD, *Commodity Statistics Volume II: Imports*, Paris: OECD, various years.

OECD 1978, *Policies for the Stimulation of Industrial Innovation: Country Reports*, Vol.II -2, OECD, Paris.

OECD, 1989. *United Kingdom,* OECD Economic Surveys, Paris: OECD.

OECD, 1997, *Ireland,* OECD Economic Surveys, Paris: OECD.

O'Donnell, M., 1997, 'The Changing Commodity Structure and Destination of Irish Exports 1972-90', Technical Paper No.97/5, Trinity Economic Paper Series, Dublin:Trinity College.

O'Malley, E., 1992, 'Industrialisation in Ireland', in P. Clancy (ed.), *Ireland and Poland: Comparative Perspectives*, Dublin: Department of Sociology, University College Dublin.

Panchamukhi, V.R., 1996, 'WTO and Industrial Policies', Study No.7 of Project on East Asian Development, Geneva: UNCTAD.

Panoutsopoulos, V., 1981, 'East Asian and Latin American Export Performance in Industrial Country Markets in the 1970s', in J. Black and L.A. Winters (eds.), *Policy and Performance in International Trade*, London: Macmillan.

Papageorgiou, D., Michaely, M., Choksi, A. and K. Kim, 1991, *Liberalizing Foreign Trade, Vol.1: The Experience of Argentina, Chile and Uruguay*, Cambridge: Basil Blackwell.

Rasiah, R., 1998, 'The Export Manufacturing Experience of Indonesia, Malaysia and Thailand: Lessons for Africa', UNCTAD Discussion Paper No.137, Geneva: UNCTAD.

Review of Industrial Performance, 1990, Dublin: Stationery Office.

Ruane, F., 1991, 'The Traded Sector: Industry', in J.W. O'Hagan (ed.), *The Economy of Ireland: Policy and Performance*, sixth edition, Dublin: Irish Management Institute.

Sachs, J., 1997, 'Ireland's Growth Strategy: Lessons for Economic Development', in .Gray [*1997*].

Song, Pyong-nak, 1994, *The Rise of the Korean Economy*, Oxford: Oxford University Press.

Sweeney, P., 1998, *The Celtic Tiger*, Dublin: Oak Tree Press.

Telesis Consultancy Group, 1982, *A Review of Industrial Policy*, Report No.64, Dublin: National Economic and Social Council.

Thirlwall, A.P. and H.D. Gibson, 1992, *Balance-of-Payments Theory and the United Kingdom Experience,* London: Macmillan.

Turner, P. and J. Van't dack, 1993, 'Measuring International Price and Costs Competitiveness', BIS Economic Papers No.39, Basle: BIS.

Tyler, P., 1980. 'The Impact of Regional Policy on a Prosperous Region.' *Oxford Economic Papers*, Vol.32, pp.151–62.

Wade, R., 1990, *Governing the Market: Economic Theory and the Role of Government in East Asian Industrialization*, Princeton, NT: Princeton University Press.

White Paper on Industrial Policy, 1984, Dublin: Stationery Office.

World Bank, 1993, *The East Asian Miracle: Economic Growth and Public Policy*, New York: Oxford University Press.

Wickham, P., 1993, 'A Cautionary Note on the Use of Exchange Rate Indicators', IMF Paper on Policy Analysis and Assessment, PPAA/93/5, Washington, DC: IMF.

World Economic Forum, 1997, *The Global Competitiveness Report*, Geneva: World Economic Forum.

4

Export Promotion in the Czech Republic

ALASDAIR MacBEAN

After an initial drop due to the collapse of CMEA trade in the early 1990s Czech exports and the current account balance proved relatively buoyant until 1995. But from then on the trade balance and the current account went deep into the red. Policies to expand exports became a clear option for paying off debt, meeting requirements for consumers, capital and intermediate imports, and job creation. This chapter seeks to evaluate the policies to promote exports adopted by the Czech government since the start of economic reform.

It begins with a section on foreign trade before 1990, then considers the reforms adopted which had a major influence on foreign trade, and finally turns to policies to promote exports through government and other institutional support for exporters. This latter section reports the results of interviews with Czech officials in the trade policy area and of a survey carried out by interviews with Czech managers in manufacturing companies engaged in exporting, and foreign trading companies (export-import companies). It also reports on surveys by others carried out in earlier years. The final section seeks to draw some conclusions for Czech foreign trade policy from our own and other studies.

PRE-REFORM FOREIGN TRADE

Pre-reform, foreign trade was, in principle, centrally planned, but in practice bureaucratically controlled by large state monopolies. Foreign exchange was under central control. Trade was mainly conducted through a few state-trading companies, which were large and specialised by sector such as chemicals, machinery or ceramics. Most trade was locked into the Soviet bloc by bilateral and CMEA arrangements. Domestic prices bore little relation to international prices. The structure of exports and imports was, at best, only loosely connected to Czechoslovakia's comparative costs. The efficient use of

---

Earlier versions of this chapter were presented at workshops in Prague (25 October 1997) and Budapest (27 March 19

the country's resources to obtain the goods and services demanded by its citizens was not the aim. Rather, as in other centrally planned countries, exporting was simply the means for paying for essential imports [*Lavigne, 1995: 67–8*].

Economic reforms introduced in the late 1960s were soon reversed, and between 1970 and 1987 no substantial changes were made to the command economy system [*Krejci, 1990: 196*]. Despite some reforms in the 1980s such as exchange auctions and a 19 per cent devaluation [*Kaminski, Wang and Winters, 1996: 7*] enterprise managers still had little incentive to improve efficiency or to seek out foreign markets for their products. State owned enterprises continued to operate mainly as administrative units of the state [*Myant, 1993: 155–60*]. In terms of its institutional arrangements the Czechoslovakian economy was more closed than Hungary or Poland [*Gacs, 1994: 3–4*]. Trade patterns were somewhat biased as compared with 'normal' trading patterns i.e. those that ought to arise from market forces under reasonably free trade and undistorted prices. The CEEC trade in the mid-80s with CMEA partners was a little too high; with market economies, especially OECD, it was too low. With developing countries it seems close to the predicted level, and CEEC trade with each other was about one third higher than predicted [*Kaminski, Wang and Winters, 1996: 11*].

These results are based on estimates of their trade potential, and are similar to results based on other gravity models. For both statistical and methodological reasons they provide rather weak evidence [op.cit.]. But, for the CEEC they accord with expectations based on casual observation. In both orientation and commodity structure the system was unlikely to produce an efficient use of the resources of the Czech economy. But, more importantly, the suppression of normal trading relations with the OECD also weakened Czech manufacturing through lack of competition and exposure to recent technologies.

POST-REFORM TRADE PERFORMANCE

Czech trade has been thoroughly reoriented from dependence on Russia and former CMEA to OECD and the rest of the world. In 1989 trade with centrally planned economies was over half of the Czech exports and imports, and the Soviet Union was the largest trading partner. Now almost 60 per cent of trade is with Western Europe, and nearly over half of that with Germany. Trade with the former Soviet Union countries and other former CMEA has fallen sharply (Table 4.1). The change in the origins of imports is similar.

Not only the direction, but also the composition of exports changed after the start of transition. The principal change was a decline in the share of machinery and transport equipment and a rise in other manufactures. In 1989

TABLE 4.1
DIRECTION OF EXPORTS 1989–98

	1989	1994	1996	1998
World	100	100	100	100
European Community(12)	26.3	45.7	58.2 (EU)	59.9
(of which Germany)	(16)	(29.4)	(35.7)	(38.5)
EFTA	8.5	10.1	n.a.	n.a.
(of which Austria)	4.0	7.1	6.1	5.9
European Transitional Economies including CIS	46.9	30.0	26.5	26.3
(of these Russia)	n.a	3.9	6.8	5.5

Sources: World Trade Organization, *Trade Policy Review, Czech Republic 1996* for data to 1994.
Table 1.3.
Czech Statistical Office, *External Trade, January to December 1996* (1997) Table 3,
p.13 and January to December 1998 (1999), Table 3, pp.13 and 15.

machinery and transport equipment formed over 40 per cent of exports and by
1994 this had fallen to 26 per cent while other manufactures had risen from
20 to 30 per cent [*WTO, 1996: Chart 1.4*]. The economy has become much
more open with the trade ratio increasing from 38 per cent in 1990 to 90 per
cent in 1996 as shown in Table 4.2.

TABLE 4.2
TRADE RATIOS FOR THE CZECH ECONOMY

	1990	1996
Exports plus imports Bil. $	12.4	49.4
*GDP bil.$	32.17	54.98
Trade ratio %	38.5	89.9

Source: calculated from EBRD, *Transition Report 1997*, p.221.
Note: * GDP converted from koruna to US dollars at the average
exchange rate for each year: 18 koruna to the $ in 1990, 27.1
koruna to the $ in 1996.

Both exports and imports have risen rapidly since reform with the current
account staying roughly in balance until 1995, but with a sharper descent into
the red in 1996 and 1997 as shown in the following Table 4.3 on the external
sector indicators. The trade balance has been in deficit every year but buoyant
earnings from tourism and other services have kept the current account deficit
minor until 1995. Some of the increase in the current account deficit is
explained by the inflow of foreign direct investment in the capital account.
There was, however, also a steep increase in short and medium term
borrowing which is reflected in the foreign debt. But compared with most
transitional and developing countries the foreign debt servicing costs are a
relatively modest proportion of the value of Czech exports.

TABLE 4.3
THE EXTERNAL SECTOR OF THE CZECH ECONOMY 1990–98
in billions of US$

	1990	1991	1992	1993	1994	1995	1996	1997	1998
Current account	−1.1	0.3	−0.3	0.1	0.0	−1.4	−4.3	−3.2	−1.7
Trade balance	−0.8	−0.5	−1.9	−0.3	−0.9	−3.7	−5.9	−4.6	−3.0
Exports	5.9	8.3	8.4	13.0	14.0	21.5	21.7	22.5	27.0
Imports	6.5	8.8	10.4	13.3	14.9	25.1	27.6	27.1	30.0
Foreign-direct investment, net	n.a.	n.a.	1.0	0.6	0.7	2.5	1.4	1.3	1.0
Gross reserves (end-year)	0.2	0.7	0.8	3.9	6.2	14.0	12.4	9.8	n.a.
External-debt, stock (convertible currency)	6.0	6.7	7.1	8.5	10.7	16.5	20.8	21.4	n.a.
Debt service as % of exports	n.a.	n.a.	12.4	6.5	13.1	9.3	10.4	15.1	n.a.

Source: EBRD [*1997, 1998: 213*].

Notes: Data for 1990–92 are for former Czechoslovakia.
n.a. not available
Data for 1997 estimate and for 1998 projection
The sharp rise in FDI in 1995 was largely accounted for by the sale of the Czech
telecommunications company.

Overall, the current account deficits were modest until 1995, and foreign investment has flowed in [*IMF, 1997: 240–45; Economist, 25 May 1996: Table: Emerging Market Indicators*]. Until recently the Czech economy could be acclaimed one of the most successful of the transitional economies. Doubts have now emerged concerning the effectiveness of its industrial reforms, particularly the lack of sufficient restructuring of many large firms. The banking system and the capital market have also shown serious weaknesses. But overall the Czech transition was remarkably successful for many years. How was this transformation and relative economic success achieved? Why have problems emerged, and what do they imply for export promotion policies in the Czech Republic?

TRADE POLICY REFORM

The reform of trade policies is a key component of transition. This is not simply in terms of its effect on international economic relations, but through its role in influencing the development of a rational pricing system, its influence on monopoly and competition, and in acting as a stabilising force on prices and wages. Equally, domestic policies on budgetary control, monetary policy, and wages, and their influence on the price level and the exchange rate affect profoundly the competitiveness of enterprises' exports.

Almost as important for international trade are policies to liberalise prices, and to privatise, or at least, commercialise, state owned enterprises so that their managers become committed to raising productivity, seeking out markets, and realising the importance of meeting customers' wants. But, recent experience in transitional economies has shown that privatisation on its own will not necessarily promote efficiency. Good corporate governance, proper relations between shareholders and management, transparency in business relations, competition and ease of entry and exit to the industry, honest and efficient commercial banking, effective stock market regulation are other necessary conditions for privatisation to produce maximum benefits, or even improvement in efficiency [*EBRD, 1997: 89–96*].

Just which economic policies promote maximum gains from international trade remain controversial. Questions such as whether, and how far governments should deliberately bias incentives in favour of some tradable goods, or should leave it almost entirely to market forces to establish which goods and services should be exported, which should compete with imports, and which should effectively be non-tradable remain unsettled [Chapter 3 above, *World Bank, 1987, 1991, 1993 and 1996; Wade, 1990, 1992; Amsden, 1989, 1995; Stiglitz, 1996 and others*].

That trade liberalisation was achieved so rapidly in Czechoslovakia from a late start in 1991 was due in part to the conservative macroeconomic policies of the 1980s. There was a history of low inflation, low foreign debt and little monetary overhang compared with most of the command economies, where endemic shortages of goods and services led to large liquid balances in the hands of the public [*Svejnar, 1995: 3–4*]. These advantages made stabilisation, though still painful, less so than in most transitional economies. Unemployment, never rose above 4.1 per cent between 1990 and 1996, and was less than three percent in 1992 and 1995, at least in terms of the official statistics. Inflation (consumer prices) peaked at 56.6 per cent in 1991 but was down to 10 per cent by 1994 and kept below 10 per cent for the next three years. Money wages increased faster than consumer prices in every year from 1992 to 1997 [*EBRD, 1997: 221*]. Low unemployment, maintenance of low rents, fuel price controls, and cheap transport, plus the method of voucher privatisation all helped to ameliorate the growth of inequality in income distribution. Measured by the Gini Coefficient income inequality was low compared with most countries in 1989 and had hardly changed by 1993 [*EBRD, 1997: Table 2.2.5*]. At least, in terms of a 'pain index' that combines these measures, the Czechs suffered much less than the citizens of the other CEEC let alone the former Soviet Union countries. There prices soared by over 1000 per cent in several post-reform years and inflation remained in at least double figures up to the present, unemployment increased and real wages, when paid, fell sharply.

The Czech economy is now regarded as at least as open as many of the OECD countries. State trading is negligible, export controls and licences govern only the same types of products such as defence equipment, or safety standards, that are found in most OECD countries. The Czech Republic joined the World Trade Organisation in January 1995. There is current account convertibility and even partial capital account convertibility. Unlike most transitional economies the official, pegged, exchange rate was generally also the free market rate. The Czech average weighted tariff is just under six per cent, and there are no serious administrative barriers to exports or imports [*EBRD, 1996: 147*].

A BRIEF HISTORY OF THE REFORMS

The Velvet Revolution occurred in November 1989. The new government immediately devalued the Koruna by 20 per cent against convertible currencies, and raised its exchange rate against the rouble by ten per cent. It also tightened budgetary policies for 1990, declared the adoption of a market economy, and the intention of integrating its economy with western countries.

In the course of 1990 Czechoslovakia started a process of reform to stabilise and liberalise the economy. In January 1991 a comprehensive programme of reforms was adopted. But earlier, in the autumn of 1990, the currency was devalued against the US dollar by 64 per cent (from 18Kcs to 29.5Kcs. per dollar). The Koruna was then pegged to a basket of five western currencies, weighted heavily by the D-Mark and the dollar, later to these two currencies only (65 per cent D-Mark, 35 per cent US$). At the same time the government made clear its determination to maintain control over the macroeconomic situation through tight budgetary and monetary policies. The government held to that determination and as a result the exchange rate, at least in nominal terms, was stable and even appreciated slightly until 1997, while foreign exchange reserves climbed to a peak of $14 billion in 1995.

THE EXCHANGE RATE AND THE BALANCE OF PAYMENTS

In the context of foreign trade one key contribution of macroeconomic policy is to maintain a real exchange rate which keeps the prices of tradable goods competitive with foreign goods (and sufficiently high relative to non-tradables as to avoid biases against production of tradables). The other main contribution is to make sure that the balance between aggregate supply and demand is consistent with long run equilibrium in the balance of payments. As long as the economy is growing and can service debt out of its rising earnings there is no need to maintain current account balance. Indeed a current account deficit is the necessary counterpart to the capital inflow required to modernise the economy. But governments need to keep a close control over their own expenditure and private expenditure to ensure that deficits do not grow out of control. This, the Czech government carried out rather successfully until 1995/96.

It was achieved by following tight budgetary and monetary policies. Czechoslovakia had a small budget surplus in 1990, and the deficits in 1991 and 1992 were kept under one per cent of GDP. After the split from Slovakia in 1993, the Czech Republic kept the budget in balance or in slight surplus or deficit, ranging from 2.7 per cent of GDP in 1993 to minus one per cent in 1997 [*EBRD, 1997: 221*]. Government expenditure as a percentage of GDP fell by 14 per cent in 1992. This was even more severe than in Poland or Hungary. Under the Czech Republic, from 1993 on, expenditure on subsidies to industry and housing continued to fall as a share of total government expenditure [*Economist, 26 Oct. 1994: 26*]. Tax reforms have boosted revenues while changing in structure to conform to OECD norms. Apart from foreign borrowing from the European Union, the World Bank and the G24, the government has kept its borrowing to a minimum. The central bank has been made independent of the government and is forbidden to cover budget deficits by lending to the government [*Klacek and Hrncir, 1994: 10*].

Some argue that the macro-policies in the early 1990s were too restrictive. Relative stability could have been attained at lower cost in terms of falling incomes and rising unemployment. But the results were impressive. Open unemployment declined to an enviable 2.9 per cent (though hoarded labour, some subsidised firms, training programmes, and withdrawals from the labour market mean that genuine jobs were less than this low unemployment figure suggests. Employment has fallen much more than unemployment has risen [*Jackman, 1994: 331–2*], and survey data show higher levels of unemployment than official registered data [*Boeri, 1994: 3*]. Unemployment rose to 5.5 per cent in 1998 [*Czech Statistical Office, 1998*], and this still seriously underestimates the true underutilisation of labour [*Schwartz, 1997*]).

Between 1992 and 1996 wages doubled, the rate of inflation fell to 8.5 per cent, and growth in GDP reached five per cent in the mid-1990s. The Czech economy performed well up to then, rather better than its CEEC neighbours [*Economist, 25 May 1996: 54*].

Monetary policy was also aimed at maintaining stable prices in the face of the major upheavals and dislocations involved in the rapid liberalisation of the economy. The authorities adopted both a monetary and an exchange rate target as intermediate variables. In 1990 the policy was extremely restrictive. This stance was held for the first half of 1991, after which it was shifted to a neutral stance. The shock of the split from Slovakia forced a reversion to a tight policy to prevent inflationary expectations growing out of control. These orthodox fiscal and monetary policies were combined with several periods, up to July 1995, when wage control policies were in force [*EBRD, 1996: 147*].

Despite these strict measures of control, the exchange rate appreciated in real terms. Taking its level in 1990 as 100 it reached about 130 by early 1995 [*WTO, 1996: Chart 1.3*] Although inflation has been low by the standards of transitional economies it is higher than in the OECD countries which form the main markets for Czech exports. Wages have risen faster than productivity and this, together with the removal of price controls and subsidies, has led to prices rising faster than in the Czech Republic's main markets (Table 4.4).

TABLE 4.4
PRICES AND WAGES, ANNUAL AVERAGE INCREASES 1990–97

	1990	1991	1992	1993	1994	1995	1996	1997	1998
Consumer prices	10.8	56.6	11.1	20.8	10.0	9.1	8.8	8.5	10.7
Producer prices	4.47	0.3	9.9	13.1	5.3	7.6	4.8	n.a.	n.a
.*Gross average monthly wages	4.5	16.7	19.6	23.8	15.7	17.0	17.4	n.a.	n.a.

Source: EBRD [*1998: 213*].
Note: * in manufacturing.

The rise in the real exchange rate, and the increase in the current account deficit, caused increasing concern among many observers. Should it? Given the great need for investment to restructure and modernise Czech industries and social infrastructure it makes sense to have an inflow of capital. The current account deficit has been financed by an inflow of direct foreign investment plus funds borrowed at commercial rates of interest and is the natural counterpart of the capital account surplus. Given a fixed nominal exchange rate, the rise in the real exchange rate through an increased domestic price level is an appropriate adjustment to the capital inflow. But does this imply that there is no need for policies to increase exports?

THE EXPORT IMPERATIVE

Several reasons for efforts to promote exports in the Czech economy are valid: First, the financing of the deficit has increasingly been through borrowing by Czech firms while direct investment in the Czech Republic has been declining. Some of this borrowing was for current inputs and some for the purchase of investment goods. Both of these will lead to increased exports and replaced imports in the future, but that depends on their effective use by Czech industry to raise productivity and improve quality, and may involve quite long time lags. Some of the capital inflow was into highly liquid assets and therefore quite volatile. Changes in perceived currency risk or changes in relative interest rates could lead to sudden outflows. Debt servicing costs at about 13 per cent of export earnings, while not critical, are not trivial either.

Secondly, there are market failures, both systemic and government-induced which have deterred exports in the past and some which continue to make it difficult for enterprises, especially those which are small to medium in size, to exploit export opportunities. Some market failures are common to most economies but for transitional economies they are endemic and more critical. Standard examples of these are lack of access to credit, and credit guarantee systems that are routinely available in OECD economies; inadequate experience of selling to sophisticated markets, and lack of good marketing information. Such factors lead to exaggerated views of the risks and difficulty of selling in foreign markets, and so divert sales to domestic markets, and cause excessive use of foreign intermediaries for financing and managing sales abroad. If these and other market failures were corrected such enterprises would be able to earn higher profits through selling some or all of their output in foreign markets, or in non-traditional foreign markets.

A third relevant market failure is in the labour market. Although the Czech unemployment figure was low by most standards, it rose to 5.5 per cent in 1998. Labour market participation rates have fallen to below average levels for OECD countries, particularly for males [*Boeri, 1994: 8; Jackman, 1994: 332*]. Some of this is due to withdrawals from the labour market by people who would prefer to be employed, but have been forced into early retirement or other government schemes which keep them off the unemployment register. Some continue to be employed in companies that have excess supplies of labour, or are being prevented from going bankrupt by subsidies or soft loans that will have to be ended soon. Bankruptcies and labour shedding are likely in the near future. Increased exports would provide real jobs for some of these workers. Reporting on, and analysing these and other market failures and difficulties faced by Czech exporters, and the attempts to support exporters made by Czech Government and other agencies form the content of a later section of this chapter.

WAGES AND PRICES

The rates of change of wages and prices affect the real rate of exchange and so influence exports, but relative prices also affect exports through their effects on incentives. If prices reflect real opportunity costs they should guide production for the foreign and home markets so as to maximise gains.

The Czech government's initial stabilisation measures were followed in January 1991 by liberalisation of about 85 per cent of domestic prices, while at the same time wage controls were imposed (to calm inflationary wage increases) and domestic currency convertibility was introduced. Later in the year further price liberalisation took place. Today, there are no wage controls and only five per cent of prices remain regulated: prices of public utility services, selected agricultural products and rents. Rents for flats which remain under controls have been raised substantially [*Dyba and Svejnar, 1995: 24–25; EBRD, 1997: 164*].

FOREIGN TRADE POLICY AND LIBERALISATION

Czech foreign trade policy is not interventionist. Until recently it was basically rather laissez faire, confining activity mainly to trade diplomacy in seeking access to EU, EFTA markets and joining the CEFTA and the WTO. Most reform effort has gone into ensuring macroeconomic stability, general measures aimed at removing biases in the system such as trade barriers and tariffs, freeing prices, and creating incentives to efficiency. The last group included swift privatisation through vouchers and direct sales to give managers incentives, and allowing income distribution to become less equal. These measures, of course, gave powerful indirect stimulus to exporting.

It could be argued that the devaluations were initially somewhat excessive. The exchange rate probably overshot what was strictly necessary to make CSFR tradables competitive. But it was almost certainly correct to err in the direction of a low exchange rate. The freeing of domestic prices, removal of subsidies and most controls could have led to a massive rise in nominal wages and rapid inflation. It was impossible to know in advance how successful the government would be in maintaining tight fiscal and monetary policies in the face of the public outrage and the rising unemployment that could reasonably be expected.

Subsequently, the inflow of capital made it easy to maintain the nominal exchange rate, but, rising wages and prices caused a substantial appreciation in the real exchange rate [*WTO, 1996: Chart 1.3*]. Czech competitiveness began to be eroded. This made itself felt in sluggish exports and rapidly rising imports which have outrun exports over the last two years. Trade deficits have been rising, reaching US$6 billion in 1996 (Table 4.3 above), nearly six per cent of GDP. Tourism and associated expenditures helped to keep down the current account deficits. But the rising trade deficits reflect weaknesses in Czech manufacturers' ability both to penetrate foreign markets, despite the relatively open markets which face them, and to hold their home markets in the face of foreign competition. The output of the economy, especially in manufacturing is lower than it could be and this represents a threat to employment in manufacturing.

The CSFR moved from a closed to an open trading economy in remarkably quick time in 1991. Most measures were adopted in January 1991 when all but four categories of imports were freed from import licensing and only 20 per cent of merchandise exports remained subject to controls. Initially, to prevent a surge in imports an import surcharge (removed at the end of 1992) was imposed on a wide range of goods and the use of trade credits was restricted to payments for certain categories of goods. Tariffs were set at a remarkably low average rate of five per cent [*Gacs, 1994: 8–10*].

The Czech Republic became a member of the World Trade Organisation (WTO) in January 1995. Before that, in 1993 along with several other CEEC and Baltic States, the Czechs signed a 'Europe Agreement' which lowered trade barriers on most trade between the country and the EU, and contained a number of other measures aimed at further integration between these countries and the EU. Since then the EU agreed to abolish all remaining barriers to imports from the Czech and some other CEEC on all industrial goods, save textiles, in the course of 1995-96. Other concessions on agricultural trade have been agreed on a bilateral basis. Similar arrangements have been made with the European Free Trade Area. The Czech Republic will probably be among the first ex-CMEA states to become a full member of the EU. The Czech Republic is also a member of the Central European Free Trade Agreement (CEFTA) since 1992. It involves the progressive liberalisation of trade among the members during the period up to 2001. Overall, it is clear that the Czech economy is now more open than the acclaimed 'export promoting' success stories of East Asia such as South Korea and Taiwan.

A major difference from them, however, lies in the approach to supporting the efforts of manufacturers and traders to sell goods abroad. The Asian Tigers have been strongly interventionist in their support of exporters. The Governments in both South Korea and Taiwan have discriminated in credit allocation in favour of exports. They have used moral and other methods of persuasion to encourage firms to export. They have created or encouraged institutions to provide a wide range of support for exporting. KOTRA, set up in the image of Japan's JETRO has been a major force in helping Korean firms to market their products and services abroad (Chapter 3 gives a more detailed account of export promotion in developing countries). China, since it opened up its economy, though remaining one of the most highly protected in Asia, has adopted many of the devices of the Asian Tigers to promote its exports. But the Czech government showed considerable reluctance to follow these examples in terms of explicit government assistance for exporting. Its approach at least up to 1993, was simply one of ensuring neutral incentives and free competition.

INSTITUTIONAL SUPPORT FOR EXPORTING

It was agreed in February 1992 to create an Export Guarantee and Insurance Corporation [*Myant, 1993: 220*]. But no measures to promote exports directly were introduced until the end of 1993 [*Sass, 1995: 63*]. At first glance this seems surprising given that all the OECD nations have various mechanisms, both public and private, whose main tasks are to support exporting. The market failures, commonly put forward to justify such help, are more likely to be serious in ex-centrally planned economies than in the developed market economies. But, given the experience of failure with government run enterprises and state trading companies, and the failures of exports in the 1980s the Czech government's unwillingness to invest much in institutional support for exporting is less surprising. Moreover, 'The modern theory of market failures recognises that government interventions may not improve matters', given the risks of 'regulatory capture' and 'rent-seeking' by officials and enterprises [*Stiglitz, 1996: 156*]. Such evidence as exists on export promoting institutions in the developing countries gives little, or at best ambiguous, support to their effectiveness in increasing exports. Some of the leading commentators take the view that until the standard package of trade liberalisation policies are in place there is little sense in developing support services for exporters. Moreover, trade promotion organisations placed in the public sector, as most are, have often proved worse than useless [Chapter 2 above; *Keesing and Singer, 1991: 17* and others cited].

On the basis of most evidence the Czech government has been right to focus first on getting the general policies correct, and to remove any explicit biases against exporting, such as an overvalued exchange rate and a protected home market. But once these objectives have been achieved there is a strong case for measures to assist exports. There are many reasons, based on various types of market failure [*Stiglitz, 1994, 1996*], why simply leaving it entirely to the market may lead to under performance. Whatever the earlier doubts of the Czech government about support for exporting, the rapidly escalating trade deficits from 1995 on led to a shift in attitudes. And even as early as 1993 the government appears to have accepted this line of reasoning for it began to create new institutions to support exporters and has gone to some lengths to publicise them to manufacturers and traders [*Ministry of Economy, 1995*].

There are far too many to even list them in this chapter. For a comprehensive description of all the governmental and non-governmental organisations which provide credit, information and other services to exporters see the Ministry of Economy's publication, 'Export Promotion in the Czech Republic', 1995. But to discover how effective they are is a main objective of this research project.

GOVERNMENT POLICIES TOWARDS INSTITUTIONAL SUPPORT FOR EXPORTING

Four areas of support for exporting can be identified in the East Asian success stories. These are: provision of infrastructure, preferential access to capital and foreign exchange for exporters, help in developing new export markets, and help in improving the reputation of the country's exports [*Stiglitz, 1996: 170–71*].

The first involved improving port facilities, transport, power and telecommunications. For the Czech Republic which already has relatively good road and rail links, electricity supplies, and telecommunications, infrastructures could be improved but are probably not a major obstacle to foreign trade. But access to credit and credit insurance is generally identified by most commentators as a real problem for Czech exporters. Given the history of bureaucratic direction of industry and protected markets Czech exporters could be expected to need considerable help with marketing goods in international and highly competitive markets. That would also be true for help to attain international standards of quality and for building a reputation for reliability and high product standards. How successful have Czech policy makers been in identifying these issues and in providing adequate support to exporters in these fields?

THE MAIN CZECH EXPORT-SUPPORTING INSTITUTIONS

Czech government policy is still evolving on this front. Proposals for reform were sent to the Parliament in March 1998 but were sent back for amendment. The following description and comments are mainly based on the institutions as they were during our surveys. The comments we received from manufacturers and traders were based on their experiences up to March or July 1997.

MINISTRIES

Up to 1996 the responsibility for foreign economic affairs was divided among three ministries: the Ministry of Economy, the Ministry of Industry and Trade, and the Ministry of Foreign Affairs. Recent policy changes have involved redirecting the responsibility of the Ministry of Economy towards regional economic policy within the Czech Republic. This left the division of responsibility for foreign economic matters between the Ministry of Foreign Affairs which is responsible for co-ordinating all foreign economic relations and the Ministry of Industry and Trade which is responsible for the stipulation of foreign economic policy. Implementation seems to be divided between them, with the more practical matters of information and trade promotion lying with Foreign Affairs and its staff at Embassies. Regulations and support for trade missions and trade fairs are for the Ministry of Industry and Trade.

CREDIT GUARANTEE AND EXPORT FINANCE

Both the Export Guarantee and Insurance Corporation (EGAP) and the Czech Export Bank are regulated by an Act of Parliament in March 1995 assigning them the functions of insuring and financing exports. EGAP is a state-owned joint stock company whose main activity is the insurance of export credits against political and commercial risks. It has a basic capital of CZK 1,300 million and started operations in 1994. Its activities have risen rapidly from rather small beginnings. A mere 3.7 billion Czech crowns of exports insured against political risk in 1994 to 14.1 billion in 1996, the last year for which data are available [*EGAP, 1996: 7*]. Just over 70 per cent of exports insured were concentrated in China, Slovakia and the United Arab Emirates. The commodity structure was almost exclusively large contracts for machinery, equipment, capital goods, spare parts and services related to these types of exports. The processes involved in preparing insurance for these large export contracts are protracted and work intensive [*op. cit.: 9*]. Both of these factors militate against widespread use of the system and must tend to discriminate against smaller and medium-sized firms.

For exports insured against short term commercial risk the volume rose from 2.7 billion CZK in 1994 to 5.1 billion in 1996. Almost 80 per cent was for exports to market economies of which 51.3 per cent were in the European Union. The largest commodity group, at 42 per cent, was machinery and transport equipment. While growing rapidly, the volume of exports supported by EGAP insurance of both types remains small compared with OECD countries. In 1996 the 19.2 billion CZK of insurance concluded amounted to about three per cent of total Czech exports compared with OECD countries where, not only are much larger shares of exports guaranteed, but export credits and aid programmes provide much more help to exporters.

The Technical Account of the EGAP gives the revenues from premiums and costs of claims and operating expenditure. The result for 1996 was a loss of 137 million CZK which implies that EGAP is doing its job of providing some subsidy to the carriage of risk for Czech exporters. The loss on the Technical Account was more than offset by profits from investments and other revenues so that EGAP made an overall profit of 243 million CZK in 1996 [EGAP, *1996: 18–19*]. EGAP has been expanding both the types of services it provides and its capacity to provide them effectively. Already, in 1996 it provided seven basic types of insurance to suit the different specific needs of exporters. It has also been preparing to move into the insurance of loans for pre-export financing, an area where, as many firms told us, lack of finance was a serious bottleneck for Czech exporters. EGAP has also extended its links with overseas institutions to improve the possibilities of re-insurance and access to information [*op. cit.: 14*].

THE CZECH EXPORT BANK

The Czech Export Bank is a state owned joint stock company charged with the preferential financing (within bounds set by internationally agreed standards) of Czech exports. Its funds are raised on money and capital markets and any losses arising from interest rate differentials or exchange rate changes are subsidised from the state budget. Its obligations are guaranteed by the state [*Ministry of Economy, 1996: 19*]. One crucial condition for obtaining finance from the Export Bank is that the risks are insured by the EGAP. The Bank provides medium to long-term credits (generally 2–10 years). Both EGAP and the Czech Export Bank are intended to conform to OECD norms for such institutions.

EXPORT MARKETING AND INFORMATION SERVICES

There are many bodies in the Czech Republic, which provide these types of services. The main ones are: Czech Trade (until late 1997 the Centre for Foreign Economic Relations), the Economic Chamber with a network of district chambers, the National Information Centre and the Confederation of Industry.

CZECH TRADE
(formerly The Centre for Foreign Economic Relations or CFER)

Previously a research and analysis centre for the Ministry of Trade, other Ministries and government organisations, this institution is being developed as the main central provider of information for exporters. It is partly supported by the Ministry of Industry and Trade, partly by the sales of its services and publications. It is described in its own brochure as providing nation-wide information services on the foreign economic relations of the Czech Republic. In the recent past its main activities were producing analytical reports and statistical analyses of Czech foreign trade, and rather broad macroeconomic studies of trends and developments in the world economy and of the economies of trading partners. It produces a range of publications on a monthly or quarterly basis. Its leading quarterly is 'The Czech Republic in the International Economy'. This provides data on a quarterly basis up to the preceding quarter giving comparisons with the same quarter of the previous year. It covers, at the broad SITC one digit level, total exports and exports by major trading partners and regional groupings. This information is likely to be useful to researchers and general policy, but is unlikely to give the export manager of a firm information of a sufficiently detailed kind to be of much practical value.

Several of its publications seem aimed more at foreigners interested in exporting to, or investing in the Czech economy. But part of its organisation is a division called INFOCENTRUM, which provides, among other services, information on projects of the multilateral aid agencies such as the World Bank and the EBRD. This includes data on tenders sought by the banks. It also provides various types of commercially relevant information on individual countries and will carry out specific commissioned research or consultancy at negotiated prices. It is intended, under a PHARE funded programme, to be the back-up source of information for the Economic Chambers which are seen as the first port of call (or 'one-stop shops') for the exporter seeking almost any information connected with exporting (see below for details).

THE ECONOMIC CHAMBER OF THE CZECH REPUBLIC

Much of the Chamber's work is aimed at general activities of businesses within the Czech economy, but both it and the affiliated district or, in the case of Prague, ward economic chambers, direct a good deal of their work towards helping businesses with foreign economic relations. The Economic Chamber seeks and develops relations with foreign chambers of commerce. It provides advice and documentation on legal aspects of foreign trade, information on trade missions, trade fairs and exhibitions at home and abroad, certification and customs documentation, collects and disseminates information from the CFER and from embassies on international tenders and similar matters. It provides information to Czech and foreign businesses through publications, workshops, conferences, telex, facsimile and email. Membership is voluntary and most finance for the Chamber is from fees for services provided. Less than ten per cent comes from membership subscriptions. It receives no Government finance. There are over 80 professional staff at the Economic Chamber in Prague. Their building also houses the World Trade Centre. There are about 15,000 members, over 90 district and ward Chambers and about 36 trade associations.

THE BRNO CHAMBER OF COMMERCE

This is a branch of the network of the Economic Chamber of the Czech Republic. Part of the long tradition of commerce in Brno, it began independent activity again in July 1993. Its activity in the foreign sphere includes research on foreign firms from local databases, catalogues and world data base centres. It assists in finding business partners, provides information on foreign events and trade fairs and it organises trade missions. The Chamber provides certification, customs advice, a complete import and export documentation service, and legal advice. It includes the EURO INFOCENTRUM, which provides information on the European Union, on PHARE programmes; tenders in the EU and an Euro Information Centre stand at trade fairs.

The Brno Chamber sees about 30 or 40 clients a day. It has an establishment of 20 staff but only 15 were in place (July 1997), and only two of them were specialised in foreign trade. Of the services they provide the most commonly used are help with customs and provision of certificates of origin. In recent times they felt that they had made the most impact in helping firms to return to selling to the former COMECON countries. They have fraternal relations with Chambers of Commerce in several cities in Central and Western Europe.

The Prague Economic Chamber is very recent (started in 1996). It is a small office with few staff as yet. Its main services are providing information and facilitating business contacts. It has several publications of which the most important is *TIPS*. It contains current information for exporters and importers, listing potential suppliers and customers for different specific products and services. They also have a computerised data bank that lists a large number of companies giving such detail as size, capitalisation, products, turnover and exports. In principle, all the economic chambers are self supporting financed by subscriptions and sales of services, but the Prague Chamber admitted to a small subsidy from the City Council in the form of a lower than market rent for their office space. The office does give some direct services to the Council in return.

THE NATIONAL INFORMATION CENTRE

The provision of export support services or even information on foreign trade issues was never a main part of its activities, and few exporters have looked to it for much help [*ACE, Jan. 1996: 35*]. It is, however, as an offshoot of the traditional Ministry of Economy, the official distributor of EU, World Bank, OECD, IMF, and other UN documents. It also contains within its structure the EURO INFO CENTRE with its regional branches in Brno, Ostrava and Pilsen. This Centre can provide assistance with information from EU countries; on EU projects such as those under the PHARE programme, business contacts, consultancy services, assistance with contacts, and seminars on European subjects.

THE CONFEDERATION OF INDUSTRY (CIT)

Established in 1990 as an organisation to represent the interests of firms in industry and transport, it is independent of government. Membership is voluntary. In 1996 it covered about 1,200 companies with, altogether, over one million workers. Its main activities are at the policy level in lobbying the government on behalf of its members, for example on tax legislation or regulations. Some of that lobbying concerns matters of international trade and trade promotion. It also puts foreign enterprises in touch with Czech businesses for such purposes as technology transfer, licensing, production, direct investment and assists them with guidance on administrative procedures, and business opportunities. It does not provide direct services to Czech exporters, but assists them in negotiations with government on legislative changes, for example in customs and tax matters, or improving access to credit guarantees and export finance. The CIT also has extensive links with similar organisations abroad and with chambers of commerce in other countries [Interviews and *ACE, Jan. 1996*]. But few exporters mentioned it as a source of help in promoting exports [*Survey 1997*].

EMBASSIES ABROAD

For many countries the commercial sections of their embassies provide a major source of support for exporting. Czech exporters today look back with some degree of nostalgia to the help they received from the commercial staff at embassies during the communist era. Such staffs were well trained in foreign languages and often had a good technical knowledge of the products that they were promoting. Sometimes the state trading companies had offices of their own in or near embassies. The commercial staffs at the embassies were often well educated with an engineering background where dealing with the machinery, equipment and technical products, which were major exports from Czechoslovakia. They often had some training in economics or business methods as well as in the relevant foreign languages. They were however tainted by association with the planned economy, the large state trading monopolies, and the belief that some of them had been agents of the secret services. They were disbanded when the country gained its freedom and a government with a strong faith in markets took over. Many of them moved into trading companies and the export offices of manufacturing companies and conglomerates.

When it was recognised just how much most of the world uses commercial counsellors in embassies and that they may serve a useful purpose in assisting exporters the Government revised its stance and the Ministry of Foreign Affairs had to recruit staff anew to reconstitute the service. Given budgetary restrictions and the shortage of people with the combination of language skills, commercial experience, or economics, business, or technical training, the numbers actually placed in embassies were few, generally only one or two professional staff. Moreover there was a tendency for ambassadors to give them political work in addition to their commercial duties. The result has been that exporters have found them of little help. Requests appear to have been ignored or replies so vague or so long delayed as to be useless [*Survey, 1997*].

The Ministry is aware of the problems, has made commercial services a high priority and is trying to increase and upgrade the staff, but up to 1997 it seems to have had little impact on business opinion.

In an attempt to arrive at an independent evaluation of the various instruments of support for exporting from the Czech Republic we interviewed officials from the relevant ministries and principal export institutions and carried out a survey through interviews of a sample of the main users of their services.

THE SURVEY

As response rates to academic questionnaires tend to be very low it was decided to interview a number of institutions and firms drawn from both trading companies (export-import firms) and manufacturers engaged in exporting. The institutions ranged from the Ministry of Industry and Trade to Economic Chambers and Industry Associations. The firms covered large and small companies with product specialisation ranging from heavy engineering

TABLE 4.5
USE OF EXPORT SUPPORT SERVICES (BY 34 COMPANIES)

	21 Manufacturers			13 Trading Companies		
	Used	Help	No help	Used	Help	No help
Export Credit Guaranteed (EGAP)	7	2	5	10	7	3
Credit, Cz.E.B. or	4	1	3	5	4	1
Commercial Bank	2	2		3	3	
Commercial Section of Embassy	8	2	6			
Infocentrum (Min. of Ind. and Trade)	3	1		3	2	1
Economic Chambers	9	7	2			
Trade Fairs (support)	9	9		4	4	
(self-financed)	5					
Phare support to achieve international standards	2	2				
Training for export (subsidised)	1	1				
(self-financed)	3	3				
No help sought from government instititions			2			2*
No help sought from Economic Chambers			2			2

Source: Survey of 34 companies, March and June/July 1997.

Notes: * One other company received government help (subsidy) to export an agricultural product. One company used EGAP once, but generally its orders were too small. Other sources of help used: Consul (active individual) 1, Trade Association 1, Trade missions 1.

to wallpaper, and dairy products. Table 4.5 on Use of Export Support Services summarises the results as viewed by the managers of firms that we interviewed in March and June/July of 1997.

The companies were chosen from a large list of firms, which exported substantial proportions of the products, they produced or handled. They were based in or around Prague and Brno. As this meant they were likely to be more in contact with Government and institutions than firms in more remote locations were, this should, if anything, have biased the results in favour of greater usage of export services. In practice few of them had made much use. EGAP, the institution providing export credit guarantees had been used by only seven out of 21 manufacturers. Of these only two had received help. 10 out of 13 trading companies had used EGAP and of those seven had been given help. Four manufacturers had sought help from the Czech Export Bank and one had obtained a loan. The others got no help. Five trading companies had approached the Czech Export Bank, four successfully. Two manufacturers and three trading companies had obtained loans from commercial banks.

These results might suggest a lack of interest in such help, but on the contrary, most firms mentioned credit risk and the need both for loans to finance exports and for pre-production as very important. They were eager to obtain such help but thought it very unlikely that they would obtain it from EGAP. But the Czech Export Bank requires a credit guarantee from EGAP for the transaction before it will provide credit. Most firms got around the problem by various means such as loans from their foreign trading partner, particularly where they were producing an intermediate good under an agreement with the foreign company. Others insisted on payment in advance or on delivery. Some managed to obtain loans from foreign banks. Generally they recognised that these methods placed them at a disadvantage compared with foreign suppliers who could give standard credit terms to their customers.

All Czech embassies have a commercial section, but they are generally small and overworked. Only eight manufacturers said that they had contacted Embassy staff for help. Of these only two felt they had received some help. None of the trading companies had even approached embassies for help.

Infocentrum is the main institution, which is a data bank and provider of basic economic information and market studies for exporters. Only three manufacturers had made any use of Infocentrum and of these only one felt it had been of any use. Three trading companies had used Infocentrum, two with success and one said that it had received no help.

There is a central Economic Chamber for the Czech Republic located in Prague and many economic chambers linked to it in cities and districts throughout the country. Very many services are advertised as being available from this leading non-governmental organisation. Nine of our sample of manufacturers had contacted their economic chamber for assistance and seven said that they had been helped.

Some 14 manufacturers had made use of trade fairs. Of these nine had contributions to their costs through an economic chamber or from the Ministry of Industry and Trade. Five had financed participation themselves. Four trading companies had taken part in trade fairs with the help of financial contributions from the Ministry.

Help in achieving international standards (ISO 9000) from a Phare programme had been used by two manufacturers. Others had done this on their own, some were still unaware that help for this was available.

Only one company admitted to having received any help for training staff, but three others had sent staff to training programmes at their company's expense. Two manufacturers claimed never to have sought help of any kind from Government agencies. Two trading companies made a similar claim, but in fact one of them had actually been given a subsidy to export an agricultural product. Two manufacturers and two trading companies also made it explicit that they had never sought help from economic chambers.

Many of these companies had entered or wanted to enter new markets. For some that was the result of lost markets in the former Soviet Union and other COMECON countries. For others it was a matter of trying to get back into markets such as Russia and the Ukraine which they had abandoned as a result of bad debts there and competition from OECD countries' goods and services. Since most of the manufacturing firms were new to competing for sales in foreign market economies they could be expected to have urgent need of help, both financial and marketing. From the results of our enquiry most got no help or were relatively dissatisfied with the help they received

In the survey managers were also asked about which export support services they regarded as most important. The measures most frequently mentioned by the managers in manufacturing companies are shown in Table 4.6 on Services Wanted.

Other suggestions made by no more than two firms were: information on markets and on regulations governing imports to foreign markets, information on useful contacts, more political support for exporting, abolition of import deposit requirements or a speeding up of the processing of imported inputs. One firm claimed that delays on getting imported inputs cleared had caused them to miss delivery dates. Two firms suggested that help for exporting should be untied to specific forms or suppliers. They wanted to be able to buy help from any approved source and then seek reimbursement for an agreed part of the costs in the form of a government subsidy. Two other suggestions were aimed more at assistance to manufacturing in general rather than to exporting: support for research, and debt forgiveness for debts incurred before privatisation.

TABLE 4.6
SERVICES WANTED (21 MANUFACTURING FIRMS)

Type of service	Number of Firms
Credit Guarantee or Insurance	8
Access to export credits	7
Access to pre-production finance	4
Better quality services from commercial section of embassies	8
Well-led (or led by high profile minister) trade missions	3

Source: Surveys of firms March and June/July 1997.

PREVIOUS STUDIES

One report, based on research carried out in the CEEC between January and October 1994, was published in November 1994 by the Trade Development Institute of Ireland (TDI) for the PHARE Programme [*TDI, 1994*]. This claimed that the Czech government decided on a 'minimal interventionist trade development policy' [*1994: 35*] The government took the view that its role was simply to provide an environment in which market forces would determine the direction and speed of trade development. The study also pointed out that in the Czech Republic no single ministry was responsible for trade development. Responsibility was divided among the Ministry of Industry and Trade for foreign trade relations and agreements; the Ministry of Economy for export promotion; the Ministry of Foreign Affairs for overseas trade representation [*1994: 37*]. But, the reluctance to create a single national agency for trade development had not barred the government from other means of helping exporters. The study says, 'There are plans to assist the network of economic chambers to provide a range of trade-related services which would eventually be entirely funded by the private sector' [*1994: 38*]. The study also noted that the Export Guarantee institution (EGAP) and later, the Czech Export Bank had been set up in 1993–94, but were not yet operational.

A second PHARE-supported consultancy study produced a report in four sections, which drew on six earlier studies, four by the institutions themselves, and two by independent consultants. All were based on questionnaires between 1994 and 1995. The PHARE study by Asesores de Commercio Exterior S.L. (ACE) was done between December 1995 and February 1996. The four sections, released between December 1995 and February 1996 were: (1) Review of Czech Exporter's Needs; (2) Evaluation of Export Service Provision; (3) Gap Analysis; (4) Czech Export Support Policy.

Table 4.7 below, which is adapted from Table 5 in the ACE study, summarises results from five individual studies. based on questions mailed to Czech firms engaged in exporting. The footnotes appended to the table give some information on the characteristics of the recipients of the questionnaires. All were carried out in 1994 except E, which was done in October 1995. The ranking of the managers' expressed needs was based on the frequency of the occurrence of the feature in the replies.

TABLE 4.7
ASSESSMENT OF NEEDS: EXPORT SUPPORT IN THE CZECH REPUBLIC

| Type of Need | Study | | | | | Evaluation | |
	A	B	C	D	E	No. of studies	Rank order
Tax relief based on export performance	2	2	3	1		4	1
Finance and credit	1	1	1	7	3	5	2
Insurance of foreign trade operations	5	3	2	6		4	3
Interest paid for Investments in pro-export production	4	4	4	5		4	4
Contribution to investment of 8-20%	3	5	7	4	5	5	5
Accelerated depreciation for outstanding exporters	6	7	5	2		4	6
Contact services	7	6	6	9		4	7
Discount from highway tax and berthages	8	9	10	3		4	8
Consulting services	10	10	8	8	4	5	9
Advertising services		8	9	10	9	4	10
Know how transfer	9	11	11	11		4	11

Source: ACE (Asesores de Commercio Exterior), 26 Jan. 1996, Task 2.
Notes: 1 represents highest priority, 11 lowest.
List of studies summarised in Table 3:
A. Results of Inquiry of Exporters covering 23 large firms (250mil.CZK or more per year)
B. Results of Inquiry covering 23 small and medium firms
C. Public Inquiry covering exporters of complete plants.
D. Public Inquiry of the CIT, Part c. External Relations.
E. EC Phare Industrial Restructuring Project. Needs Analysis Phase.

Preferential tax relief for exporters in proportion to their volume of exports is given the top rank, and finance for exports came a close second, with credit insurance against risks of default third.

TRAINING FOR EXPORTING

The ACE study also reported an enquiry into export management training in the Czech Republic that took place in April 1995. The method used was 'Inquiry by comprehensive questionnaire used in meetings/contacts with the companies, independent secondary research sources consultations'. The study was based on replies from 91 small, medium and large companies within nine sectors, 32 support organisations (banks, chambers of commerce, business and public support organisations), and 35 Czech trainers/consultants. The conclusions of this study identified the training needs of Czech exporters as, in order of importance: marketing, general management, finance, production, human resources management, and administration.

In our own enquiry we found only four manufacturing companies which had used externally provided training, only one of them with government assistance. They had found it of some help. But none of the firms in either the manufacturing or the trading companies mentioned training in exporting as a service that they wanted. Some managers expressed doubts as to the quality of training available.

The Asesores study also used four workshops in November 1995: one organised by the Confederation of Industry and Transport, one by the Centre for Foreign Economic Relations, one by the Economic Chamber, and one by the National Information Centre.

Among them these included as participants 43 companies, covering small, medium and large organisations, weighted more to large (ten with under 250 employees, 13 with between 250 and 1000, and 19 with over 1000 (actually sums to 42), all engaged in exporting. The workshops focused on the types of export support that Czech companies deemed necessary such as information, promotion, consultancy or advice to companies and support abroad. The method was, open discussion led the by ACE experts. The discussions also covered current efforts of the government and other institutions to meet these needs.

Their conclusions were that most of the participating companies were confused about which institution could provide comprehensive export services and would prefer a 'one stop shop'. Firms were uncertain about what they could reasonably expect from the Czech government as compared with the generous support Western competitors could expect from their governments. The participants regarded insufficient export financing as a major problem, particularly for capital goods exporters. They put a low value on services provided by existing export support institutions. Support abroad (from commercial sections of embassies) was accorded a high priority and the current support abroad was thought to be nearly non-existent as compared with the help available before 1990 or with what their Western competitors receive.

The second part of the Asesores de Commercio Exterior (ACE) study was 'Evaluation of Export Service Provision' [*26 Jan. 1996*]. This covered the Centre for Foreign Economic Relations (CFER), the Confederation of Industry of the Czech Republic (CIT), the Economic Chamber of the Czech Republic (EC) and the National Information Centre of the Czech Republic

(NIC). They approached the Czech Centres, but the Centres declined to participate in the project. Their main activities, in any case, are directed to cultural matters and tourism. None of the manufacturing or trading firms that we interviewed mentioned them as a source of commercial information or other help.

The conclusions of the ACE study were that the Chamber of Commerce (Economic Chamber), the Confederation of Industry, and Infocentrum enjoyed a positive image among Czech firms. The National Information Centre, however, was not well known and its image was not very positive. But, in our survey few firms had used these institutions and only the Economic Chambers emerged as having helped a significant number. They looked to the Confederation of Industry, or to their particular trade association, more for lobbying services to draw Government attention to problems than for marketing or other information.

From their earlier studies ACE concluded that the key requirements (other than financial) for Czech exporters were market business information, information on international tenders, promotional tools, support abroad, and advisory/consultant services. In 'Gap Analysis' [*26 Jan. 1996*] they reviewed the current tasks and facilities of the existing institutions. They pointed out that the Centre for Foreign Economic Relations and the Economic Chambers operating together provided the best prospects for holding and disseminating information on markets/business, and international tenders. The Economic Chambers formed the only organisation currently doing significant promotional activity. At present there was little effective support abroad, nor any effective provision of advisory/consultant services. Upgrading the existing Commercial Sections of the Embassies would, in their view, require a specific programme with the participation of the Ministry of Foreign Affairs who currently administer them. A new service would have to be created to provide consultant/advisory services for exporters. The institution most likely to serve as the base for such services would be, in their view, the Economic Chambers, but the CFER and the Confederation were other possibilities.

The Asesores de Commercio Exterior S.L. study [*20 Feb. 1996*] made a number of recommendations. As it had dealt only with non-financial aspects of export promotion: information, promotion, advice, and support abroad it made no recommendations on insurance or finance. Their study had identified the overlap in services of different export support institutions (ESIs) and confusion among exporters as to where to go for advice as a major problem. This leads to their main recommendation that one organisation should be responsible for co-ordinating the whole effort to support exports, and that there should be 'one-stop shops' as the main contact point for firms seeking information on any topic connected to exporting.

They also recommended that an Advisory Committee for Export Support be created and charged with the task of guiding and assisting in the implementation of an overall national export strategy. This committee should be chaired by the Minister for Trade and Industry and should have representatives from all the ministries, official and private institutions, and export finance institutions. Policy should be further refined by an autonomous government institution such as the Centre for Foreign Economic Relations with the assistance of users of export support. Final approval would lie with the Advisory Committee. Private sector bodies selected by the CFER would provide the services to exporters: Economic Chambers, private companies, the Confederation of Industry and Transport and so on.

Their recommended one-stop shops should be based in district economic chambers with staff from the chambers, supplemented by staff from relevant ministries and the Czech Export Bank. An intensive training effort for the staff is recommended. They also recommend a pilot programme to establish export assistance centres run by the private sector and aimed at small businesses.

They recommended that Infocentrum within the CFER should become the single information office, which would co-ordinate the existing specialised export information offices. It should disseminate information through the existing network of district economic chambers. The CFER would also become responsible for organising trade events (trade fairs, missions, exhibitions) after they had been selected by the Ministry of Industry and Trade from proposals for a given year from the various export support institutions. None should be allowed save those that have been approved in a review at a specified time so as to enable evaluation and ranking by priority to take place. The number of events should be limited and duplication eliminated.

They recommended that commercial work should have a much higher priority in embassies and Czech centres and should be of a higher standard. They suggest that there should be a strategic plan for countries with market potential. They make many detailed recommendations for improving the effectiveness of the support for exporters abroad.

Finally, the ACE study recommended that there should be an export support institution's Advocacy Co-ordinating Network within the Advisory Committee. The Minister for Trade and Industry should chair it, and it should develop aggressive advocacy along with the private sector and within the context of Czech foreign policy to give similar support to Czech exports as foreign countries such as the United Kingdom and Germany give to theirs.

IMPLEMENTATION

The Czech government appears to have accepted the main recommendations of this report and has also proposed other measures to promote exports such as additional funds for export credit, accelerated depreciation for export relevant machinery and equipment, and tax preferences. The Ministry of Industry and Trade has become the leading Ministry in setting policy for institutional support for exporting. Czech Trade (formerly the Centre for Foreign Economic Relations) has become the central agency for providing all kinds of information in support of exports, and is the central backup for the one-stop shops located in the district economic chambers.

An EU-PHARE project set up an Exports Support Fund to provide grants of between 50 per cent and 75 per cent of the costs of users of various services that assist exporting. The grants were to cover 75 per cent of the costs of buying information products from Infocentrum in the CFER or from the Economic Chamber of the Czech Republic up to a maximum per firm of 15,000 ECU (about $16,500). The grant would also make a contribution of 50 per cent of promotion costs incurred by a firm in, say, participating in a trade mission, trade fair or promotion campaign, up to 20,000 ECU. Fifty per cent of the costs of buying services connected with obtaining product certification up to a maximum of 5,000 ECU per product and 10,000 ECU for each firm that received a grant. Firms could also get a grant of 75 per cent of the cost of entry into the Czech Subcontracting Exchange (up to 1000 ECU).

The assistance was limited to firms with less than 1,000 employees (with priority given to small and medium companies). Payment was to be to the export support institution providing the service, and applicants had to meet various conditions. These are not onerous, but the procedures to be followed seem time-consuming. The Project was to run until December 1997 when it would be reviewed and might be extended. The total funds made available were quite small. If each grant recipient purchasing information services used the full 20,000 ECU, less than 40 companies could use the service.

CONCLUSIONS ON CZECH SUPPORT FOR EXPORTING

It is clear that the Czech government has become much more convinced of the need for increased exports and that institutional support for exporters can make a significant (even if small) contribution to this objective. The weaknesses in the provision of support in the recent past outlined in the various studies, including our own, have been recognised. From our interviews with officials in the Ministry of Industry and Trade, the Centre for Foreign Economic Relations, and the Ministry of Foreign Affairs over the last year (1998), it was clear that there was no complacency about the situation. All were keen to strengthen the means of providing export support. But the Czech Parliament raised objections to the government's proposals and this has caused some delay. The system continued to be in a state of flux, and it is really too early to evaluate whether the reforms will be adequate to provide

Czech exporters with worthwhile support services. Probably the best that we can do at present is to raise a number of questions about the reforms.

One fundamental question is whether the chosen institutions can recruit staff with adequate skills and experience to provide the services. The salary levels in the Ministry of Foreign Affairs may be too low to attract staff for their commercial sections with the language fluency, business experience, and technical competencies to assist firms in finding markets and contacts in foreign countries. Successful private firms in manufacturing, banking and tourism will be able to offer much higher salaries for such people. At present the commercial sections of the embassies have very few staff. Budgetary considerations are likely to prevent a large expansion with well-qualified staff. This is also likely to be true for the one-stop shops.

Although Infocentrum may be able to put together and make available all the information which can be obtained on calls for international tenders by multilateral banks and governments it is much less likely that they could carry out a market research study on highly specialised manufactures in a foreign country. For this type of assistance it may only be a specialised local consultancy firm or a large foreign consultancy firm which would be capable of providing useful results. It was a very frequent comment by the managers that we interviewed that their products were too specialised for a general researcher to give help. Some had commissioned Czech or foreign consultants to find trading partners or market information. The satisfaction expressed about the results was certainly higher than those expressed about services of Czech official agencies.

An interesting experiment would be to have a fund in parallel to the Phare Exporters Support Fund. This fund would reimburse half of exporters costs of buying export support services against invoices from any agency, public or private, local or foreign as long as the agency was bona fide and there could be checks on actual expenditure. As firms would be meeting at least half of the costs themselves they would have an incentive to seek the most cost-effective means of obtaining the support they wanted. Competition among the suppliers of such services would tend to keep up quality and reduce costs. It is not clear why the existing Exporters Support Fund limits the use of its grants to the purchase of services to the existing Export Support Institutions.

It was also clear from our study that the main interest among firms was in finance and insurance against commercial and political risk. Pre-production finance was singled out by several as a key bottleneck. While information about markets and contacts was valued by some, others, which had solid foreign partners with relatively integrated production, had no need of marketing help. Their products were even displayed for them at trade fairs by their foreign partners. Large companies in defence or power industries stressed the importance of high-level trade missions to counter the pressures put on foreign governments by ministerial visits from OECD countries. They seemed to have little need of help in finding out about tenders. Their own offices and agents abroad, or membership of international associations for their industry gave them access to such information.

It will be interesting to see whether the Czech Subcontracting Exchange proves helpful to Czech firms. Some managers expressed the view that for their industries the current and potential suppliers were easily known. The Czech economy is not large so most managers have a good knowledge of possible suppliers. In their view it would not be difficult for a local or even a foreign firm to find out such information. But their views may be biased by their particular industry. The problem may be greater in others.

Overall, it seems that the Czech Government has responded to the trade deficits and the criticisms of the policies and institutions that were in place up to 1996/67. The major questions which remain are whether given stronger exports due to the depreciation of the Czech Crown enthusiasm wanes, and whether enough resources have been put into the new system to make it work. It would be a great pity if Czech companies were to be encouraged to have high expectations of what could be provided in the immediate future when it may take some years to build up an effective export support programme.

REFERENCES

ACE (Asesores de Commercio Exterior S.L.), 1996, 'Design of Czech Export Programme', mimeo, Prague.
Amsden, A., 1989, *Asia's Next Giant: South Korea and Late Industrialisation*, Oxford: Oxford.
Amsden, A., 1993, 'Structural Macroeconomic Underpinnings of Effective Industrial Policy: Fast Growth in the 1980s in Five Asian Countries', Geneva: UNCTAD Discussion Papers, No. 57.
Boeri, T., 1994, '"Transitional" Unemployment', Paris: OECD, *Economics of Transition*, Vol.2.
Centre for Foreign Economic Relations, 1995, 'The Czech Republic in the International Economy', Prague, May.
Czech Statistical Office, 1998, *Indicators of the Social and Economic Development of the Czech Republic*, Prague: CSO.
Dyba, K. and J. Svejnar, 1995, 'A Comparative View of Economic Developments in the Czech Republic', in J. Svejnar (ed.), *The Czech Republic and Economic Transition in Eastern Europe*, New York: Academic Press.
(*The Economist*), various issues, London: The Economist Newspaper Ltd.
EGAP (Export Guarantee and Insurance Corporation), 1996, *Annual Reports*, Prague.
European Bank for Reconstruction and Development (EBRD), 1995, 1996, and 1997, *Transition Report*, London.
Gacs, J., 1994, 'Trade Policy in the Czech and Slovak Republics, Hungary and Poland in 1989–1993. A Comparison', in CASE, Studies *and Analyses* 11, Jan., Warsaw.
Gacs, J., 1997, 'Government Policies in Support of Exports in Small Transition Economies', Ch. 9 in R.N. Cooper and Janos Gacs, *Trade Growth in Transition Economies: Export Impediments for Central and Eastern Europe*, Cheltenham, UK and Lyme, US: Edward Elgar.
Gaspar, P. 1995, 'Exchange Rate Policies in Economies in Transition', in Gaspar (ed.) [*1995*].
Gaspar, Pal (ed.), 1995, *Changes and Challenges: Economic Transformation in East-Central Europe*, Budapest: Akaemiai Kiado.

Gelb, A. and C. Gray, 1991, ' The Transformation of Economies in Central and Eastern Europe: Issues, Progress, and Prospects', mimeo, Washington, DC: World Bank.

IMF (International Monetary Fund), 1997, *International Financial Statistics*, Washington, DC.

Jackman, R. 1994, 'Economic policy and employment in the transition economies of Central and Eastern Europe: What have we learned?', *International Labour Review*, Vol.133, No.3.

Kaminski, B., Wang, Z., and A. Winters, 1996, *Foreign Trade in the Transition: The International Environment and Domestic Policy* (Studies of Economies in Transformation), Washington, DC: World Bank.

Keesing, D., 1988, 'The Four Successful Exceptions: Official Export Promotion and Support for Export Marketing in Korea, Hong Kong, Singapore, and Taiwan, China', Washington, DC: UNDP-World Bank, Trade Expansion Program, Occasional Paper 2.

Keesing, D. and A. Singer, 1991, 'Development Assistance Gone Wrong: Failures in Services to Promote and Support Manufactured Exports', in P. Hogan *et al.*, *The Role of Support Services in Expanding Manufactured Exports in Developing Countries*, Washington, DC: Economic Development Institute of the World Bank, EDI Seminar Series.

Klacek, J. and Hrncir, M.1994, 'Macroeconomic Policies: Stabilisation and Transition in Former Czechoslovakia and in the Czech Republic', Prague: CASE, *Studies and Analyses*, March.

Krejci, J., 1990, 'Eastern Europe', in A. Seldon, *Government and Economies in the Post-War World*, London: Routledge.

Lavigne, M., 1995. *The Economics of Transition*, London: Macmillan.

McAleese, D. and O' Donnell, 1996. 'Institutional Support for Exporting: Issues and Evidence', mimeo, paper presented to Phare Workshop, Warsaw.

Ministry of Economy of the Czech Republic, 1996, *Export Promotion in the Czech Republic*, Prague: Ministry of Economy.

Myant, M., 1993, *Transforming Socialist Economies: The Case of Poland and Czechoslovakia*, London: Edward Elgar.

Sass, M., 1995, 'Developments in Foreign Trade and Trade Policy in the "Visegrad Countries"', in Gaspar (ed.) [*1995*].

Schwartz, A., 1997, 'Market Failure and Corruption in the Czech Republic', *Transition*, Dec.

Stiglitz, J.E., 1994, *Whither Socialism*, Cambridge, MA: MIT Press.

Stiglitz, J.E., 1996, ' Some Lessons from the East Asian Miracle', Washington, DC: World Bank, *Research Observer*, Aug.

Survey, 1997, Interview with Czech Ministries, Agencies and Companies, March and June/July 1997 in Prague and Brno.

Svejnar, J., 1995, *The Czech Republic and Economic Transition in Eastern Europe*, New York: Academic Press.

Trade Development Institute of Ireland (TDI), 1994, 'Phare Multi-Country Programme Trade Development: Preliminary Study ', Final Report to DG1-Phare, Nov.

Wade, R. 1990, Governing *the Market: Economic Theory and the Role of Government in East Asian Industrialisation*, Princeton, NJ: Princeton University Press.

World Bank, 1987, 1990, 1991, 1996, *World Development Reports*, Oxford: Oxford University Press.

World Bank, 1993, *The East Asian Miracle: A World Bank Policy Research Report*, Oxford: Oxford University Press.

World Trade Organization (WTO), 1996, *Trade Policy Review: Czech Republic*, Geneva: WTO.

5

Export Promotion in Hungary: Rebuilding the System

In each transitional economy some aspects of change are common and others are unique. For Hungary the unique aspect lies in its early start on economic reform. This brought both advantages and disadvantages to developing a market directed, open, export promoting economy as opposed to a protected, administratively regulated one. Although some progress towards decentralisation and increased trade with OECD nations was made after 1968 the main developments were after 1989. The stimulus to increased exports came mainly from general macro and market directed reforms that brought in foreign direct investment. Indeed, the major source of increased exports has been those companies with substantial foreign direct investment in their plant. That is particularly true in the latter half of the period

Government institutional support for exporting made only a small contribution. The most important contribution was indirect: by attracting (export-oriented) foreign direct investments. Most of the support actually went to large companies. Most of these were former state owned enterprises whose exports continued to be to the countries of the former Soviet Union (FSU). Limitations on government support for exporting will tighten as Hungary takes on the responsibilities of membership of the World Trade Organization (WTO) and moves closer to membership of the European Union. But, in our view, more vigorous policies and more effective instruments should be used by the government to assist exporters, particularly small and medium-sized indigenous firms.

HUNGARY'S EXPORT PERFORMANCE, 1991–97

For Hungary, as a small open economy, foreign trade is crucial. The openness of the country (in terms of exports plus imports divided by GDP) has grown steadily from 67 per cent in 1991 to 81 per cent in 1996. Table 5.1 reports the most important developments in Hungary's foreign trade. After 1994, in US$ terms, the annual growth rate of exports exceeded 20 per cent in each year. On the other hand, the growth rate of imports, at less than 18 per cent, helped to reduce the foreign trade deficit.

TABLE 5.1
HUNGARIAN FOREIGN TRADE, 1991–98 (million US$)

	1991	1992	1993	1994	1995	1996	1997	1998
Export	10186.9	10705.1	8906.9	10700.8	12867.0	15703.7	19099.9	23005.3
Import	11382.1	11078.9	12530.3	14533.8	15466.3	18143.7	21234.0	25706.4
Balance	–1195.2	–373.8	–3623.4	–3853.0	–2599.3	–2440.0	–2134.1	–2701.1

Source: Ministry of Economic Affairs.

One of the most striking characteristics of Hungarian foreign trade was its massive reorientation. The demise of the CMEA and economic transition acted as push factors, more liberal trade with the developed countries – due to preferential trade agreements and trade liberalisation in Hungary – played the role of pull factor in the reorientation of foreign trade. Already in 1991, most exports were directed towards developed economies. Their share, and within that group, the share of the EU, continued to grow up to 1998, as shown in Table 5 2.

TABLE 5.2
THE DESTINATION OF HUNGARIAN EXPORTS, 1991–98 (%)

	1991	1992	1993	1994	1995	1996	1997	1998
Developed countries	67.9	71.2	67.6	72.0	69.5	76.3	77.5	80.3
– EU	45.7	49.7	46.5	51.0	62.8	69.7	71.2	72.9
Developing countries	8.4	5.3	5.4	3.9	3.9	3.2	2.7	3.2
former CMEA	23.1	22.5	24.7	22.1	23.3	19.8	19.2	16.5

Source: Ministry of Economic Affairs.

The geographical reorientation was followed, especially after 1996, by a restructuring of exports in product composition. Table 5.3 shows the Finger similarity indices of the partner and product composition of Hungarian foreign trade. While changes in partner composition are more characteristic in the first part of the analysed period, the product composition of exports changed more significantly in the second part.

Table 5.4 shows the share of 'traditional' export products, like food and beverages falling throughout the period while there has been a gradual but marked increase in the share of machinery and transport equipment, which accelerated in 1996 and 1997. The change in the product composition is even

TABLE 5.3
SIMILARITY INDICES (FINGER) OF HUNGARIAN EXPORTS

Composition	1997/96	1996/95	1995/94	1994/92	1997/92
Product	0.75359	0.89018	0.87900	0.84260	0.67304
Partner	0.89080	0.93188	0.91913	0.76848	0.79080

Source: Partners: 119 countries
Products: 310 (SITC, Rev. 3., three digit) product groups
Notes: (1) Finger similarity index: $S_{ij}=[SUM|sh_i^k-sh_j^k|x\ sh_j^k]$
(where: i and j are years; sh is the share of the sector k in total export.
The larger the index the more similar the trade structure to the base year.
(2) data for 1996 do not contain export from the industrial free trade zones. According to calculations based on two-digit data containing export of the industrial free trade zones in 1996, a significant change in the product composition started already in 1996, and correspondingly, was less pronounced in 1997.

more obvious in exports to the EU: here, in 1997, the share of food and beverages diminished to 7.4 per cent, and the share of machinery and transport equipment amounted to 53.6 per cent.

TABLE 5.4
THE PRODUCT COMPOSITION OF HUNGARIAN EXPORTS 1991–98

	1991	1992	1993	1994	1995	1996	1997	1998
Food beverages agric. products	23.2	21.8	19.2	18.5	20.2	15.2	12.9	10.6
Raw materials	7.6	6.7	6.6	6.1	5.5	4.4	3.8	2.9
Fuels, energy	3.0	3.4	4.0	4.0	3.2	3.4	2.6	1.9
Manufactures	44.8	47.4	46.6	45.8	45.5	40.8	35.5	32.7
Machinery, transport equipment	21.4	20.7	23.6	25.6	25.6	35.2	45.2	51.9
Total	100.0	100.0	100.0	100.0	100.0	100.0	100.0	100.0

Source: Ministry of Economic Affairs.

Three specific features of Hungarian exports need special attention from the point of view of later analysis. The reason is that they affect a high share of Hungarian exports, and – for different reasons – the exports involved usually do not need the export promoting services discussed later in this study.

First, foreign direct investments (FDI) play a very important role in the Hungarian economy. The stock of FDI (without reinvested earnings) reached 20 billion US$ by 1999. While the absolute level of stock and annual inflow is higher in Poland than in Hungary after 1997, the Hungarian per capita stock and inflow is still the highest in the region. Companies with foreign participation in 1997 accounted for 14 per cent of GDP and 70 per cent of exports (data from the Joint Venture Association). The majority of the companies with foreign participation has close ties or is closely controlled by the foreign company, and their trade relations with foreign headquarters or other foreign affiliates substantially facilitate their trade. Some of them conduct trade almost exclusively with other affiliates of the controlling foreign company. Thus they usually do not need and do not use export-promoting services.

Second, the activity of companies in the industrial free trade zones has become important, particularly since 1995. Liberal regulation increased the attractiveness of these zones, especially for companies with foreign participation, who carried out basically assembly activities. Companies in customs free zones belong mainly to the machinery and car industry. Already, in 1997, 26 per cent of Hungarian exports derived from industrial free trade zones; by 1998 this had risen to 36 per cent (Ministry of Economic Affairs, Website). These companies, operating in industrial free trade zones, and carrying out mainly assembly activities [*Antalóczy, 1998: 12*], usually have no need for export promotion services.

Third, approximately one-fourth to one-fifth of Hungarian exports is given by outward processing trade (OPT). The share of OPT in total exports was 21 per cent in 1998 (Ministry of Economic Affairs, Website). OPT activities are most important in the clothing and machinery industries and are prevalent in trade between Hungary and Germany, Austria and Italy. Companies, carrying out especially clothing OPT (with that as the main source of their revenues) have close relations (secured market, payments agreements, etc.) with their foreign partners [*Antalóczy, Sass, 1998: 747–70*], thus they rarely use services to promote exports.

Of course, the above three segments are closely related. Most of the companies in the industrial free trade zones have foreign participation; companies with foreign participation also carry out some of the OPT activities. Some companies in each group may use some of the export promotion services, but the majority of the companies seldom need them.

THE FRAMEWORK

The rate of change in Hungary's trade policy in the nineties has been dramatic compared to the eighties. Three factors determined the main direction of the changes. First, the reform of the inherited, somewhat reformed socialist system needed to be completed. Second, the reform of the foreign trade system formed part of an overall reform and liberalisation of the economy. Third, changing international obligations (membership in international organisations, international trade agreements, concluded in the period) also greatly restricted the room for manoeuvre in trade policy.

Export Promotion in Hungary

The Past System of Foreign Trade and its Reform

During the planned economy, foreign trade, foreign exchange and credit were state monopolies in Hungary. Foreign trade activities were conducted through specialised foreign trade companies and foreign exchange control did not allow companies to retain foreign currencies. Administrative import controls were in force. Most trade flows took place among CMEA countries, mostly with the Soviet Union. Foreign trade patterns did not reflect the comparative advantage of the economy.

After 1968, economic reforms were gradually introduced. These had significant effects on foreign trade. Due to the reform steps, the Hungarian foreign trade system became less monopolised and more liberal compared to other planned economies [*Gács, 1993*]. The main characteristics of foreign trade (and export promotion) were as follows.

Between 1968 and 1991 exports were still determined by the two most important characteristics of foreign trade in Hungary's planned economy, the state monopoly of foreign trade and restrictions on foreign currency holdings. Foreign trade was controlled and regulated by the Finance Ministry and the Hungarian National Bank (through multiple exchange rates, subsidies attached to them, and differential credits), the Foreign Trade Ministry (through diplomatic activities, institutional support and regulations), and the Hungarian State Insurance Company.

In the 1970s, after the initial reforms, and due to the foreign exchange needs of the country because of the high foreign debt burden, the importance of trade with developed countries grew. The character and regulation of foreign trade with CMEA and OECD countries, however, differed a great deal. Within the CMEA (which still involved most foreign trade), trade was conducted on the basis of bilateral trade agreements, which included fixed prices, and mandatory export-import quotas [*GATT, 1991: 11*]. At the company level there were almost no direct connections with the foreign partners, insurance was not required. But, in trade with developed market economies, economic factors such as exchange rates, credits and interest rates and profits played a greater role, and after 1968, some of the companies most heavily involved in foreign trade were allowed individual foreign trading rights.

The financing of exports and imports was regulated by the agreement between the Finance Ministry, the Foreign Trade Ministry and the Hungarian National Bank (Tripartitum). Exports were financed by the National Bank until the currency actually reached the country. The companies could finance short-term export credits without special permission. However, middle and long-term credits were refinanced by the National Bank and special permission from the Foreign Trade Ministry was required. This system worked until 1991. The only difference was that after the two-tier banking system was introduced, credits were given by commercial banks, and the National Bank automatically refinanced them [*Antalóczy, 1997*].

The export credit insurance system was introduced in 1968, and elaborated by the Finance Ministry, on the model of the German Hermes Kreditversicherung AG. The State Insurance Company handled the business (after 1984: Hungaria Insurance Company). Defaults were financed by the state budget. These mainly occurred in trade with developing countries. From then Hungarian companies could insure economic, political and exchange rate risks [*Antalóczy, 1997: 5*]

The Foreign Trade Ministry organised the elements of the so-called institutional export promotion: participation in trade fairs, providing information on markets, business counselling, training, and organisation of trade missions. Local trade representatives in the most important markets provided help and information for foreign trade activities. Foreign trade companies, specialised by sector (the so-called impexes) handled foreign trade on behalf of those domestic companies that had no special right to trade internationally [*GATT, 1991: 12*].

These elements of export promotion in its narrow sense played only a marginal role in promoting exports in the planned economy. The most important incentive for the companies to export was the exchange rate, and the system of subsidies connected to the exchange rates applied in foreign trade. In the eighties, because of the high foreign debt accumulated during the seventies, this system of subsidies, connected to exports to 'hard currency' countries had been continuously widening. The most important institution from this point of view was the Finance Ministry and it can be considered the most important organ of export promotion [*Antalóczy, 1997: 12*].

In agriculture, prior to 1989, direct export subsidies were the key means of promoting exports. The subsidies were differentiated according to transferable rouble and non-rouble trade. In general, lower rates were applied to hard currency trade, while much higher rates had to be granted for transferable rouble trade. This was in order to close the gap between the Hungarian price and the very low and strictly controlled prices in the former Soviet Union and other CMEA member countries [*Kiss, 1997: 5*].

At the beginning of the transition process, Hungary had a 'reformed' planned system of foreign trade. While distortions existed, compared to other planned economies, the share of foreign trade with market economies was higher and the number of economic agents with first-hand experience of trading with companies that operated along market principles was also higher. But, in the CMEA trade, the 'old' foreign trade system survived until transition began [*Sass, 1997: 172*].

Reform of the foreign trade system had two main goals: the gradual liberalisation and deregulation of exports and imports, and at the same time, building up the organisational structure along market economy principles, including the tariff system, export promotion, financing of exports and so on. From the first of January 1991, Hungary's two-tier trade system (CMEA versus market economies) was replaced by a unified one [*GATT, 1991: 11*].

Hungary's reform process was gradual. The preparation of the liberalisation of imports started as early as 1985 [*Nagy, 1993*] and the actual programme was introduced in 1988. Its implementation was speeded up in 1990, due to the political changes. Critics of the excessive speed of import liberalisation claimed that it created too fierce competition in the domestic market in some sectors, that some exporters lost their domestic market shares and thus scale economies could not be realised and costs rose [*Gáspár, 1994*]. The progressive liberalisation of imports was aimed at encouraging competition and allowing imports of materials and products necessary for restructuring. Over 93 per cent of products can be imported now without an import licence.

Most licensing of imports was abolished in 1989 [*GATT, 1991: 13*]. Hungary still applies import quotas on some consumer and industrial goods. But there are plans to eliminate quotas on cars, footwear and household detergent in the near future, and those on textiles, clothing and other industrial products should go by 2004 under the WTO agreement [*GATT, 1998: 42*]. The system of determination and allocation of the quotas, however, still seems to be rather unclear and *ad hoc* [*Sapir, 1994: 44*]. Hungary's average import duties have been cut from 50 to eight per cent during the reform period. The tariff structure reflects fiscal considerations to a smaller and smaller extent. The ratio of unbound to bound tariff rates is low (they can be found among industrial tariff lines). Further cuts will be implemented as a result of the Uruguay Round. The previous statistical fee (two per cent) and customs clearance fee (one per cent) are no longer applied to WTO members [*GATT, 1998: 33–41*]. Liberalisation of foreign trade in Hungary is now probably at least at the same level as the average among the OECD countries.

There are no export prohibitions and export transactions were subject to licensing only up to the end of 1990. Licensing served mainly to verify that exports were undertaken only by authorised enterprises to market economies and remained within bilateral quotas to CMEA. Licensing is maintained for a few items in order to control exports of products covered by specific non-commercial regulations, to regulate exports of military products and to implement export restraint agreements [*GATT, 1998: 48*]. A duty drawback scheme for imported products used in export production is operated, as in market economies, but from July 1997, due to the participation of Hungary in the Pan-European Free Trade Area, the system has been modified [*GATT, 1998: 39*].

The organisational structure of foreign trade has changed considerably since the abolition of the foreign trade monopoly of the state. Specialised foreign trade companies were privatised or went bankrupt. Often their management established their own small foreign trade venture outside the company and brought the know-how and part of the clientele with them. Any legal person or business organisation, registered in Hungary, is free to engage in foreign trade activities [*GATT, 1998: 33*].

During transition, the reform of the system and the position of the budget limited the opportunities for 'classical' export promotion. In the field of institutional export promotion, first, the system of foreign trade representatives continued up to 1997. In the same year, this was partly merged with the foreign embassies, partly transferred to the ITD (Investment and Trade Development Public Benefit Company) which is100 per cent owned by the Ministry of Economic Affairs, but with an intention of privatisation in the near future.

Second, different funds were created from budgetary sources. These funds promote exports directly, through an Export Development Fund of the Ministry of Economic Affairs. Since 1996 supports from this fund have been called 'targeted allocations'. Exports are promoted indirectly as well, through other funds, both at the Ministry of Economic Affairs and at other ministries: regional development at the Ministry of Transport and small company credits at the Finance Ministry. The financial resources of the 'targeted allocations' have been rather limited, in 1996 only 15 billion HUF (US$ 98.3 million) [*GATT, 1998: 49–50*]. Assistance included profit tax preferences, refund of the value-added tax paid on export-oriented inputs, research and development support, promotion of market research and participation in fairs and exhibitions abroad.

The role of commercial banks became greater and greater. But, finding finance for 'risky' foreign trade proved difficult. Those companies with liquidity problems due to the inflated exchange rate and high interest rates also had financial problems. One result of this was a surge in trade handled by intermediaries. As for 1991, an estimated 15 per cent of Hungarian trade with former CMEA countries was realised through Austrian, Swiss or German intermediaries [*Sass, 1993*], the present level of intermediary trade is still estimated to reach five per cent of total foreign trade. Second, some companies could not finance their exports (or production for exports) which contributed to the decrease in exports in 1992–93. At the same time, some still state owned companies with financial reserves effectively had forced exports to survive. Their 'forced' exporting was unprofitable, and could be realised only in the short run. But this contributed to the surge in exports to developed countries at the start of the transition period. Later many of the products involved disappeared from Hungary's exports.

According to Hungarian law, insurance and other financial activities can not be carried out in the same organisation. Two institutions, the Eximbank and Export Credit Guarantee Agency, were accordingly established in 1994. But, both only started work at the end of 1995 [*Botos, 1996: 49*].

In agriculture, since 1989 the value, rate and extent of export subsidies have all been cut in Hungary. At the end of the 1980s the maximum rate was 75 per cent, at the beginning of the 90s the average was around 12-13 per cent, with the highest 30 per cent for products such as beef, chicken and dairy products. By 1995 the average for agricultural exports was 13 per cent compared with an average 19.8 per cent for other subsidised products [*Kiss, 1997: 9*].

The Reform Process

Clearly, in foreign trade some components of a market economy already existed at the beginning of the transitional reform process. But this was also true for the whole economy: a two-tier banking system was set up in 1987, the company act was passed in 1988, the liberalisation of imports started in 1989, some companies were already privatised before 1990.

The restructuring of foreign economic relations as well as rapid structural changes inside the economy due to the liberalisation of imports, the introduction of the bankruptcy law, the acceleration of privatisation and so on created an environment in which companies had to adapt themselves quickly. As a result of the break-up in CMEA relations, exports to transition economies fell by 28 per cent between 1989 and 1991. This sudden drop in external demand as well as a fall in domestic demand led to a significant decline in total output. Double-digit inflation also emerged as a consequence of the liberalisation of prices, the reduction of price subsidies and the effects of freer finances. Consumer prices rose by 31 per cent in 1991 and 25 per cent in 1992. Due to the low domestic demand, 'forced' exports (exports at a financial loss) enabled some companies to survive, and due to the decline in the net borrowing requirements of companies, the external balance of the country improved. The current account balance showed a surplus in US$ of 127 million in 1990, 267 million in 1991 and 324 million in 1992, almost one per cent of GDP [*Sass, 1993*].

After these processes, economic policy-makers assumed at mid-1992, that the necessary structural changes had already been achieved. To restore growth the money supply was allowed to become excessive, the real interest rate became negative and the real effective exchange rate appreciated. The exchange rate, the exceptionally bad weather (which reduced agricultural exports) and the recession in the main foreign markets caused a sharp fall in Hungarian exports in 1993, by more than ten per cent decline in real terms compared to the previous year. Moreover, a decline in savings and an increased budget deficit resulted in greater domestic disequilibrium.

Consequently, the balance of payments went into the red showing a deficit of $3.5 billion at the end of 1993.

Economic conditions had deteriorated further by 1994, an election year. The budget deficit grew to 8.4 per cent of GDP, excluding privatisation receipts. Companies kept on borrowing, domestic credit grew by more than 16 per cent both in 1993 and in 1994. Exports recovered to their 1992 level, but together with the growth of imports, the current account deficit amounted to $3.9 billion (9.5 per cent of GDP). Hungary's net external debt grew by $5.5 billion between 1992 and 1994 [*Hungarian National Bank, Annual Report, 1995*].

It became obvious by the end of 1994, that if these developments continued, the country would face a Mexican-type crisis. The main aim of the economic programme introduced in March 1995 (the so-called Bokros programme) was to reduce the current account deficit and that of the general government to a sustainable level. Its main elements were a cut in domestic demand and in the public sector's borrowing requirement. Together with a nine per cent devaluation of the currency a crawling peg exchange rate regime was introduced and a temporary import surcharge of eight per cent (abolished by July 1997). The outcome was that the balance of payments' deficit was reduced to the planned $2.5 billion (5.6 per cent of GDP). Exports grew by more than 15 per cent while imports remained at the same level. However, inflation remained at two-digit level (28.3 per cent), and economic growth slowed (1.5 per cent real growth compared to 2.9 per cent in the previous year).

1996 was a year of a further improvement in external (and domestic) equilibrium. In correspondence with the above processes, export industries were first to recover. But, the recovery spread to the whole economy later than expected. This delay helped to reduce the trade deficit to $1.7 billion because it suppressed import demand. This caused further differentiation among companies: those producing for export markets developed vigorously (the majority of them newly established companies with foreign participation), while others stagnated. 1997 witnessed a similar performance, with the exception of much higher rate of GDP growth (3.5 per cent), the main source of which was invariably the growth in exports [data from *Hungarian National Bank, Annual Report, 1997*].

Policies affecting the supply side of tradable goods did not contribute significantly to the above processes, with the notable exception of policies affecting the inflow of foreign direct investments. Industrial policy was minimal in this period. Its main aim seemed to be to support the big, non-profitable state-owned companies. Agricultural policies created an uncertain environment for agricultural activities, mainly because of unclear property rights. This contributed to a decline in production in this sector as well as to declining exports. Policies to induce foreign direct investments can be judged successful in this period. The relatively advanced stage of transition compared to other countries in the region, the need to sell state companies for cash, and some special arrangements such as customs free zones and special benefits for investors, resulted in the highest inflow of foreign direct investments in the region. Newly established and restructured companies contributed to a great extent to the growth of exports: about 80 per cent of Hungarian exports now come from companies with foreign participation.

From the above it is evident that foreign trade and exports played a special role during the so-called 'transformation recession'. In this period, only increased exports (and imports) could compensate diminishing domestic demand (both for finished products and, because of the disruption of former company linkages, for raw materials and semi-finished products). Exports played a role in restructuring: first, because exports are the most reliable way to select 'winners' and 'losers', second, many non-competitive companies went bankrupt. Moreover, exports paid for the indispensable imported inputs, machinery and investment goods, some incorporating (high) technology, which are of crucial importance from the point of view of restructuring the economy.

While the above elements underline the importance of exports and imports, the actual policies adopted in Hungary's transition process seem anti-export or at best neutral, reflecting the preferences of the reform policy package. For example, the exchange rate was used as a nominal anchor, which resulted in its real appreciation. During the reorganisation and restructuring of existing capacities, the restructuring of the financial sector can result in inter-enterprise arrears that can hinder the financing of production for export even in cases where the export would be competitive. The same can happen to companies with high debts at the beginning of the reform process, which – due to the underdeveloped financial sector – face a growing debt burden, and are sometimes unable to finance their day-to-day production and refinance exports. Moreover, disruptions of former export relations with other economies in transition can also act as a drag on exports.

The transition also coincides with the rebuilding of some institutions, among them those in connection with export promotion. Sometimes this can result in severe inconsistencies across sectors or even inside a sector. But macroeconomic instability, as in Hungary where growth of domestic demand due to the expansive fiscal policy in 1992 also hindered exports, had a larger effect on the actual export performance than specific trade policies.

External Constraints on Foreign Trade Policy

External constraints on one hand narrowed the scope for trade policy. On the other hand, they helped to maintain the liberalisation achievements attained by the trade policy, and could be used to prevent attempts to reverse trade policy changes. In this respect, membership of international organisations (like the WTO and the OECD), and preferential trade agreements played an important role.

The Uruguay Round narrowed the opportunities for latecomers to apply the same export promotion tools, which were widely, and successfully used by the newly industrialised countries of south east Asia. The conclusion of the Uruguay Round (UR) and the establishment of the World Trade Organisation (WTO) limit the policies that can be used for export promotion in the countries in transition. While the UR widened export opportunities for the contracting parties due to the considerable tariff reductions and removal of non-tariff barriers to trade, some policy tools are now restricted [*UNCTAD Trade and Development Report, 1996*].

First, subsidies are defined; disciplines on subsidies are tightened and extended to all WTO members. Non-actionable subsidies are also defined, including those, which are intended to promote basic research, agriculture and regional development. Second, the TRIMs Agreement identified those investment measures, which were incompatible with GATT articles, like local content requirements. Third, the General Agreement on Trade in Services involves binding commitments on market access and national treatment though only when these have been specifically negotiated on a sectoral and subsectoral basis and included in the schedules of commitments. Fourth, the TRIPs Agreement establishes the basic intellectual property norms, and limits the use of certain policy tools. Ongoing negotiations may result in further international regulations.

OECD-membership includes obligations, which indirectly influence export performance and limit export promotion tools. By adopting the IMF clause VIII exports are facilitated through introducing (limited) currency convertibility. Another obligation, opening the domestic market for financial services, has also contributed since 1998 to a more efficient organisation of exporting activities. On the other hand, entering the OECD means taking on obligations that limit scope for export promotion. Participation in the export credit group of the OECD 'Arrangement', or the Multilateral Agreement on Investments add to obligations which narrow the use of direct and indirect instruments of export promotion.

The most important limitation on export promotion policy may result from participation in the so-called 'Arrangement'. Hungary would have to abide by its disciplines. The main fields affected are: *ex ante* and *ex post* notification of official support for export credit transactions, the disciplines on maximum repayment terms, minimum cash payment, minimum interest rates, repayment profile, minimum premium bench marks and also on terms and conditions of concessional finance. But, on the other hand, the country gets access to the confidential transparency network established between participants on case-by-case application of the above-mentioned disciplines for officially supported export credit transactions.

The most important part of the Association Agreement (AA) concluded with the EU is a schedule of trade liberalisation in bilateral trade. Its importance is underlined by the fact that already in 1994, the majority of Hungarian foreign trade was conducted with the member countries of the European Union (Table 5.2). Moreover, the agreement put a limit to those safeguard measures (including infant industry), that can be used in bilateral trade as an argument for raising tariffs and thus providing (temporary) protection for some industries. Another element is the limited scope for refunding import duties on goods needed for export production due to the establishment of the so-called cumulative pan-European zone. Basically, the agreement provides EU companies with 'national' treatment, effectively the same as for domestic companies. Compared to the WTO obligations, the extra obligations due to the AA are different for the trade of industrial and for agricultural products. In the area of industrial products, the use of trade policy tools such as tariffs and quotas is strictly limited after 2001. But, for agriculture, the agreement covers a much smaller part of trade. Moreover, the control over the implementation of the resolutions is likely to be much closer than for WTO obligations.

Future membership in the EU can further limit the tools available for export promotion. For example, common foreign trade policy, common standards, health and environmental regulations, and harmonising FDI policy will limit the scope of tools previously available. But, other tools such as for regional policy may broaden the scope for certain kinds of action. Some existing export promoting institutions and regulations such as duty free zones are to be abolished if derogations are not negotiated. Because the most important aim of Hungarian foreign policy at present is accession to the European Union, the approximation of Hungarian regulations, laws and legislation to that of the EU has already started. The new Customs Law, adopted in 1995, is aimed at the harmonisation of Hungarian customs procedures to that of the EU. EU standards are gradually being adopted in Hungary. Thus, the direct and indirect effects of the future accession on the export promotion policy can already be traced. Generally, the effects on exports seem positive, especially for exports to the EU or other developed countries and to a lesser extent to those other transition economies that are also in the process of joining the EU.

Preferential trade agreements (PTAs) were concluded by another set of countries (EFTA, CEFTA). In the short to medium run, differences in the timetables of reduction of tariff barriers can result in an uncertain economic environment for exporters. This can continue until the total elimination of tariff barriers is realised [*Jánszky and Sass, 1993*]. Other PTAs constrain trade policy similarly to the AA, in respect of trade with the signatory countries. But, by providing freer access to foreign markets, they help exporters. Due to the resolutions of the PTAs concluded by Hungary (with the EU, EFTA, other CEFTA countries, Turkey and Israel up to April 1998), about four-fifths of Hungarian foreign trade is already basically duty and quota free, particularly in industrial products.

THE PRESENT SYSTEM OF EXPORT PROMOTION

The three most important elements of the export promotion system in most market economies are the following.

- The VAT drawback system;
- the activities of the export credit and export credit insurance and guarantee agencies;
- the other elements of institutional export promotion such as information, assistance with product design and marketing.

As agriculture differs so much from the other sectors, export promotion in it will be analysed separately. And as policy concerning foreign direct investments has been particularly important as a special export-promoting factor, it too will be analysed separately.

The VAT Drawback System

Its mechanism differs among countries. The most important facet of its effectiveness as an incentive for the exporter is the time needed for claiming and receiving the money. In some countries there is a long delay. In the French or English systems, the transfer is realised before the product is finally sold, which enables the exporter to buy inputs for the export production at the price less VAT. The Hungarian system is actually relatively quick and therefore delay poses no problems to the exporter [*Somogyi, 1993: 24*].

Export Financing

Financing of exports is carried out partly by commercial banks (mainly 'non-risky' exports to developed economies and to CEFTA), and by the EXIMBANK (to CIS, and other 'risky' directions). From interviews with three commercial banks (all the three joint banks with foreign capital), it is evident, that they usually concentrate on their main clientele (which are important consumers of other services of the given bank), when they finance exports.

Both the Hungarian EXIMBANK and the Hungarian Export Credit Insurance Ltd (MEHIB) are state-owned share holding companies, which were established in 1993[*Antalóczy, 1997*]. The major activity of the first is to finance Hungarian exports, mainly to the markets of the Commonwealth of

Independent States (CIS), to the states of ex-Yugoslavia and to the developing countries. Besides this, the EXIMBANK provides and manages export credit guarantees from its own assets, grants prefinancing and refinancing export credits, and takes part in cofinancing. The main advantage of the credits given by the EXIMBANK lies in their terms, which are better than those prevailing on the financial markets. MEHIB promotes exports through guarantees in areas where the political, economic and exchange rate risks are unusually high, as in the CIS, some Central, East European and developing countries.

When established the base capital of the EXIMBANK was 1 billion HUF or $9.5 million. This was later raised to 5 billion HUF, $27 million by 1997. Further sources from the budget include 45 billion HUF guaranteed credit line for credits offered by commercial banks. A growing number of Commercial banks, with state backing, also have a special credit line for short term export financing with reduced rates (50 per cent of the cost of the credit is paid by the state).

The non-profit institute, MEHIB, which has a base capital of 3 billion HUF, $16 million in 1997, covers political and commercial risks. A special budgetary cover is given for the financing of insurance on political risks, the value of which is 110 billion HUF, $588 million in 1997.

After a relatively long period of 'non-activity', two new directors were appointed to the two latter organisations. One of them was an expert, with extensive experience in export finance and insurance in developing countries as an employee of the UN. Partly due to the activity of the two new directors, partly because Hungary showed signs of recovery, and restructuring at the company level was proceeding well, the two institutes started their real activity at the end of 1995.

The base capital of both institutes was raised significantly, and the number of employees grew as well: at the EXIMBANK from 66 in 1995 to 96 in 1996, and about 130-140 by 1997. At the MEHIB, staff numbers grew from 40 to 54 between 1995 and 1996. The coverage of exports with prefinancing credits grew from 8.2 per cent in 1994 to 9.2 per cent in 1995 (1996 data were not available). The insurance by the MEHIB covered 0.6 per cent of exports in 1995 and one per cent in 1996. But, this coverage does not seem so low if we take into account, that only a fraction of exports can qualify for insurance against political risks (those to former socialist countries, former Yugoslavia, and some developing countries). On the other hand, commercial risks can only be covered for exports to stable countries such as OECD and CEFTA members.

The present system of export financing needs some modifications in view of the future membership of Hungary in the European Union. First, the two categories of risks (political and commercial) are minimal in the developed economies. The trend, both in the EU and the OECD is that the state should resign from insuring against marketed risks. Non-marketed risks are those, which can not be sold on the normal insurance market, and this is the area, where the state can take up some responsibilities. Such a change needs modifications of existing laws and regulations in Hungary.

Second, the present Hungarian system is quite unique. In the Anglo-Saxon–American system, one institute carries out both activities (financing and insurance), in other Western European countries EXIMBANKs do not exist, only insurance institutes. The Hungarian system is not EU-compatible.

Third, from the point of view of improved effectiveness of export financing, the following points should be taken into account. The relations between the EXIMBANK and commercial banks have to be improved. The MEHIB has to take up activities in connection with providing insurance for domestic trade activities – as is common in other (developed) countries. Moreover, it is equally important to advertise the activities of the two institutes to small and medium-sized enterprises, which, as can be seen later, are not aware of the opportunities provided by the two institutes.

Institutional Export Promotion

An important difference from market economies' export promotion systems is that the system of institutional export promotion in Hungary is still highly centralised. While in industrially developed countries, regional and local authorities' organisations play a substantial role in providing information and other help to the producers/exporters of the given locality, in Hungary, the most important organisations all remain centrally organised and financed.

During transition, however, local authorities have been playing a much larger role in promoting (foreign) direct investments – which also promote exports, as many are export-oriented. Examples in Hungary are Székesfehervár and Tatabánya.

Moreover, private, self-organised institutions also provide useful information and assistance in meeting potential business partners. For example the Hungarian Chamber of Commerce, foreign-Hungarian chambers of commerce, small foreign trade companies, and other organisations of companies and managers are becoming much more important in this sphere

The state, while still the most important provider of the services of this type, has been playing a diminishing role. The most important state organisations, institutions that are directly or indirectly involved in export promotion, apart from finance and insurance, are the following: the commercial section of Hungarian embassies or commercial representatives abroad; OMFB (Hungarian Technical Development Committee), ministries (targeted allocations) and ITD Hungary (the Investment and Trade Development agency). In some cases, especially for big Hungarian companies, trade missions organised by ministries are also important for trade development.

ITD Hungary is the Hungarian government's Investment and Trade Development Agency, established by the Ministry of Industry, Trade and Tourism in 1993 to promote international economic relations and business. ITDH has representative offices in seven regional centres of Hungary, where most of the company's services are also available (source of information: http://www.itd.hu/).

ITD Hungary concentrates on the following activities: export promotion, trade consulting, FDI promotion, a special information service on the European Union, publications, business matchmaking and services. Hungarian exporters may receive logistical, financial and professional support to carry out efficient marketing and increase exports. ITD tries to target new Hungarian SMEs. Priority sectors are selected: food processing, pharmaceuticals, and herbal products, wine producing, engineering, textiles and garments, and software development. Investment consultants provide general information on the investment scene, seek partners for the different parties and participate as consultants in the legal and financial preparation of joint companies. ITD's targeted investment programs currently focus on greenfield investments with special regard to the following sectors: electronics and software, automotive parts and tourism.

The Euro Info Centre offers a wide range of information covering legal, trade, financial, employment and regional aspects of the European Union to the Hungarian business community and supplies the Europeans with relevant business information about Hungary. ITD Hungary develops and distributes business guides, trade directories and information booklets. ITD Hungary's business newsletter contains business offers and demands that ITD Hungary receives from abroad through Hungarian trade offices, foreign embassies, trade promotion organisations and directly, from the various business entities. ITD Hungary arranges business programmes for individual visitors and delegations, organises conferences, exhibitions, product displays and other business events. Its activities correspond to that of the institutions providing export-promoting services in most market economies.

In 1996 the government created the 'economic development targeted allocation' managed by the Ministry of Industry, Trade and Tourism with a total budget of HUF 15 billion ($98.3 million). This fund supports both domestic and foreign entrepreneurs. They can be assisted in the form of non-repayable grants, interest-free loans, and interest subsidy or equity participation by the state. Eligible activities include: promotion of capital investments, particularly large-scale; expansion of the manufacture of up-to-date products; integration of industry suppliers into the production networks of major foreign investors; development projects improving the competitiveness of small and medium-sized businesses; implementation of quality assurance systems in conformity with EU rules.

Resident legal entities, business organisations that are not legal entities and individual entrepreneurs may benefit from repayable or non-repayable grants from the Targeted Allocation. The amount of the grant may extend to 33 per cent of the combined costs of investment in infrastructure and investment in production facilities to a maximum grant of HUF 200 million ($1.1 million in 1997) provided that the investments in production facilities do not exceed HUF 1 billion ($5.4 million in 1997). The grants can be obtained by applying to take part in competitions offered by the Allocation Fund.

Other 'targeted allocations' help exports indirectly. The Ministry of Traffic and Regional Development operates the Territory Development and Regional targeted allocation. Subsidies can be given to areas where unemployment is fifty percent above the national average. The importance of this fund will be increased during the negotiations on Hungarian membership in the European Union. The Finance Ministry operates a special credit line for small and medium sized enterprises. But this scheme has no export requirements. The Ministry of Environment operates the system of industrial parks in Hungary, some of which attract large capital inflows, with mainly export-oriented production. These industrial parks offer full infrastructure, different services and reduced local taxes for both domestic and foreign investors.

Export Promotion in Agriculture

There are important reasons for handling agriculture separately. The most important is the different nature of agriculture from the point of view of export promotion. Given the highly distorted markets facing them export subsidies play a key role in raising their competitiveness [*Kiss, 1997*].

The Market Regulation Office of the Ministry of Agriculture runs the present Hungarian agricultural export subsidy system, according to the rules of the Agricultural Market Regulation Act that has been in force since the first of March 1993. This body approves the levels of export subsidy for the various product groups. Export subsidies are available to all domestic firms and legal entities, including joint ventures with foreign participation, which are conducting export activity either directly or via commissioned merchants. Re-exporting and subcontracting are not eligible for export subsidies. Export subsidies are paid to the recipients entitled to them on the basis of export sales and supplying the requisite data to the authorities.

Up to 1996 export subsidies were provided on a fixed *ad valorem* basis and the rates were set as percentages of free Hungarian border export receipts in US dollars, and persisted over a period of time regardless of price changes. This system was not only inefficient, but led to the abuse of agricultural export subsidies as well. The system was inefficient in the sense that export subsidies continued to be paid to exporters even after world market prices had risen above the domestic prices, or conversely, that the rate of subsidy could no longer cover the price gap if world prices happened to fall.

The abuse of agricultural subsidies was practised by overpricing exports, by the repeated export of the same shipments, by fictitious exports, by indicating higher quantities and by claiming subsidies for product categories other than those actually exported. The Hungarian police started inquiries into several cases of suspected fraud involving agricultural export subsidies. According to the figures of the Hungarian Tax Office, irregular use of such subsidies amounted to HUF 5.4 billion ($42.9 million) in 1995 and HUF 5.2 billion ($34.1 million) in 1996 which equalled ten per cent of the total export subsidies.

In order to eliminate the above deficiencies, since 1996 direct agricultural export subsidies have been levied on the quantity of the exported goods expressed in fixed amounts of HUF. This change was aimed at eliminating overpricing. But it failed to increase the efficiency of export subsidies, as subsidies were still granted on a normative basis. In order to overcome the continued shortcomings, under a new decree of tenth January 1997, agricultural subsidies have been opened to tender, and controls over the appropriation of subsidies have been tightened.

The efficiency of export subsidies is further strengthened by the regulation that the amount of export subsidy would change in line with seasonal and market developments. In order to increase the efficiency, the responsibility for granting agricultural export subsidies was transferred from the Ministry of Industry, Commerce and Tourism to the Ministry of Agriculture at the beginning of 1997. The efficiency of the Hungarian agricultural export subsidies did increase. This is shown by the rise in the ratio of export sales to subsidies. In 1995 export subsidies of HUF 35 billion ($278 million) resulted in HUF 152 billion ($1209 million) return from sales. But in 1997 less subsidies (HUF 24 billion, or $128.5 million) resulted in a higher return from sales (HUF 240 billion, or $1285 million).

Since the beginning of April 1998 an EU-conforming Agricultural Intervention Agency was erected within the Ministry of Agriculture with the intention to manage and co-ordinate Hungarian agricultural exports with due regard to the revised export subsidy system. The tenders for agricultural export subsidies should be submitted to this Agency which evaluates and registers them. The Tax Office pays the granted export subsidies.

Financing of exports for agricultural products has more or less the same problem as for other products. The most common form of financing exports is through commercial banks. However, this type of financing, and especially the willingness of the banks to finance the transactions, greatly depend on the profitability of production. As agricultural production in Hungary is characterised by low profitability and ownership relations are burdened with legal uncertainties, commercial banks are usually reluctant to finance agricultural production for domestic markets as well as for export purposes. The risks of financing (agricultural) exports, and consequently the interest rates, have increased due to the abolition in April 1993 of refinancing by the Central Bank (the Hungarian National Bank) of export credits granted by commercial banks. Consequently, the commercial banks provide export credits from their own resources up to 70–80 per cent of the value of the export for a duration of one year at an interest rate higher than the 11 per cent of the abolished refinancing credit. As a result, export credits are generally too expensive for most Hungarian enterprises, especially the small- and medium sized ones. Besides commercial credits, both Lombard credits, provided on the basis of the activity of public warehouses, and mortgage credits can be used for financing agricultural exports.

Besides funds financing all segments and branches of the economy, there is also a newly formed organisation which specialises in promoting agricultural exports. The Hungarian Institutional Agricultural Marketing Centre (AMC) Public Benefit Company was founded by the Minister of Agriculture on the first of June, 1996 with a funding capital of HUF 10 million ($0.07 million).

The AMC collects and distributes information on Hungarian and foreign food markets. It prepares analyses on the main tendencies of different food markets, and collects rules and sanitary regulations that relate to food markets in different countries. It also helps product development and research work for the Hungarian food industry. It organises regular scientific forums and food displays, connecting them to different cultural and tourist programmes. It helps distributing and/or acquiring state subsidies in a new, GATT/WTO-conforming manner. The institutional marketing managed by the AMC is connected to the companies' individual marketing activity, as – according to the AMC's philosophy – harmonised, institutional work strengthens both sides and can lead to outstanding results. The institutional marketing program of the AMC for 1997 includes marketing activity on the one hand, and product-and country programmes as well as regional campaigns on the other. The country programmes are organised for countries that maintain traditional commercial relations with Hungary.

The financial means for the individual programmes are agreed in advance between the AMC and the concerned product councils and trade associations, and are approved by the Agricultural Marketing Board. This system will work as long as the programmes are financed from state resources. In the first three years, AMC's finances have been granted from budgetary sources, but it has to prepare a plan for its partial direct financing, including resources from the producers. In 1996 the AMC's budget was around HUF 100 million ($0.6 million) which has increased to HUF 300–400 million in 1997 ($1.6–2.1

million), and was expected to increase to HUF 500–600 million ($2.4–2.8 million) by 1998. Because of its relatively short history of export promotion and its initial low funding, its efficiency cannot yet be appraised.

Promoting Foreign Direct Investments: an 'Indirect Way' of Promoting Exports

As previously stated companies with foreign participation play a crucial role in Hungarian exports. Thus, through promoting (export-oriented) foreign direct investments, exports can be indirectly promoted.

Compared with international norms Hungary gave very generous incentives for foreign investments between 1990 and 1993. Moreover, in privatisation policy, preference was given to selling for cash, which in practice meant selling to foreigners. While the generosity of incentives has been reduced since 1993, large-scale investments still enjoy substantial tax reductions and other help. Whether, these incentives play a significant role in attracting FDI to Hungary, and whether the revenues lost, due to the tax incentives, are at least matched by the benefits emerging from the investments in the economy remain subject to debate.

Now, foreign and domestic investors are basically treated equally. Large investments, investments in depressed areas and in research and development can receive government support in the form of tax holidays, and as previously mentioned, in the framework of the Economic Development Targeted Allocation, direct financial support for (large) investments is available.

The rules governing special customs free zones provide incentives as each individual company can set up its own customs free zone. This especially attracts companies that are mainly assembly operations and have to transfer expensive production equipment to Hungary.

The stock of foreign direct investments in Hungary is about $20 billion (data supplied by the Ministry of EconomicAffairs), which amounts to 40 per cent of total foreign direct investments realised in the CEEC region (excluding CIS). About 40 per cent of these investments targeted the manufacturing sector, 60 per cent went to services. Within the manufacturing sector, the chemical, machinery and food industries attracted most. According to sector data, companies with foreign participation are more export oriented in each sector, than their Hungarian counterparts [*Eltetö and Sass, 1997*]. However, the export orientation of the individual sectors differs a lot, for example, the food industry is basically domestic market oriented, while the machinery industry (especially electronics and the car industry) export most of their production. The contribution of these companies to Hungarian exports is highlighted by the fact, that in 1998, companies with foreign participation produced 80 per cent of total exports. FDI has certainly boosted Hungary's exports.

Basically Hungary's system of export promotion has the same elements as in most of the developed market economies. But the role of private institutions is smaller and the system in Hungary is more centralised. The future may see a move towards a greater role for private export supporting institutions. Our survey, which follows, shows that a demand for such a move exists.

THE SURVEY

Characteristics of Companies in the Sample

Questionnaires were sent out to 100 companies of which 26 replied. Nine of the companies that replied were located in Budapest and 17 in the countryside. Ten were established before 1989 and 16 later. None of the companies in the sample operated in a customs free zone and only four were in an industrial park.

The breakdown by sector was: five in the food industry; six in light industry; seven in machinery; four in chemicals: two in building and two in other sectors. When classified by number of employees: three were in the group of smallest companies (1–9 workers); four had 10–49 workers. In the medium-sized group there were seven companies with 50–249 workers, and eight companies with between 250 and 2,000 workers. Four big companies (more than 2,000 employees) complete the sample.

Grouping the companies according to their base capital produced a similar distribution: three had the smallest base capital of one to five million HUF, and four others had also a small base capital (5–50 million HUF). Five with 50–200 million HUF were medium-sized, as were 11 with 200 to 1,000 million HUF. Five with more than 1,000 million HUF fell into the category of big companies.

In the sample there were nine 'big' exporters, whose share of exports in total sales is more than 50 per cent. For seven companies, the share of exports in total sales was below 20 per cent. Ten companies imported less than 10 per cent of their total inputs and 18 less than 30 per cent.

While the European Union was the most important market for eight companies (the EU's share in total exports was above 80 per cent), ten had negligible exports to this area. For 12 companies, the CEFTA relation is relatively important (more than ten per cent). The same was true for the CIS in the case of eight companies.

There were two majority foreign owned companies and three with 100 per cent foreign ownership in the sample. The others were state-owned (six) or privately owned by domestic owners (18, out of which eight have a minority of shares in foreign ownership).

From the characteristics shown by the firms in the sample, it is not representative of the total population of Hungarian companies. The companies that answered the questionnaire were outside customs free zones, with, at most, minority foreign ownership and which exported to more 'risky' areas like the CIS and CEFTA rather than the European Union. On comparing the results of the questionnaire survey with those of the interviews, it appeared that those companies which answered the questionnaire were either relatively active in using export promotion or had encountered serious problems when they tried to use export promotion services.

Survey Results

The companies in our sample were quite active in using export promotion. Only six had never used any of the services listed in the questionnaire. One of them was a company in 100 per cent foreign ownership and another had majority foreign ownership. Neither needed any of the services because of their close contacts with their foreign owner. Three other companies that were in Hungarian private ownership (two of them small), considered these services to be too expensive and insufficiently advertised. The sixth company operated in a relatively small market segment (health products) with a small export relative to total sales, destined to the European Union. All the other 20 companies made relatively frequent use of the export promotion services listed.

The services listed can be grouped according to the source of financing. Eighteen companies used directly or indirectly state-financed services, and two companies financed from their own sources all of the export promoting activities that they used. Of these two companies one was 100 per cent Hungarian privately owned and the other Hungarian majority owned. The first company self-financed its participation in a fair, while the second one used export credit from a commercial bank, also to finance participation in a trade-fair. Both types of export promotion services were used by 14 companies. Among these companies were the nine most active users of export promotion services, each with a higher than average number of services used.

According to Table 5.5, the companies in our sample found that the services that they actually used were useful and efficiently provided help for their exporting activities. The most frequently used instrument was a trade fair, financed by the companies. (Companies can ask for financial help in this field from ITD.) Almost every second company participated in trade fairs.

Companies in our sample were also active in using the 'targeted allocation' from the ministries. They used different types of services, offered in this framework. Among these were: preferential credit to establish further exporting capacities or to improve the quality of the export product; part financing of participation in trade fairs; establishment of a representative office in their most important export market; obtaining the ISO 9002 certificate; publishing advertising material.

Equally popular among the companies in the sample was the use of export credit insurance against political risk. Nine out of the 26 companies used this kind of service from the Hungarian Export Credit Insurance Ltd. Eight of them were satisfied with the quality of the service. These were all companies with a relatively high share of exports to other transition economies (especially the CIS) or developing countries.

Relatively many (almost every third company in the sample) used the commercial sections of Hungarian embassies or trade representatives. The services provided included market information, on products, on competitors and potential partners. But many companies felt that this 'information-providing' element of export promotion needs further improvement and development.

It is worthy of note that self-financed training for exports was the next most popular form of export promotion. Together with the most popular- trade fair participation financed from the company's own sources- it signifies that companies are ready to pay for services that they believe help their exporting.

TABLE 5.5
EXPORT PROMOTION SERVICES USED BY COMPANIES IN SAMPLE

	Used	Help	No help
Export credit from the EXIMbank	5	4	1
Export credit from a commercial bank	5	4	1
Export credit insurance against commercial risks	3	2	1
Export credit insurance against political risks	9	8	1
Export credit guarantee	4	4	0
Export guarantee	3	3	0
Commercial section of embassy	8	8	0
ITD	4	4	0
Economic chambers of commerce	6	5	1
Hungarian-foreign economic chambers of commerce	2	2	0
Trade fairs (self financed)	12	12	0
OMFB support for achieving quality standards	5	5	0
Ministry support from funds or targeted allocations	9	9	0
Training for exports (self financed)	6	6	0
Other government financed help	1	1	0
Other private financed help	0	0	0
Other	2	2	0

Source: Replies to questionnaires by 26 companies out of 100 sampled, 1996.

Economic chambers of commerce were equally important, almost every fourth company in our sample used their services. The chambers provide mostly information, introductions to potential business partners and advertising in their publications. Similar services were provided (but used by only two companies in the sample) by Hungarian-foreign economic chambers of commerce.

Five companies used export credits from the Eximbank and from commercial banks. Out of these only four found that the service provided helped their exporting activities. The support from the OMFB for obtaining quality certificates is equally important for the companies in the sample. The companies in question operate in the paper (2), machinery (2) and food (1) industries.

Four companies used the services provided by ITD Hungary. The types of services used are the same as in the case of the commercial representatives or the commercial sections of Hungarian embassies abroad. Because the network of foreign representatives now belong to the ITD Hungary, the use of the export promotion services of the agency will become more frequent in the future.

While the composition of the sample does not allow us to carry out sophisticated statistical analyses, we can compare the likelihood of a company using export promotion services with the characteristics of that company. The results were the following: companies exporting mainly to the European Union were slightly less likely to use export promotion services; companies exporting mainly to the CIS and the CEFTA were more likely to use them. Large companies, both in terms of their number of employees and their base capital, were more likely to use export promotion services. And finally, companies in the machinery sector were more likely to use export promotion services than their counterparts in other sectors. In other respects, there were no significant differences among the different groups.

Companies were asked to indicate on the questionnaire, which export promotion services were missing, who should provide these services and who should finance them. Twenty companies indicated their choice. For most of them (12), information on markets was very important. Ten companies indicated their opinion on the potential provider of this type of service. Six of these thought that the government must provide these services free of charge or at preferential prices, while four claimed to be ready to pay market prices for market information.

Access to pre-production finance hindered exports in the case of ten companies and made exporting impossible for one company. Most of the companies thought that there was a larger role for government in this field. Nine companies were not satisfied with the current level of export credit services and of the information available on trade barriers. The majority of them expected a greater role for government institutions in providing these services. Eight companies listed problems in obtaining information on competing products. Two were prepared to pay for this and three wanted free provision by government. Eight mentioned information on quality standards in the foreign market as an important gap. Three were willing to pay for it, but four wanted it free. Only in the case of three companies (one state-owned, one

TABLE 5.6
EXPORT PROMOTION SERVICES USED BY THE COMPANIES

	Effect of the lack of export promotional tool		Possible povider of the missing export promotion tool	
	Hindering exports	Making exports impossible	Government (free)	At market prices
Export credits	9	0	5	2
Access to pre-production finance	10	1	6	1
Information on markets	12	0	6	4
Information on competing products	8	0	3	2
Information on trade barriers (tariff and non-tariff)	9	0	6	0
Lack of knowledge of languages	3	0	1	2
Information on quality standards on the market	8	0	4	3

Source: Survey 1996.

where the state owned the majority of the shares and one in Hungarian private ownership) was lack of knowledge of foreign languages listed as hindering exporting.

Interviews

Six companies were interviewed to supplement the results of the questionnaires. They were selected as typical of particular categories. Cases A and B present two companies with minority foreign ownership and with relative independence from their foreign headquarters. That means, they had to 'organise' a relatively safe way of financing (in some cases: prefinancing) exports. They found the service of the EXIMBANK slow and usually avoided using it. On the other hand, they did use the services of the Ministry's Targeted Allocation. Their opinions differ about its effectiveness. During the interviews it was suspected that the second firm had too high expectations and was therefore disappointed with the outcomes, while the first company was quite stubborn in applying and in the end was more successful. Comments made by some companies in answers to the questionnaires tended to support that view. Firms that persisted in applying sooner or later got some help from the Ministry's fund.

Company A, actually the affiliate of a British based multinational, financed its exports from its own working capital and payments from clients in advance of delivery. It needed continuous financing from its clients. Normally they paid 30 per cent on signing the contract, 30 to 40 per cent before completion and the remainder on delivery. It made no use of state credit guarantees, state credit or commercial credits from banks for financing exports. They had, however, applied many times for other types of help from state funds and succeeded on three occasions: once they got finance on preferential terms to develop a new product, once for preparing and printing a new prospectus and once for starting production of a new product. They thought well of these examples of state help and believed that persistence in applications pays in the long run.

Company B was a German–Hungarian joint venture that also finances exports mainly through advance payments from its clients in all of its external markets. Their only use of bank services in international trading was for imports where a supplier demanded a bank guarantee. The company had applied to the EXIMBANK for credit. This took eight months, but was considered quite swift compared to the norm. They had also applied to the Economic Development Fund of the Ministry, but the decision took so long that they had obtained the required credit from the EXIMBANK and therefore renounced the state support. They intended to apply for targeted allocations in the future.

Company C is typical of most of the companies that are engaged almost exclusively in outward processing trade (OPT) in the clothing, footwear and furniture making sectors. It is a Hungarian owned co-operative in clothing. In common with most Hungarian OPT firms it is in outward processing co-operation. Ninety per cent of its revenues come from this activity. It has French and German partners with whom it has had close relations for the last four to five years. Consequently its markets are secured for its exports. Prepayment from its trading partners meets the costs of production. The company therefore has no need of support for its exporting activities and made no applications for loans or state incentives. There are disadvantages in such relationships. There is a lack of security when the main reason for the relationship is low wages in the sector. The foreign partners can easily shift their allegiance to firms in other countries if Hungary loses its low labour cost advantage. The management of company C expressed these worries. There is a case here for export support policies that reduce Hungarian companies' dependence on foreign trading partners. There is some evidence that the OPT system has worked better in the machinery sector where firms have been able to upgrade their relationship with foreign partners by increasing the amount of local value added [*Antalóczy and Sass, 1998*].

Companies D, E and F are representative of the most important users of export support services. They are large and usually in the machinery industry. In the past they mainly served the Soviet or CMEA markets and that still remains largely the case today. As formerly large state owned companies they were familiar with state provided finance for exporting. All were aware of the roles of the EXIMBANK and the MEHIB and used them frequently. One of the three firms said that the services of these organisations were indispensable to their ability to export. With their help they could establish business relations with western banks. But the second company had criticisms of the two institutions. It had been let down by a last moment change in conditions for insurance from MEHIB for exports to Yugoslavia. The third company had another complaint against the EXIMBANK. It lost an order from Romania as a result of a demand by the EXIMBANK that the Romanian partner should put up 10 to 15 per cent of the payment. This, the Romanian company was unable to do. The EXIMBANK was apparently under the impression that this was an absolute OECD condition for state financing of exports. But in some circumstances it can be waved. The Dutch competitor for the order was aware of this possibility and secured the contract.

Clearly large companies can secure support for financing exports. Indeed it seems that in Hungary it may have been used as a part of industrial policy to keep certain old state owned companies in business. Small and medium sized firms, however, felt somewhat excluded. But those who were very persistent usually did succeed in getting some assistance and did find it useful.

All in all, the companies in the sample were quite active in using export promotion services, even if it was financed entirely by their own resources or private borrowing. Many companies feel that special information to assist exporters is missing from the market. The majority thinks that the state must play a greater role in that respect, but some are ready to pay market prices for better services. This indicates that small private agencies could fill a gap in the market. Many companies also feel that the present system of export credits and pre-production financing must be supplemented to a greater extent with state-finance.

CONCLUSIONS

1. From the point of view of export performance the role of export promotion, in the narrow sense of institutional support, is quite limited. But, in the special circumstances of transition, there should be a role for export promotion institutions. They can smooth the process of trade reorientation, and possibly reduce its social costs. Shortage of budget resources and the time taken to reorganise the system, however, severely limited export promotion activities financed and organised by the state. Also, it takes time to get private institutions established and in action.

2. Besides the special characteristics of the transition process, international obligations (Uruguay Round, WTO membership, the Association Agreement with the EU, other preferential trade agreements, OECD and

future EU membership) at present limit the tools, which can be used for export promotion in Hungary. This will be even more pronounced after joining the European Union.

3. By now, the institutions characteristic of export promotion in most market economies exist and are working in Hungary. Now that the system has stabilised somewhat, it is important to disseminate the information about the services, which can directly or indirectly help exporters, regardless of the kind of institution or agency providing these services.

4. The system of export promotion is still relatively centralised and relies heavily on financing from the state budget. But, private institutions and especially non-profit organisations seem gradually to be getting a greater role in providing export promotion services. It is especially encouraging from the survey that there exists a demand from companies for services provided at market prices by private institutions and agencies. Such a demand will quicken the process of filling this market gap.

5. The system of Hungarian export financing and insurance is clearly out of line with international norms. This situation is aggravated by the fact that the future EU (and the present OECD) membership of Hungary will make some changes necessary in order to be compatible with their rules.

6. Small (and medium-) sized enterprises seem to be more or less bypassed by the system of export financing. Most are simply not aware of the opportunities provided by the institutions, or believe that they would apply in vain. On the other hand, large (formerly) state owned companies seem to obtain relatively easy access to these services. However, in the case of small (and medium-) sized companies, success is somehow determined as well by the approach of the management. Persistence gains rewards in terms of some help for export promotion.

7. Some sectors of Hungarian exporters make little or no use of the various services of export support institutions. This is true for both those companies, which exist predominantly on outward processing activities, especially in the light industries and some of the partly, or wholly, foreign-owned companies. They rely on their relations with their foreign headquarters or their headquarters' relations with other companies. But, in some instances they do use official bodies such as chambers of commerce and bilateral chambers for information.

8. Agricultural exports were adversely affected by the instabilities caused by

the transition process through lack of institutions, lack of financing, and unstable ownership rights. They were also affected to some extent by international treaties. The level of export subsidies in Hungary is now significantly lower than in most OECD countries, particularly to the critical market, the EU. Moreover, Uruguay Round obligations (and miscalculations made in preparing for accession) made the situation in agriculture more difficult. These factors may be some of the causes of the decline in Hungary's agricultural exports.

9. More than two thirds of the companies in the sample used at least one type of export promotion service. The majority was well informed about the available services. The most frequently used services were the following: participation in trade fairs, export credit guarantee against political risks, support from the 'targeted allocation' of the ministry, information from the commercial section of the Hungarian embassy abroad.

10. Usually, the companies evaluated the services received as being of high quality, useful and helpful. But, they criticised the length of the processes in some cases.

11. In the opinion of the companies who answered the questionnaires, lack of certain information (such as information on markets, competing products, trade barriers and quality standards) is now an important barrier to their exporting activity. While some expect a greater role for the government in providing this information, some companies are ready to pay market prices. The ITD Hungary (with the help of foreign representatives) could now play a greater role in this respect. Some smaller companies would like access to preferential pre-production finance to help their exporting.

REFERENCES

Antalóczy, K., 1997, 'Vámszabadterületek Magyarországon' (Customs Free Zones in Hungary), manuscript (in Hungarian).
Antalóczy, K., Sass, M., 1998, 'Bérmunka Magyarországon és a világgazdaságban' (Outward Processing Trade in Hungary and in the World Economy), manuscript (in Hungarian).
Botos, B., 1996, 'Beruházás- és exportösztönzés a magyar iparpolitikában' (Investment and Export Promotion in Hungarian Industrial Policy), Ipargazdasgi Szemle, Nos.1–2–3. pp.45–50.
Éltető, A. and M. Sass, 1997, 'Motivations of Foreign Investors – FDI and Foreign Trade: The Hungarian Case: Results of an Empirical Survey', in S. Wysokinska and J. Witkowska (eds.), *Motivations of Foreign Direct Investors and Their Prosperity to Exports in the Context of European Integration Process*, University of Lodz, pp.77–105.
Gács, J., 1993, 'Trade Liberalization in Eastern Europe: Rush and Reconsideration – Experiences of the CSFR, Hungary and Poland', in J. Gács and G. Winckler (eds.), *International Trade and Restructuring in Eastern Europe*, Vienna: IIASA.

Export Promotion in Hungary

Gáspár, P., 1994, 'Az exportösztönzés gazdaságpolitikai feltételei' (Economic Policy Conditions of Export Promotion), manuscript, Budapest: Institute for World Economics of the Hungarian Academy of Sciences.

GATT, 1991, 'Trade Policy Review: Hungary', Geneva: GATT.

GATT, 1998, 'Trade Policy Review: Hungary', Geneva: GATT.

Jánszky, Å., M. Sass, 1993, 'A visegrádi országok gazdaságpolitikája, a preferenciális szerzôdéseikbôl fakadó versenyelônyök és -hátrányok.' (The Economic Policy of the Visegrad Countries, and Competitive Advantages and Disadvantages Resulting from their Preferential Trade Agreements), Budapest: OMIKK.

Hungarian National Bank, 1995, 'Annual Report', Budapest.

Hungarian National Bank, 1997, 'Annual Report', Budapest.

Kiss, J., 1997, 'Export Promotion In Hungary', manuscript, Budapest: Institute for World Economics of the Hungarian Academy of Sciences, May.

Nagy, A., 1993, 'Import liberalization in Hungary', Discussion Paper No.17, Budapest: Institute of Economics, Hungarian Academy of Sciences.

Sapir, A., 1994, 'A társulási megállapodás kereskedelemszabályozási és intézményi alkalmazása' (The Trade Regulation and Institutional Application of the Association Agreement) Struktúrák, szervezetek, stratégiák, Ipargazdasági Szemle, No.3, pp.26–50.

Sass, M., 1993, 'A piacvédelem, iparvédelem és az exportösztönzés lehetôségei Magyarországon' (The Possibilities of Market Protection, Industry Protection and Export Promotion in Hungary), Budapest: Institute for World Economics of the Hungarian Academy of Sciences, Series: Kihívások (Challanges). No.23. (in Hungarian).

Somogyi, D., 1993 'Az exportorientált gazdaságpolitika lehetséges eszköztára' (The Possible Tools of an Export-Oriented Economic Policy), Külgazdaság, No.5, pp.23–9 (in Hungarian).

UNCTAD, 1996, 'Trade and Development Report', Geneva: UNCTAD.

Papers prepared in the framework of the project:

Antaloczy, Katalin, 1997, 'The System of Export Financing and Export Credit Guarantees in Hungary', mimeo (in Hungarian).

Elteto, Andrea, 1997, 'Export Promotion in Hungary. Results of Company Interviews', mimeo (in English).

Kiss, Judit, 1997, 'Agricultural Export Promotion in Hungary', mimeo (in English).

Sass, Magdolna, 1997, 'Export Performance and Export Promotion in Hungary', mimeo (in English).

Sass, Magdolna, 1998, 'The System of Export Promotion in Hungary', mimeo (in English).

Sass, Magdolna, 1998, 'Export Promotion in Hungary. Results of a Questionnaire Survey', mimeo (in English).

6

Export Promotion and Institutional Change in Poland

ANNA WZIATEK-KUBIAK

The process of creating new institutions is at the heart of the transition to a market economy. This is certainly true for the foreign trade sector, which in Poland has been developing rapidly since 1989. Much has been written on institutional change in the Polish economy, but little attention has been paid to the impact of export promotion on institutional change in the foreign trade sector. This chapter addresses that issue. It begins by describing changes in the export pattern, both in commodity and in geographical composition. Compared to the Czech Republic and Hungary, on the threshold of its transformation, the Polish economy had certain special features. They affected the specific nature of the Polish transformation strategy, including the position and role of the export-stimulating policy in the transformation and development of the export sector. The second section presents specific features of this strategy. The third section deals with trade policy reforms and with the direction of the policies intended to stimulate exports. The general evolution of trade policy reform has been supported with the results of research in Poland and with experts' opinions on its effectiveness. The fourth section portrays the main institutional changes in the export sector and the role of newcomers. The fact that newcomers are the most dependent on the availability of export services means that they generate the strongest demand for them. In the final section, we summarise the results of a survey based on questionnaires sent to providers and users of export promotion services and instruments. It points to deficiencies in Poland's institutional support for exporting.

DEVELOPMENT AND STRUCTURE OF POLAND'S EXPORT PATTERN DURING TRANSITION

Over the years 1990–97 the dollar value of Poland's exports (in current prices) almost doubled (Table 6.1). In constant prices the export increase was less pronounced. The volume of exports increased by 60 per cent, while

TABLE 6.1
MAIN INDICATORS OF POLAND'S EXPORT PERFORMANCE IN 1990–97

	1990	1991	1992	1993	1994	1995	1996	1997
Export value [bill. US$	14.3	14.3	13.2	14.1	17.2	22.9	24.4	25.8
Share in the world trade [per cent]	0.44	0.42	0.36	0.36	0.37	0.41	0.43	0.45
per capita value	374	390	314	368	447	593	633	666
share of export in GDP [per cent]	16.5	19.2	15.7	13.7	15.0	19.4	18.2	19.0
share in industry sales [per cent]	14.2	21.2	23.0	22.2	20.6	21.5	22.4	Na
volume indices, constant prices, previous year = 100	113.7	97.6	97.4	97.6	118.3	116.7	109.7	113.7
trade balance [billion USD]	4.8	-0.6	-2.7	-4.7	-4.3	-6.2	-12.7	-16.6

Source: Central Statistical Office, Warsaw, 1998.

imports increased by almost 300 per cent. Per capita exports grew at a lower level than in the Czech Republic and Hungary. In 1996 Czech exports per head were about 3.6 times higher than Poland's.

As the foreign trade performance determines the current account balance in Poland, its position deteriorated. In 1996–97 the current account deficit as a proportion of GDP increased from 1.4 per cent to 4.2 per cent. So for Poland raising export growth is important.

During transition the performance of exports was uneven over time. A spurt over 1990 (including the first half of 1991) was followed by stagnation over the next three years. This was accompanied by a decline in the size of the

TABLE 6.2
POLAND'S EXPORTS BY GROUPS OF COUNTRIES

	Developed countries			Developing countries	CEECs and the former Soviet Union	
	Total	EU	EFTA		Total	CEFTA
1989	43.0	27.9	8.7	19.8	37.2	
1990	58.6	44.3	9.3	18.2	23.2	
1992	71.9	58.0	10.3	12.7	15.4	–
1993	75.1	63.0	7.9	11.6	13.3	4.8
1994	75.4	62.7	8.2	10.1	14.5	4.8
1995	75.0	70.0[a][b]	1.6[a][c]	7.7	17.3	5.4
1996	71.7	66.2	2.2	7.8	20.5	6.1
1997	69.0	64.0	1.5	6.6	24.4	6.8

[a] In real conditions
[b] In comparable conditions – 63.8 per cent
[c] In comparable conditions – 7.8 per cent

Source: Central Statistical Office, Warsaw, 1998.

export sector (Table 6.1). Exports increased substantially over 1994–95 but again slowed over the next two years.

The major changes in geographical and commodity structure that occurred in Poland's exports' during transition took place before 1993. The shift in trade and progress in transition to a market economy quickly revealed a new pattern of comparative advantage in Poland's foreign trade. The commodity composition of Poland's exports changed. But after 1993, though volume increased, no radical changes occurred in Poland's export pattern at branch level (Table 6.3).

Up to 1994 there were radical changes in the geographical structure of Poland's exports (Table 6.2). The share of European Union countries increased, while Central and Eastern European countries (including former USSR countries) decreased. During this period Germany became Poland's main export market. In 1990-94 its share in Poland's exports increased from 25.1 per cent[1] to 35.7 per cent, while the share of Russia decreased from 15.3 per cent in 1990[2] to 5.4 per cent. So Poland's exports became highly dependent on Germany. 1993 completed the shift from traditional (CMEA) markets to EU markets. Since then more than two thirds of Poland's exports have been directed to EU markets. EU countries' demand dominated Poland's export pattern and performance even though since 1993 a new trend in the geographical structure of Polish exports has been emerging. The share of Germany fell to 32.9 per cent in 1997 while that of Russia increased to 8.4 per cent. The share of Russia, the Baltic and other countries of the former Soviet Union in Polish exports was much higher than other advanced reformers. It seems that some revival of old geographic relations is occurring.

TABLE 6.3
COMPOSITION OF EXPORTS BY BRANCH GROUP
[constant prices 1990]

	1989	1990	1992	1993	1994	1995	1996	1997
fuels and power	10.9	10.1	9.9	9.7	9.3	8.9	7.3	6.1
metallurgical	11.7	14.6	19.8	17.0	17.1	14.4	13.2	8.6
electro-engineering	34.3	29.3	21.4	21.7	20.5	23.0	23.1	34.6
chemical	9.9	12.0	13.3	11.0	10.5	10.8	11.5	10.9
mineral	1.5	1.7	2.7	3.1	3.1	3.0	3.0	3.3
wood and paper	4.0	4.1	8.9	10.1	11.2	11.7	11.9	11.2
textile, shoes	7.2	6.4	7.0	13.9	13.8	14.6	14.6	12.0
food	9.8	10.0	9.4	9.1	10.8	9.8	11.5	9.4
other	0.4	0.6	0.6	0.7	0.7	0.7	1.1	1.4
agriculture	3.8	5.4	6.0	3.4	2.7	2.9	2.4	1.2
forestry	0.3	0.4	0.5	0.3	0.3	0.2	0.2	0.3
Other	0.8	0.6	0.5	0.0	0.0	0.0	0.2	1.1

Source: Central Statistical Office, Warsaw, 1998.

Poland also increased its share in EU imports but at only 2.2 per cent in 1996 that share remains small, while the EU has the dominant share in Poland's foreign trade. A shift in trade towards the EU was completed in 1993. But this redirection was only minimally due to the implementation of the Interim Agreement with the EU in 1992. Regional liberalisation has caused only small trade creation and trade diversion effects. In 1992 the trade diversion effect for Poland's exports was estimated at ECU 39 million and in 1993, at ECU 50 million [*Komitet Integracji Europejskiej, 1996*].

Comparing Table 6.2 with 6.3 we can see that changes in the export commodity structure, accompanied the shift in the geographical structure of Poland's exports. The scale of these changes in so short a time demonstrates the fragility of the previous specialisation when confronted with market forces.

Between 1991 and 1993 the new commodity structure of Poland's exports (Table 6.3) emerged. Exports previously directed to CMEA on non-market rules appeared uncompetitive on new EU markets. Electrical and machinery exports, geared mostly to CMEA countries in the past, diminished sharply because of the collapse of these markets. Up to 1994 this fall in engineering exports to the former USSR[3] was not compensated by increases to the EU. The trade reorientation in response to new conditions influenced Poland's comparative advantage in three branches of industry: minerals and mineral products, wood products, paper and textiles and shoes. Their share in Poland's exports doubled over 1990–93 (Table 6.3).

After 1993 changes in the branch structure of exports were much smaller. Only the shares of wood and paper products, and electro-engineering in Poland's exports were higher in 1997 than in 1993, while metallurgical, agriculture and fuels have been decreasing.

What was the role of 'newly' introduced products in Poland's export performance during transition? Under the previous system the extent of product differentiation was limited. The central planning system and the absence of competition provided no incentive for producers to differentiate goods in exporting or for intermediary agents to find 'new' products for exporting. The collapse of CMEA markets and the need to redirect trade forced exporters to introduce 'new' products for new markets. In Poland's exports to the EU these 'new' commodities show increasing importance. Between 1992 and 1995 the number of 8 digit (of the EU Combined Nomenclature) items exported to the EU increased by 10.9 per cent (author's calculations). This calculation should be supplemented by the value of upgrading exports, as a result of trade reorientation. Hoekman and Djankow [*Hoekman and Djankow, 1996*] using 2-digit level of the Standard International Trade classification (SITC) for 1988–94 estimated that no more than 15 per cent of Poland's exports to non-CMEA markets comprised exports 'diverted' from CMEA countries. Simple re-direction of trade from CMEA to EU markets played a limited role in export growth to EU. New products played the significant part. These changes in Poland's exports reflect restructuring and adjustment of the Polish economy.

Poland's exports during transition shifted from capital intensive towards labour intensive goods. The share of textiles and shoes, food and furniture in Poland's exports increased considerably. Part of electro-engineering production, such as TV sets, radio sets, and computer assembly is also labour intensive. If we include unregistered exports, which consist mainly of labour intensive goods, probably about 50 per cent of Poland's exports can be categorised as labour-intensive. The reorientation of trade, which accompanied transition to a market economy, revealed that Poland has a comparative advantage in labour-intensive goods. While developing a strong specialisation in labour-intensive activities Poland still also specialised in resource-intensive sectors: agriculture, raw materials, wood, paper and non-ferrous metallurgy. But the share of high-technology intensive goods in Poland's exports is only about five per cent.

From 1994 Poland appears relatively specialised in engineering products, transport equipment and electrical machinery, paper and furniture. Benefiting from foreign direct investment and subcontracting, the share of machinery in intra-industry trade increased.

Polish exports are mainly inter-industry. In 1994, using the Grubel/Lloyd measure, the indicator of intra-industry trade between Poland and the European Union was the lowest among CEFTA countries [*Pluciñski, 1998*]. The only sector in which intra-industry trade increased was electro-engineering (from 41 per cent in 1989 to 50.5 per cent in 1994). Intra-industry trade stimulated the growth of electro-engineering's share in Poland's exports in the last two years.

Changes in Poland's commodity and geographical exports were the result of transition to a market economy including trade liberalisation. It was due to radical changes in the domestic and international conditions facing exporters. Liberalisation of foreign trade created the conditions for the de-monopolisation of foreign trade and the entry of new agents. As a result the institutional (organisational) part of Poland's export sector changed radically (see below).

INITIAL CONDITIONS IN POLAND

Foreign trade plays a crucial role in the transition to a market economy. It is an objective of transition (the reintegration into the world economy) and an instrument in transition through its instrumental role in stabilisation and structural adjustment.

Many factors influence changes in the foreign trade sector. Change comes not only from export promotion and trade policy, but also from industrial policy. The success of export promotion programmes depends on many factors and policies: domestic, such as macroeconomic stability and liberalisation, and international. Changes in the export sector can be a side effect of progress in transition to a market economy rather than a direct effect of any specific policy. So it is difficult to distinguish between effects on exports of the export promotion policy and of other types of policies, for example macroeconomic, technological and industrial. If these were not successful the success of the export promotion policy would be doubtful.

Post-socialist countries are commonly treated as a homogenous group. They shared a similar institutional design of communism. This reflected a system of organisation and incentives that are fundamentally different from a market directed system. In all post-socialist countries the foreign trade sector was characterised by state monopoly, the administrative management, the insulation of domestic producers operating in foreign trade from changes in world market prices, inconvertibility of currencies, strong tendencies towards bilateralism, subordination of foreign trade to plans and centralisation of external relations. The structure of foreign trade was shaped with little reference to comparative advantage.

Despite the common legacy, the Visegrad group of countries inherited different macroeconomic, structural and systemic situations. These differences influenced their subsequent development. They initiated their foreign trade reforms from different basic conditions. These included the degree of openness of the economy, the state of macroeconomic destabilisation and the degree of liberalisation.

Up to the end of the 1980's the degree of central control over external relations differed among the three countries. In the 1980s the most liberal policies were pursued by Poland and Hungary, the most centralised by Czechoslovakia. Poland and Hungary inherited a more advantageous institutional economy than most post-socialist economies. In Poland there were foreign trade reforms as early as 1982. They, as in Hungary, were more comprehensive than in other CEECs.

In the 1980s the policy of the Polish authorities aimed at creating conditions for the state owned enterprises (SOEs) to expand exports. This policy comprised the following reforms: allowing SOEs to conduct foreign trade, transforming the foreign trade organisations (FTOs), implementing a new exchange rate policy and adopting hard currency retention schemes [*Kamiński, 1993; Biessen, 1996; Rosati, 1989*]. In Poland from 1988 the private sector was granted the same rights as state-owned firms [*Bak and Kawecka-Wyrzykowska, 1991; Lavigne, 1992*]. But increased openness as measured by exports per capita or the share of foreign trade in GNP did not accompany differences in the degree of decentralisation of foreign trade relations in Poland.[4]

As a much larger economy with a bigger internal market, Poland was traditionally less open than Hungary and Czechoslovakia. This influenced its competitiveness. A more open economy tends to engage more in international division of labour. The gap between supply and demand in the domestic market is also smaller. So in the case of the more open economy it is easier to establish realistic prices which reflect supply and demand. Such prices also help macroeconomic stabilisation.

Poland, unlike Czechoslovakia and Hungary, faced an urgent internal destabilisation problem at the start of reforms. The rising macroeconomic imbalances driven by growing consumption in Poland resulted in 640 per cent inflation in 1989. The situation was different in Czechoslovakia and Hungary. In 1990 in Czechoslovakia inflation was 16 per cent, in Hungary — 35 per cent [*Balcerowicz and Gelb, 1995*]. Their more stable pre-reform situation enabled more continuity in reforms than in Poland, where open inflation was far more serious.

The broad outline of transformation strategy in the Visegrad group was similar. It consisted of: the liberalisation of prices and markets, entry of new firms and foreign trade, macroeconomic stabilisation and institutional change. The differences in initial conditions among the three countries influenced the priority accorded to problems to be solved in the short and medium run. The emphasis on various components in each country was somewhat different from that in Poland. This resulted in a different transformation strategy and trade policy in each country.

Poland faced hyperinflation and global shortages. In Czechoslovakia and Hungary inflation was relatively low, shortages were structural rather than global. At the start of the reforms, Poland's situation was bleak with severe macroeconomic disequilibrium. As a result the 'cost' of creating relative stability was high. In Poland macroeconomic stabilisation was central to the transformation strategy. Foreign trade was more an instrument than an objective of transformation policy.

Nevertheless foreign trade liberalisation was one major part of Poland's transformation strategy. It included the following reforms:

– de-monopolisation of foreign trade,
– import liberalisation,
– foreign exchange liberalisation,
– exchange rate policy,
– changes in trade relations (foreign payments and pricing mechanism).

These reforms were introduced from 1990. Nowhere in the developing world have such comprehensive and deep trade reforms been accomplished so swiftly. Several decades have been the norm for such reforms in most developing countries. That is one reason why there have been such important differences among the factors influencing the changes in the export sector between third world countries and the post-socialist countries in Europe during transition.

Export promotion policy in Poland was a part of transformation strategy in the form of de-monopolisation, liberalisation of foreign trade activity, privatisation and adjustment of domestic prices to world ones. But relatively little attention and resources, even less than in the Czech Republic and Hungary, were directed to institutional support for exporting. Lack of budget finance, and the high priority given to macroeconomic equilibrium contributed to this attitude. But it was also due to the belief that the major source of export development is improved competitiveness and institutional change. Without stabilisation it is impossible to reach this aim. As a result the principal focus of the Polish transformation strategy was macroeconomic stabilisation. It was left to market forces to influence exporting.

Reforms at the Beginning of the 1990s

In 1990 there was a sharp increase in Polish exports. In the literature three explanations are given for this spurt in exports: (1) the effect of radical devaluation, leading to undervaluation of the zloty [*Plowiec, 1994*]; (2) changes in monetary and fiscal policy [*Zielinski, 1995*]; and (3) as a side effect of the systemic reforms, mainly liberalisation of prices, entry of new firms, markets and foreign trade [*Kamiński, 1993*].

The export boom in 1990 probably resulted from the combined effect of the systemic reforms and the sharp devaluation. They stimulated not only rationalisation of production, and entry by new firms, but led to 'crowding-out' of production from domestic to foreign markets as well. Due to the immediate liberalisation of prices and foreign trade, and sinking domestic demand, fierce competition evolved in the domestic marketplace. Both local companies and traditional suppliers from other CMEA countries were suddenly exposed to the previously unknown competition. This exposure of firms to external competition together with the cut back in domestic demand constrained domestic enterprises. Increasing imports from the West displaced goods previously purchased from domestic and CMEA suppliers. Increasing competition on the domestic market sharpened the effect of the market opening. It created an incentive to rationalise production and exercised discipline on the highly concentrated Polish state-owned enterprise sector. For the first time domestic producers in Poland faced a demand constraint. No longer did they have a comfortable sellers' market at home. The shortage economy was transformed into a surplus economy. In order to maintain production at an acceptable level, local enterprises were forced to seek foreign outlets for their production. The sharp initial devaluation of the Polish zloty also gave strong incentives to domestic firms to sell abroad.

The export boom in 1990 resulted from the combined effect of several factors, which were the result of systemic reforms plus a large devaluation. These factors complemented each other. But which factors were decisive? Without radical liberalisation of the economy the effect of devaluation on exports would have been much weaker. Trade liberalisation without price liberalisation would have led to misallocation of resources and distorted export decisions. Since 1990, the first year of systemic reforms, all economic parameters have changed. That makes it impossible to evaluate precisely the role of each factor in explaining the surge in exports.

The 1990 reforms eliminated the major distortions that hampered export growth. Deep devaluation not only neutralised anti-export bias but also stimulated exports. In March, the tariffs on most goods were at least partially suspended. The average customs tariffs were reduced to about 5.6 per cent. But internal and partial convertibility of the zloty increased the level of protection.

The obligation imposed on exporters to convert their hard currency earnings instantly into zloty increased their transaction costs from two per cent to four per cent, putting up the cost of exports, especially for those exporters, who used imported inputs. It biased incentives against export growth. Yet this policy was continued right up to 1996 when at last it was suspended.

In 1990 domestic circumstances favoured a rise in exports. But, factors, which stimulated exports in 1990, were not operating in 1991. And factors, which had not been operating in 1990, started to influence changes in the subsequent period. The exchange rate policy was targeted more towards its anti-inflationary role than towards export growth. Due to the continuous appreciation of the zloty in real terms exporting became far less attractive. The restoration of tariffs in August (the average import duty rose to 9.65 per cent in 1991, but after the first of August, to 14.27 per cent) resulted from pressure from domestic producers: both old and new lobbies. They came from the sectors most exposed to foreign competition. Most were weak players in the market game and so sought protection. The threat of large budget deficits created pressure on the government to increase revenues.[5] The persistence of old state-owned monopolies was supplemented by activities of new lobbies: foreign subsidiaries and newly emerging local firms. The increase in tariffs eased home sales and the weakening of foreign competition decreased the incentive to rationalise production. The rise of real wages in 1991 further decreased the competitiveness of exports.

Trade shock caused by the collapse of the CMEA and the full switch to hard currency was at least partly compensated by increased exports to the Soviet Union and the West. Heightened protection, appreciation of the zloty in real terms, productivity lagging behind the rate of growth of wages decreased the profitability of exports. The change in fiscal and monetary policy influenced the increase of effective demand in the domestic market. As a result of these factors the growth of exports fell.

The period 1992–93 was characterised by a continuation of the tendencies that had emerged in 1991. The continued real appreciation of the zloty, and increases in average tariffs (to 11.52 per cent in 1992 and 14.13 per cent in 1993)[6] improved the domestic producers' conditions for selling at home. As A.P. Lerner's 'symmetry theorem' demonstrates a tax on imports is equivalent to a tax on exports. Thus the more protected is the domestic economy, the less export-oriented it becomes. This tendency was supported by monetary and fiscal policy, which stimulated domestic demand. 1992 was the first year of economic recovery (when rising GDP pushed up domestic demand). The combination of all these factors resulted in increased disincentives to export.

With trade reorientation almost complete Poland signed the European Agreement which started the liberalisation of trade with the EU. Its impact was actually quite small. The major influence was the number of export goods for which a zero duty was introduced. But the rate of increase of these exports during 1992–95 was little higher than for all exports. Over 1992–95 the share of liberalised exports in total Polish exports to the EU increased merely from 51 per cent to 53 per cent. External circumstances, however, were generally worsening. The recession and falling demand for imports in Western markets – Poland's major trading partners, hampered Polish exports. The commodity structure of Polish exports to the West [*Beers and Biessen, 1995*] makes them sensitive to fluctuations in western markets. But, although the volume of German total imports decreased in 1993, Polish exports to Germany actually increased. This suggests that, but for the recession in Germany, Poland's main trading partner, Polish exports would have grown significantly faster.

Sluggish growth in Polish exports over 1992–93 increased the trade account deficit. Lack of a proper export promotion policy and adequate export institutions form part of the explanation. Progress in creating these was too slow. Almost no credits were available for financing exports. Created only in 1991, the export insurance agency was undercapitalised and was able to insure only a negligible (0.1 per cent in 1993) part of Polish exports. While officially registered exports were declining unregistered, 'grey market' exports were soaring.

At the end of 1993 the government recognised the importance of a programme of export promotion through direct institutional support for exporters. Flagging exports stirred the government to adopt pro-export policy guidelines. It laid down the rules, methods and tools for pursuing a more active export promotion policy in Poland. An export promotion programme was accompanied by continuous liberalisation (the average duty was 11.8 per cent on the first of January 1994 and fell to 9.3 per cent on the first of January 1995), but unfortunately there was also an appreciation of the zloty.

Exchange Rate Policy in Poland

High inflation, a large external imbalance and distorted relative prices were pressing problems at the start of the economic reform. Consequently, the initial choice of the programme accompanying trade and price liberalisation was to introduce a fixed exchange rate as a nominal anchor to brake the emerging hyperinflationary pressure,[7] while fixing the parity at the level that would restore and maintain international competitiveness. Towards the end of 1989 the zloty was devalued ten times and the official fixed exchange rate was introduced. As the nominal exchange rate was maintained at a fixed level for a year and a half, the real effective exchange rate appreciated sharply during 1991 and most of 1992 relative to 1990. This was despite two devaluations and the subsequent switch to a crawling peg regime (October 1991). The official exchange rate against the chosen basket of currencies would appreciate 1.8 per cent per month at first and at 0.5 per cent in 1998. Poland's Central Bank intervened on the exchange market to prevent the zloty from appreciating too much, especially after 1996.

Comparison of changes of the real effective exchange rate with export performance during transition in Poland suggests that the changes were not crucial [*Dabrowski, 1997*]. Despite the real appreciation of the Polish zloty over 1991–96, the growth rate of Polish exports was quite fast. Although the strengthening of the zloty should have had a negative effect on exports, it was obviously not the only factor. During the period of sharp increase in the value of exports the real effective exchange rate of the zloty grew faster than during periods of slower export growth. There seems to be about a one-year delay in the impact of the zloty appreciation on the growth of Polish exports.

The major force behind Poland's export growth was progress in transition. Restructuring of the economy brought growth in both manufacturing and productivity. During 1993–97 the growth of productivity neutralised the anti-export bias of the zloty appreciation up to 1996. Since 1995 joint ventures and companies with foreign capital have contributed increasingly to the growth of exports.

Instruments and Methods of Export Promotion Programme in Poland

An export promotion programme is relatively new to Poland. It began in 1994 with the aim of supporting the modernisation and restructuring of the export sector. It concentrated on the support of production for export. But the policy was limited to export credit guarantees, insurance and co-financing exporters' participation in trade fairs, duty drawback schemes, investment and tax relief. There have been no changes in the scale of export support since 1994, though in 1997 a new programme introduced new elements: tax relief for exporters operating in Special Economic Zones and a government guarantee for exporters.

Duty Drawback Schemes

In Poland the drawback scheme, unlike many countries, is not based on estimated technical input-output coefficients that show how much of a given imported input is used on average in manufacturing a given product. The duty drawback scheme as implemented is rather cumbersome. Exporters have to document the purchase and use of all the imported inputs. Each shipment needs separate entitlement. As the export infrastructure is underdeveloped and the efficiency of customs administration is inadequate, this procedure has been time consuming. In an economic environment of high inflation and high interest rates, with a shortage of trade finance, the duty drawback scheme is much more costly for exporters than an exemption scheme would be. Drawbacks involve financial costs for exporters because duty payments on imported inputs are reimbursed only after exports have taken place. The time lag between the customs' clearance of the imported input and the time the certified document reaches the exporter-manufacturer is expensive as no interest is paid to the exporter to compensate for the delays. The costs of imported inputs to exporters are consequently higher than international prices. Thus, these inputs incur extra cost (equal to the monthly rate of inflation multiplied by the number of months between customs clearance of imports and the actual export of the processed goods). As a result many small and first-time exporters made no use of this scheme. It has failed the group who probably most needs such help. Yet up to 1995 this group of exporters was the most dynamic.

Investment Relief and Tax Policy

Since 1994 an important part of export promotion has been tax policy. The policy of returning VAT and import tax charges paid on the imported components for export-oriented production has been applied. The normal international standard of a zero VAT tax rate is applicable to all exports. As with the drawback scheme, tax refunds are conditional on customs clearance documentation, that is, upon proof of actual export. Up to 1995 the exporter often had to wait more than two months to have custom duty and VAT refunded, the costs of exporting were raised by at least by two to three months' rate of interest. This means additional costs resulting from frozen funds and becomes particularly onerous for exports that require a long production cycle.

Manufacturers of exports are favoured over producers for the domestic market in investment allowances. The former can deduct a larger part of taxable income than the domestic market producer. Those manufacturers whose export incomes either exceed 50 per cent of their total income or whose annual export value is above ECU 8 million (from 1995, in 1994 it was ECU 10 million) can deduct documented investment expenses of up to 30 per cent of their pre-tax income.

As most exporters cannot meet these conditions, this instrument, at least in 1996, was still largely unused. In 1997 only 1,681 exporters out of over 42,000 had met the conditions. As the Foreign Trade Research Institute (FTRI) survey state, in 1996 only 16 per cent of respondents used income tax allowances based on investment. Most of the exporters surveyed made no mention of those allowances.

These tax policies support the development and modernisation of a part of the export sector. But, clearly there is a problem of incentives for newcomers to exporting. They cannot meet any of the required conditions. They do not benefit from the allowances unless they become specialised or large exporters. The policy fails to encourage new entrants and the lack of such entrants has been one of the major problems of export development since 1995.

Export Credit and Insurance

Poland has never had an export credit agency (ECA) or even a separate fund for this purpose. The high rate of inflation, the weak financial position of Polish exporters of investment goods and lack of officially supported direct export credit explains why only about one per cent of Polish exports were sold on credit terms. Polish exports of capital goods were handicapped. The fact that most of world trade in capital goods is on credit, forced Polish exporters to reduce prices to potential customers in order to compete.

Export guarantees and insurance are provided but the insurance agency did not deal with export financing. It concentrated solely on insurance coverage for exporters and banks. The major specialised institution for export credit insurance has been the Export Credit Insurance Corporation (KUKE). Established in 1991, it was able to cover just less than 1.5 per cent of Polish exports. In 'the Federal Republic of Germany only seven per cent of the total export volume is protected against certain economic and political risks by government guarantees and assistance. In comparison, the corresponding figures for Great Britain and France are about 35 per cent, and for Japan the proportion is nearly 48 per cent' [*Dichtl and Koglamayr, 1987: 111*]. The level of Polish government guarantee as compared to the level in market economies is extremely low. In 1996 about nine per cent of the FTRI exporters who responded used export credit insurance, 15 per cent did not know about it and

24 per cent said that the cost of these instruments was too high. In a survey of INE-PAN which covered 200 enterprises only 7.7 per cent used export credit insurance [*Wziatek-Kubiak, 1999: 16 and 42*]. In our survey (see section below) which covered mainly large exporters only 20 per cent respondents had used export credit guarantees and 37 per cent – had used insurance (in the FTRI – three per cent). This suggests that export credit guarantees and insurance are used mainly by large exporters. For smaller exporters these instruments are too difficult or costly.

The KUKE has concentrated on insurance covering short-term commercial risk. It covers bankruptcy, insolvency and long term delays in payments from private foreign trade offices of OECD and Visegrad countries. Up to now, the Corporation has only been able to offer coverage for risk after shipment of goods or performance of services.

By insuring export transactions KUKE tries to increase exporters' access to credit. Under the agreement between the KUKE and some of the largest Polish commercial banks, the exporter who insures their transactions with the KUKE is able to obtain credit on preferential terms. This could give exporters, especially small and medium sized enterprises (SMEs) including newcomers, the possibility of obtaining export loans on preferential terms. The scheme could ameliorate somewhat the deficiencies of export promotion. But the problem is that it is still not effective.

PRELIMINARY EVALUATION OF THE POLICY FOR EXPORT DEVELOPMENT

During the first years of transition the major sources of export growth came from the general transformation strategy: liberalisation of prices, entry, markets and foreign trade, and the macroeconomic policy. Stabilisation and liberalisation offset most of the institutional and market imperfections, which hampered exports. It also seems that up to 1995 the major sources of export growth were more the result of progress in enterprises' adjustment to market economy conditions and improvements in economic conditions in EC markets than of direct support for exporting.

The duty drawback scheme, for example, could only be used effectively by large exporters who used imported inputs for export-oriented production. It did not support new entrants nor the development of entry by small manufacturers. As for investment relief only a few firms for which exports were a major source of income, were able to meet the conditions for income tax allowances. Insurance of export credits benefited only 1.3 per cent of Polish exports in 1997. These facts reveal the feeble impact of export promotion policy on Polish exports.

Policy to support exporting in Poland focuses on improvement of the availability of capital for export production. Financial markets in Poland are more incomplete than distorted. Yet export promotion policy is mainly directed towards offsetting incompleteness of these markets. The labour market, unlike the financial, is more distorted than underdeveloped. Taxes on labour and on human capital (income taxes, taxes paid by employers for the Employment Fund, the Fund of Salary Guarantee and the Fund for Pensioners) are very high. Taxes paid by employers amount to 50 per cent of salary. These government-induced distortions are not neutralised for exporters at all. In contrast to the governments of the fast growing Asian countries, the Polish government distorts the functioning of the labour market and thus the export sector. As about 50 per cent of Poland's exports are labour intensive, government policy severely distorted the functioning of much of the export sector and indirectly constrained export development. In Poland the role of factors of production other than physical capital for export development are still underestimated. This is certainly true of human capital. No allowances are given for spending on workers' education, improvement or introduction of new manufacturing techniques for export-oriented production. Numerous imperfections still impede the market process in Poland. Information remains scarce and costly. The foreign trade infrastructure needs to be developed (see section below). This includes physical [*OECD, Report on Poland, 1997*] and non-physical infrastructure (such as human capital).

In Poland the export promotion policy supports only large and specialised exporters. There are almost no efforts to support newcomers to the export sector or to create favourable conditions for new entry into exporting.

INSTITUTIONAL CHANGE IN THE EXPORT SECTOR

Post-communist countries lack many of the markets and institutions common in advanced market economies. That is why institutional changes are at the heart of transition.

Until 1982, the export sector in Poland was monopolised and highly concentrated. Only state or co-operative legal entities could deal with foreign trade in Poland. Export and import licenses in the sphere of intermediation were granted to specialised Foreign Trade Organisations (FTOs) for specific goods. Given their well-developed international relations, FTOs monopolised information on foreign markets, as well as any contacts with foreign purchasers of goods manufactured in Poland.

On the one hand, domestic firms producing for export did not have direct contacts and trade relations with foreign counterparts. Settlements between domestic manufacturers of exported goods and FTOs were made in the Polish currency on the basis of domestic prices. On the other hand, the settlements between FTOs and foreign customers were made in foreign currency on the basis of negotiated prices. The differences between receipts from foreign customers and payments to domestic suppliers were budgetary revenues or subsidies on account of exports. This system of settlements meant that the providers of exported goods were separated from world market prices and the changes in export prices did not reflect changes in the efficiency of production of exports. Consequently, domestic manufacturers of exports became more and more isolated from the world market and foreign customers. They lacked information about foreign markets and knowledge about market economy rules. Export manufacturers were passive and formal rather than actual participants in export sector development. FTOs were the only actors which – being in touch with world markets – possessed knowledge about foreign markets and had experience of operating there. But, although FTOs were the only organisations allowed to conduct foreign trade generally, they did not have production facilities nor did they trade domestically in home-produced goods (as, for example, Japanese General Trade Companies did). All this changed in the 1990s.

Formally the state monopoly of foreign trade in Poland came to an end at the beginning of 1982 when rights to exports were extended to some individuals and partnerships. Simultaneously, some FTOs were transformed into joint stock companies with the Ministry of Finance holding at least 51 per cent of the shares. The remaining shares were distributed among the enterprises dealing with these FTOs. The bank sector was monopolised and concentrated. Bank Handlowy had a monopoly of financial services for foreign trade. Transport services were also monopolised.

In 1989, the system of centrally planned foreign trade was further dismantled. Under the law on economic activity (December 1988) all economic agents are permitted to engage freely in foreign trade and any can operate in foreign trade with equal rights. The character of the relationship between FTOs and producers has changed. The traditional arrangement was replaced by new arrangements or completely abandoned. But the past monopoly over information left a legacy that hampered export development for many years.

Liberalisation and de-monopolisation in the foreign trade sector took place in two areas that emerged during the period of planned economy:

- export infrastructure: those institutions that provide export services;

- production for export: those institutions that supply goods for foreign markets and create the demand for export services.

The infrastructural part of the export sector covers institutions which provide export services. In the planned economy there were specialised institutions for foreign trade transactions. In transitional economies this part includes some institutions which operated before 1989 such as ministries, embassies and old foreign trade organisations as well as institutions which were established after 1989 like new banks, transport entities, new intermediaries, especially small ones, trade fairs and chambers of commerce. Newly emerging actors in export infrastructure were newcomers to this sector. Most of them lacked experience in dealing with foreign trade and were not sufficiently creditworthy. Since many of the old institutions of export infrastructure failed to adjust to new conditions, the importance of the role of the newly emerging institutions increased.

The manufacturing part of the export sector covers enterprises producing goods for export, as well as manufacturers that export indirectly. Both generate demand for export services emerging in the export infrastructure. Also, some newly-established firms, commercial intermediaries, especially small ones, not only provide export services for manufacturers, but also generate demand for such services provided by the chambers of commerce, which were themselves newly created organisations.

The formal abolition of licenses for conducting foreign trade, de-monopolisation and liberalisation of foreign trade sparked off two kinds of new processes: new entrants into the export sector and 'crowding out' of the previous monopolists from this sector. New entrants into the export sector included:

- new entities manufacturing for export and simultaneously acting as export intermediaries;

- entities, which previously only sold their output on the protected domestic market but now also, exported;

- manufacturers that previously manufactured goods for exports handled by FTOs but now took over the intermediary role themselves;

- new entities acting as commercial intermediaries (new FTOs);

- new market institutions, such as chambers of commerce and exporters' associations.

These processes crowded out many large post-communist FTOs that under the centrally planned economy used to monopolise export intermediation. As a result of these changes, by the middle of the 1990s the export sector in Poland had undergone radical restructuring. These changes covered:

- a radical increase in the number of firms engaged in foreign transactions, from some hundreds to over 30,000 in 1992;

- the privatisation of the Polish export sector. By 1996 the share of private companies in Polish exports had increased to over 60 per cent. This was the result of new private firms' entry to the export sector as well as privatising of state owned enterprises;

- de-concentration and de-monopolisation of the export sector which led to

150

the fragmentation of activities and to changes in the share of various groups of enterprises in exports and an increased role for newcomers in Polish foreign trade.

The disintegration of the former system of links (FTOs-manufacturers) was accompanied by the emergence of a new system in terms of the composition (as a result of new entries) and the degree of concentration.

In 1987 there were 670 enterprises (including 370 private ones) that enjoyed foreign trade licences. A year later their number increased to 1,731 (815 private). But the share of new exporters was only about 0.1-0.2 per cent. By 1996, over 40,000 enterprises were engaged in foreign trade. But most of them were only occasional exporters. Among 20,000 enterprises reporting to GUS (the Central Statistical Office) only about two percent declared earnings from exports.

Since the 1990s the newcomers have played an increasing role in Polish exports. These newcomers were firms which entered the export sector as well as those which previously had been exporting through the foreign trade organisations and later started to export directly. This last group were newcomers in the sense that they had no previous experience with foreign markets. Before 1990 their activities had been limited to production. They did not export directly to foreign markets and knew little about the profitability of exports. They lacked information about the world market, about the wishes of potential buyers as to the quality, design and prices of products and about laws in the importing countries. Like newly emerging firms, such firms although experienced producers, were newcomers to exporting. In 1989 most of them had little market potential or knowledge about operating in foreign markets. So, exporting was a new challenge for them. This group gradually gave up using the FTOs and began to create a large new demand for basic export services. According to the INE-PAN survey covering 200 large enterprises in 1990, 74.9 per cent of the sample used an FTO for exporting, while seven years later – only 32 per cent. In 1990 only 18.2 per cent of the number of enterprises exported directly, while in 1997, 54.5 per cent were direct exporters. As much as 25.5 per cent of these enterprises said that lack of information about the foreign market was the major obstacle to export development [*Wziatek-Kubiak, 1999: 34*].

New Entrants to the Export Sector

In a market economy entry is only part of a larger process of the dynamic movement by which the economy is being continuously, but gradually, restructured. In a transitional economy, especially in the first stage of transition, the role of entry for institutional change is large. During the socialist period the number of firms operating in the foreign trade sector was strictly limited in Poland and new entrants were few. That is why liberalisation was crucial for both entry and organisational restructuring of the foreign trade sector.

The first period of transition was characterised by a surge in the numbers of exporters. It increased from about 1,700 in 1989 to 30,084 in 1992. This trend continued in the next three years. After 1995 the entry rate slowed considerably. In 1997, as compared to the previous year, the increase in exporters dropped to about one-sixth of the increase in 1994. Since 1995 fewer and fewer enterprises have been interested in internationalising their production. This suggests that liberalisation has ceased to stimulate entry into the export sector. Improved conditions on the domestic market in 1996–97, mainly due to monetary policy, effected a shift of enterprises' activities from foreign to domestic markets. Although there was a huge surge in the number of exporters in the first three years of reform, the domestic market has remained of primary significance for most exporters. In 1997 there were only about 1,650 specialised and large exporters (defined as exports more than 50 per cent of total revenues and worth over eight million ecu). Not only were relatively few companies engaged in exporting but also only a small fraction of them specialised in exporting. If liberalisation and de-monopolisation stimulated and created new conditions for entry into exporting, nevertheless most Polish companies did not plunge into export markets.

During transition the organisational structure of Polish exporters has changed considerably. First, during the first three years of reforms there was a large surge in the number of micro-exporters, those exporting up to $0.5 million and of small exporters, exporting from $0.5 to 2.5 million. Both groups played an important role in the development of Polish exports, in changes in its commodity structure and especially in the geographical redirection of Poland's exports during the first period of transition. This trend changed in the second half of the 1990s. In 1994 micro-exporters completed their important role in Polish export development. Since then their share in the number of exporters and in the value of Poland's exports has decreased. Some micro exporters even quit the export sector in 1996. The decreasing entry rate of micro exporters into the export sector indicates the decreasing propensity to export of most of Poland's enterprises. They have switched to concentrating on the domestic market. The major role in Poland's exports shifted to middle-sized and relatively larger exporters within the group of small exporters.

Another important feature of the structure of Poland's export sector was the continuous decline of the share of large exporters in Poland's exports. It resulted from diminishing export activity by 100, especially the 50 largest exporters (Table 6.4). This process was accompanied by an increase in the share of the relatively smaller exporters within the group of large exporters. The radical change within the group of large exporters whose share in

152

Poland's exports exceeded 60 per cent partly reveals a new phenomenon in Poland's exports: the increasing role of companies with foreign capital. Between 1995 and 1997 their share increased from 20 per cent to almost 50 per cent [*Durka and Chojna, 1998: 49*]. The increasing share of the smaller exporters within the group of large exporters resulted mainly from the activity of companies with foreign participation. As they concentrate on activity in these sections of Poland's exports which are increasing, these companies stimulate the growth of Poland's exports. They were major beneficiaries of the trade liberalisation of Poland's trade with the EU [*Wziatek-Kubiak, 1999: 27–8*]. The impact of this liberalisation on the export performance of domestic companies was negligible.

Table 6.4 points to a large decline in the share of the group of 100 largest Polish exporters in the value of Polish exports. The group covers two sub-groups: 18 old FTOs and some 80 exporter-manufacturers. By 1996 the share of exports from old FTOs in Polish total exports had declined to 12.2 per cent.[9] The steepest fall in the share of FTOs in Polish exports actually occurred in the period of the fastest increase in total exports (1995). Most probably, many SMEs, that previously used FTOs' intermediation, were able, as a result of the improvement of external exporting conditions, to take over the functions of trade intermediaries from the old FTOs. But, also many FTOs switched some effort away from intermediation to production.

TABLE 6.4

CHANGES IN SHARE OF DIFFERENT SUB-CLASSES OF EXPORTERS WITHIN THE GROUP OF LARGE EXPORTERS DURING 1993–97

	1993	1994	1995	1996	1997
First hundred of largest exporters	51.6	47.2	45.0	41.6	39.2
Of which:					
The first fifty	[43.7]	[40.3]	[37.9]	[34.7]	[31.9]
The second fifty	[7.0]	[6.9]	[7.1]	[6.9]	[7.3]
Second hundred of largest exporters	8.0	7.9	7.8	8.0	8.3
Other large exporters selling abroad goods of value above $6 million	7.9	8.7	9.4	14.6	14.9

Large exporters – firms exporting goods of value of above $6 million.
Source: Rutkowski [*1997: s. 6*] and author's estimates.

Clearly the old FTOs and the other largest exporters were the least active in the development of Polish exports. But it was these organisations that met statutory conditions for export-support, especially for tax incentives. They did receive such help, while SMEs who really needed such help made almost no use of export support services.

INSTITUTIONAL CHANGE IN INFRASTRUCTURE AND MANUFACTURING
FOR FOREIGN TRADE

In the era of central planning the export sector infrastructure was strongly monopolised. This was true for finance, banking, transport and commercial intermediation. They used to be monopolised by FTOs. They were specialised in branch groups.

Liberalisation provided opportunities for entry to the export infrastructure by firms that previously had not been involved. On the one hand, this created new entities and, on the other hand, led to existing firms developing activities of a new kind such as foreign trade. This has led to reduced concentration and monopoly in the export infrastructure.

The following processes have shaped institutional changes in the export infrastructure:

- new entries, mostly of SMEs, especially into trade intermediation;

- manufacturers of exported goods assuming the role of trade intermediaries, with banks taking over financial services for exporters;

- crowding out of FTOs from export activities, especially from trade intermediation;

- emergence of new market institutions, such as chambers of commerce and exporters' associations.

During the first six years of transition the number of entities operating in trade intermediation rose sharply. In 1995 the number of SMEs was 1,450 [*Wolodkiewicz-Donimirski, 1996*]. A declining share of FTOs in Polish exports accompanied the rise in SMEs' share in trade intermediation. In 1988, they covered 81 per cent of exports in transferable roubles and 88 per cent in hard currencies. A year later these shares declined to 73 per cent and 79 per cent respectively. In 1992, the share of FTOs in Polish exports decreased to about 32 per cent and in 1996 to about 12 per cent. Today the share of FTOs in Polish exports has dropped below that of SMEs. It should be remembered that FTOs are no longer only trade intermediaries but also became manufacturers of exports. The staff of these firms used the knowledge of market economies gained in earlier international contacts and their insight into production capacities of domestic suppliers of exported goods. As their economic position declined FTOs started to acquire stakes in these manufacturing enterprises and expanded their activities by entering manufacturing. FTOs did not give up being trade intermediaries for their own firms and other producers, especially smaller ones. Rather it was the strong manufacturers of exports who resigned from the services provided by FTOs. Over seven years of systemic transformation the institutional part of the export sector has been totally restructured due to de-monopolisation and fragmentation. Few of the old FTOs survived. In 1996, only 17 old FTOs were on the list of 100 major Polish exporters. Apart from them, a dozen or so smaller old FTOs are still in operation, but their market position has deteriorated.

Most of the large, old FTOs (Animex, Agros, Hortex, and Rolimpex) operate in the food-processing industry. They play a leading role in the production of selected commodity groups of this industry, especially juices, confectionery products and meat products. Moreover, FTOs also play a significant role in the metal products industry (Stalexport, Impexmetal), in the shipbuilding industry (Centromor), electro-engineering and power engineering industries (Elektrim) and in the chemical industry (Ciech). In most of these firms exports account for no more than 30 per cent of revenues. This figure is the sum of the companies' operations as export intermediaries and as manufacturers of exports. At present, the sphere of trade intermediation consists of the following segments: the group of SMEs, the group of large trade intermediaries (major FTOs, both old and new) and the group of manufacturer-exporters selling their own products. The former system of FTOs' links to manufacturers has been virtually replaced with a new network of links and interrelationships. The infrastructure of the export sector is still subject to restructuring. At present, newcomers largely dominate this part of the export sector.

Processes of fragmentation are also present in the sphere of financial services for exporters. The share of Bank Handlowy, which prior to 1989 monopolised financial services linked to export transactions, fell to 33 per cent in 1996. At the same time, the shares of old and newly established banks in these services have increased.

SMEs' competitive advantages on foreign markets are based largely on cheap labour, with exports dominated by elementary processed products. Industrial exports of SMEs are concentrated on a small group of branches. In 1995, they had more than 50 per cent of wood exports (excluding furniture) and publishing. At the same time, their share in exports of food processing, textile and apparel, metal industries and footwear as well as in the manufacture of plastics and office equipment ranged from 33 to 42 per cent. In the remaining branches SMEs' exports were occasional rather than regular. During 1992–96, except for footwear and some branches of food processing, the share of SMEs in Polish exports decreased.

Subcontracting is a significant element of export strategies of many SMEs. Their exports based on outward processing show a particularly fast growth rate. Most active SME exporters in four industries in which SMEs had the largest export shares signed subcontracting agreements with foreign partners, accounting for a major share of SMEs trade. 'For many SMEs subcontracting and other forms of work commissioned by foreign customers are an attractive strategy of entering foreign markets, which provides such advantages as: increased stability of sales, reduced marketing requirements and know-how transfer.'[10]

Summing up, the export sector in Poland has been subject to large structural changes. The most dynamic part was constituted by enterprises that were the last to benefit from export-stimulating policies; small and medium-sized enterprises and companies with foreign participation. Some large firms, enjoying tax incentives on account of their export activity were able to record fast export growth. On the other hand, exports were stagnant in the group of old FTOs and that of the largest Polish exporters. The latter, despite being entitled to export-stimulating incentives, did not contribute to rapid growth of Polish exports.

INSTITUTIONAL SUPPORT FOR EXPORTING

This section reviews supply and demand for export services. It differs from earlier evaluations of export-stimulating policies presented in the Polish scientific literature in terms of the set of aspects of the policies and the export institutions which are assessed.

Neither receivers nor providers of export services have been surveyed before. Also our attention is focused on the evaluation of the quality (as seen by exporters) and availability of export services. These include counselling on the requirements to be met by exports, and on the evaluation of availability and quality of the market information, for example, information on relevant business practices and regulations. The effects of exchange rate, tax and customs policies towards exporters are not covered here. They are covered at length in publications of the Foreign Trade Research Institute, which were summarised above.

This assessment of the development of the export infrastructure in Poland and its perceived deficiencies reveals weaknesses in the policies to stimulate exports. It points to barriers encountered not only by large established firms, but which were new to exporting, but also to problems met by newly established companies in attempting to develop exports. This research concentrates on one specific aspect of transition, the need to support institutional change in the export sector.

CHARACTERISTICS OF THE EXPORTERS SAMPLED IN OUR SURVEY

This analysis concerns two groups of exporters: mid-sized and large exporter-producers, and FTOs. After 1989 the activity of both groups changed radically. Today the difference between the two groups is that the first do not act as trade intermediaries for other companies while FTOs do. If, as we concluded earlier, the activity of the export sector in Poland is dominated by newcomers, the question is were their demands for export services met? In other words have the new institutions which emerged and expanded in the export sector, especially in export infrastructure substituted for some of the services formerly provided by FTOs?

Our sample of exporter-producers covers 46 companies.[11] The average value of exports of the sample firms was 53.4 million zloty, about US$ 20 million in 1996. All employed above 100 staff. Unfortunately, no small exporters replied, so the exporter-producers' sample represents only medium and large exporters. But they cover a large part of Polish exports.

The medium and large firms became important clients of the export promotion institutions. In many countries chambers of commerce provide much of the support services sought by exporters. Questionnaires were sent to 100 chambers of commerce but only seven replied, despite reminders. From these few replies it seems that the share of large and small foreign FTOs in the chambers of commerce activity was a little over one-third, while the exporter-producers was just over two-fifths. Probably most of the users of the export services provided by chambers of commerce would be small firms. Large FTOs would be unlikely to use them.

On the basis of several characteristics, our sample of exporter-producers seems typical of this part of Poland's export sector that covers medium and large enterprises.

(1) The ownership structure of the sample is broadly similar to the ownership structure in Polish exports. 23 companies, that is, 50 per cent of the sample are private, 15 firms (33 per cent) are state-owned. The total share of the private producer-exporters in the sample's exports was 42 per cent and for state owned enterprises it was 39 per cent. In 1996 the share of the private sector (including producers and FTOS) in Polish exports was 63 per cent. All the FTOs included in the survey were private.

(2) The average export value of the sample's firms was 53.4 million zloty. For the state-owned enterprises it was 64.3 million zloty, while for private ones, 44.9 million zloty. It is typical for the Polish export sector that the export value of private companies is smaller than for state-owned enterprises. This is the result of the socialist heritage, when major suppliers of exports were large and state-owned. The exports of the state-owned enterprises are still dominated by large exporters. But the size of private exporter-producers has been increasing rapidly.

(3) The branch structure of the sample is similar to the branch structure of Polish exports in general.

(4) The sample covers the more active part of the Polish exports sector. For 61 per cent of the sample's exporter-producers their share of exports in sales is higher than average for Polish exporters. The export share of sales intensity of the private companies is much higher than the state-owned enterprises. Interestingly the export intensity of the FTOs in the sample was quite low. For two of them it was only 10 per cent, for the next two FTOs, 30 per cent and 40 per cent. They diverted their foreign sales to the domestic market.

(5) The sample covers producer-exporters who seem to have made real efforts to improve their export performance and create the base for further export development. Half of them have a marketing department, 82 per cent started to export to the new foreign market in the last 5 years. Even though only 15 per cent of them train staff to improve exporting, this happens more often than in other groups of exporters. Of the firms in the sample, 46 per cent use the services of export promotion organisations. Only 13 firms, that is, 28 per cent, export on the basis of outward processing. Most of them were private.

In conclusion: Our sample represents a relatively active, export-oriented group of medium and large exporter-producers. The branch and ownership structure of the sample is typical for exports of enterprises with local capital domination.

Use of Export-promotion Measures and Services by Producer-Exporters in Poland

The firms in the sample are very active in Polish exports. 82 per cent of them started exporting to the new markets in the last 5 years. But most (85 per cent) of them made no use of institutional support for exporting when they tried to enter the new markets. Entry into new foreign markets was the result of their own unassisted efforts. Why did most exporter-producers seeking foreign markets not use institutional support? What kind of export services did they use and which did they neglect? What is their opinion about the export promotion services and instruments in Poland?

Different countries have different export promotion programmes [*Diamantopoulos, Schlegelmich and Katy Tse, 1996; Seringhaus and Rosson, 1990; Bell, 1997*].[12] Polish export promotion programmes can be classified as five categories of services:

(1) product developments;

(2) information about foreign market and contacts;

(3) marketing;

(4) financial support;

(5) training.

The first category, product development, includes product planning, export packing, information on quality control, product selection for exporting, product design and handling documentation. The second category, export information includes market information, information on relevant business practices and information on regulations. The third category involves marketing, mainly exhibition and trade fairs and contacts with foreign buyers. The fourth – financial support, includes export credit guarantees, credit finance for exports and insurance. The last category is mainly training for exporting.

The most popular items were among market information and marketing. The least used categories were financial support and product support. Nine services, that is 60 per cent of the total number that we asked about, were used by less than 37 per cent of exporters.

Why were most of the export promotion services used by only one third of exporters? What are the reasons for the differences in the intensity of use of different services by newcomers? Are they the result of: the differences in the availability of services for exporters in Poland, poor knowledge of exporters about this availability or differences in quality of the export services?

Regional discrepancies in the availability and quality of export support services and instruments are likely in different regions of Poland. Compared to the Czech Republic and Hungary, Poland is relatively big. In our survey some regional chambers of commerce got positive comments, good marks, from the exporter-producers. These chambers of commerce turned out to be the ones that also answered our questionnaires. But the vast majority of chambers of commerce did not even acknowledge our questionnaires. Some of these were pointed out by the exporters as poor sources of advice and help. They got the lowest marks for their export services.

Table 6.5 shows product support and export information services were seldom used. The fact that most of the firms started exporting to the new markets in the last five years and many only started direct exporting in the last seven years implied that they should have had urgent need of information on products and markets. Our survey confirms this. The lack of information about foreign market demand as well as the lack of marketing specialists was recognised by our respondents as the most important barriers to exporting. Only 26 per cent of our exporter-producers indicated services they would have liked but which are not currently available in Poland. This suggests rather little awareness among exporters, both about the available export services, and about other possible services for supporting exports in a market

TABLE 6.5
INTENSITY OF USAGE OF DIFFERENT EXPORT SERVICES BY
PRODUCER-EXPORTERS

Category of export promotion services	number use	dintensity of use [% of the sample]
1. Product support and development:	[76]	
product design	10	22
information on quality control	15	33
export packing	15	33
handling documentation	22	48
product selection for exporting	14	30
2. Export information:	[62]	
market information	28	61
information on relevant business practices	16	35
information on regulation	18	33
3. Marketing:	[78]	
trade fairs	31	67
contacts with foreign buyers	29	63
4. Financial support:	[33]	
credit finance for exports	7	15
export credit guarantee	9	20
Insurance	17	37
5. Training for exporting:	[26]	
training for exporting	26	46

Source: The Survey [June/July 1997].

economy. Many exporters may not have looked for some types of export services on the market simply because they were unaware of them.

The Major Suppliers of Export-Promotion Services in Poland

According to our survey the major suppliers of export promotion services for exporter-producers were the chambers of commerce. Every fourth exporter-producer used their services.

Our sample of chambers of commerce covers only seven (questionnaires were sent to 100). None had foreign representatives, only one co-operated with a foreign partner. Their major activity covers different aspects of information, trade fairs, help in obtaining contacts and training for exporting. Their services, as for other chambers of commerce in Poland, were not free of charge. Most were created in 1989–92 so they are new organisations. Their potential for providing specialised export services is rather limited. The reluctance of chambers of commerce to reply to our questionnaires may reflect an awareness that they had little of value to offer to exporters.

On the one hand, the chambers of commerce are suppliers of export support for middle size and large exporter-producers. On the other hand, according to our survey of chambers most chambers of commerce's clients were actually small firms. Only 21 per cent the chambers' clients were middle size and big exporters. This suggests that many middle-size exporter-producers made no use of export promotion services from the chambers.

Second on the list of major suppliers of export support is the export credit insurance corporation S.A. – KUKE. But its services were used by only 16 per cent of the exporters. These point firmly to the relatively small role played by the KUKE in the Polish export promotion scheme. But compared to the Polish average, the firms in our sample were relatively frequent users of KUKE.

The next major suppliers of export services are foreign trade organisations (11 per cent were used by the exporters), Polish Embassies (eight per cent), Ministry of Foreign Trade and other foreign trade institutions including banks (each below five per cent). The minor role of banks in export support revealed by our survey is typical for Poland. Export credits cover only 0.8–1.3 per cent of Polish exports (Ministry of Economy).

The relatively small role of the FTOs in the exports of the medium and large producer-exporters is noteworthy. It means that the previous use of the FTOs by mid-sized and large producer-exporters has been substituted by their own activity. The FTOs specialise in trade in selected products. They buy products from producers for exporting or sell them on commission. In foreign trade operations the FTOs now concentrate on the exports of their own subsidiary companies, but also continue to play the intermediary role for many smaller firms. As our survey showed only a few middle size exporter-producers have been using FTOs.

The high availability and quality of trade fairs indicates that they are important sources of information for exporters in our survey. According to FTRI contacts with foreign customers in Poland and abroad were the major source of information for three-quarters of exporters.

Conclusion: Our survey of exporter-producers and FTOs indicates that few used export promotion services to assist their entry into new markets. Most of the services we listed were used by only a third of exporters. The major sources of export promotion services for our sample of companies were chambers of commerce and KUKE.

THE EVALUATION OF QUALITY

We suggest two ways of appraising the quality of export services:

(1) by averaging the marks that they got from exporters (Figure 1);

(2) by indicating preferred instruments and services, that is, these which got high marks of 4 and 5 as compared to the lowest marks 1 and 2 (see columns 3 and 4 in Table 6.6).

We employ an additional indicator, which indicates the difference in the quality of services that were delivered by different institutions. From the sum of the percentage of instruments which got marks 4 and 5 we subtract the percentage of instruments which got a mark of 1 and 2 (column 5, Table 6.6). Almost 70 per cent of the services were given an average mark of 3 and only 12 per cent a 4 and 18 per cent got below 3. Most medium and large exporter-producers seem satisfied with export services available in Poland.

The most appreciated services (Table 6.6) were product selection for exporting, contacts with foreign buyers and credit finance for exporting. Over 70 per cent of exporters gave marks 4 and 5 to these. They got fewest grades 1 and 2.

Marks 1 and 2 were given to the following export services (Table 6.6, column 4): information on relevant business practices (from 50 per cent of exporters), export packing (40 per cent) and information on quality control (34 per cent). They also earned marks 4 and 5. Besides product design and handling documentation they were the least appreciated services.

To evaluate the quality and availability of export services used by our sample of firms we employed our additional method. From the sum of the proportion of instruments given marks 4 and 5 we subtract the percentage of instruments given marks 1 and 2. This measure suggests the differences in quality of services delivered by different export promotion institutions. The lowest differences in quality were for credit finance for exports, contact with foreign buyers, product selection for exporting, trade fairs, trade representatives abroad and export credit guarantee. The bigger differences were in the case of information on relevant business practices, information on regulations, export packing, information on quality control and product design. On quality control, export packing, market information and information on regulation many good as well as bad marks suggests that there were some institutions which are able to supply good quality of services and other institutions which deliver poor quality.

As data from Table 6.6 indicate, with some exceptions (insurance, training for exporting, trade fairs and handling documentation) the group of newcomers (exporter-producers) and experienced exporters (FTOs) have a similar opinion on the quality of export services and instruments which were delivered by the export promotion institutions. We can expect that their opinions reflect the deficiencies of export promotion policy in Poland.

The few chambers of commerce that replied stated that they provided contacts, information about foreign markets and general information. But the chambers of commerce are good suppliers of only some types of export services. Our sample's chambers of commerce as well as an EXPROM [*Polish Export Promotion Programme, EXPROM, 1996*] survey confirm a high demand for product support, market information and marketing. In the

TABLE 6.6
EVALUATION OF THE QUALITY OF EXPORT PROMOTION SERVICES AND
INSTRUMENTS

		Opinion of 46 exporter-producers				FTOs' opinion	
		sum of per cent of marks 4 and 5	sumof per cent of marks 1 and 2	[4+5] - [1+2]	ranking given by exporters	sum of per cent of FTOs marks	Ranking given by FTOs
1	2	3	4	5	6	7	8
1	**Product support and development**						
	product design	40	30	10	11	5	14
	information on quality control	40	34	6	12	9	10
	export packaging	27	40	13	13	8	11
	handling documentation	27	32	5	14	15	3
	product selection for exporting	72	21	51	3	15	4
2	**Export information**						
	contacts with foreign buyers	72	14	58	2	15	5
	market information	46	21	25	7	13	8
	information on regulations	45	33	12	10	8	12
	information on relevant business practices	13	50	37	15	5	13
3	**Marketing**						
	trade fairs	65	16	49	4	12	9
	treade representatives abroad	63	27	36	5	15	7
4	**Financial support**						
	credit finance for exports	71	0	71	1	16	2
	export credit guarantee	56	22	34	6	15	6
	insurance	42	18	24	8	18	1
	Training for exporting						
	training for exporting	46	29	17	9	5	15

Source: The Survey [June/July 1997].

opinion of the FTOs weakness in the above services, as well as the lack of specialists in marketing, form the major barriers to exporting in Poland.

Classification of Export Promotion Services According to Availability and Quality

Comparison of the data from Tables 6.5, 6.6 and Figure 6.1 leads us to the following classification of the export promotion services which are used in Poland.

I. Export promotion services which were often used (above 46 per cent) by exporters and got good average marks (above 3.5) were four out of 15 services: contacts with foreign buyers, foreign representatives, market information and trade fairs,

II. Exporters often used export promotion services (about 48 per cent), but that category got a low average mark (below 3). Only handling documentation fell into this category.

III. Export promotion services rarely used (below 37 per cent) but given a good average mark (above 3) eight out of 15 services; insurance, credit guarantee, credit finance, information on regulation, information on relevant business practices, information on quality control, product selection for exporting, training for exporting.

IV. Export promotion services and instruments were rarely used by exporters (below 33 per cent) and given a bad average mark (below 3): two services: product design and export packing.

The above classification indicates that the quality and quantity of the supply of the four services: contacts with foreign buyers, trade fairs, market information and foreign representation were deemed good.

Even though 48 per cent of the sample's exporters used the assistance with handling documentation they were dissatisfied with the quality of this service. It got more marks 1 and 2 than marks 4 and 5. Perhaps some institutions delivered good quality of services but more delivered poor quality.

Noteworthy is group III which shows services with good average marks but that were not popular among exporters. This group covers all but one (marketing) category. As in group II there are differences in supply of these services between different export promotion institutions and possibly also between regions. There are also differences among exporters in their knowledge of existing export services in Poland.

Group IV covers two types of services whose quality is criticised by exporters. They are not popular and may not be commonly available.

The worst situation is in the supply and the quality of the first and second export promotion category: product support and information about foreign markets.

Our survey covers only medium and large exporters. The major sources of information for them were similar to these for small exporters: foreign buyers, 56 per cent, trade fairs, 32 per cent, newspapers, 29 per cent, informal contacts with companies, 26 per cent. They seldom used business-supporting organisations, four per cent, joint venture's partners, 11 per cent or market research, 18 per cent.

FIGURE 6.1

CLASSIFICATION BY PRODUCER-EXPORTERS OF PROMOTION INSTRUMENTS BY AVERAGE MARKS

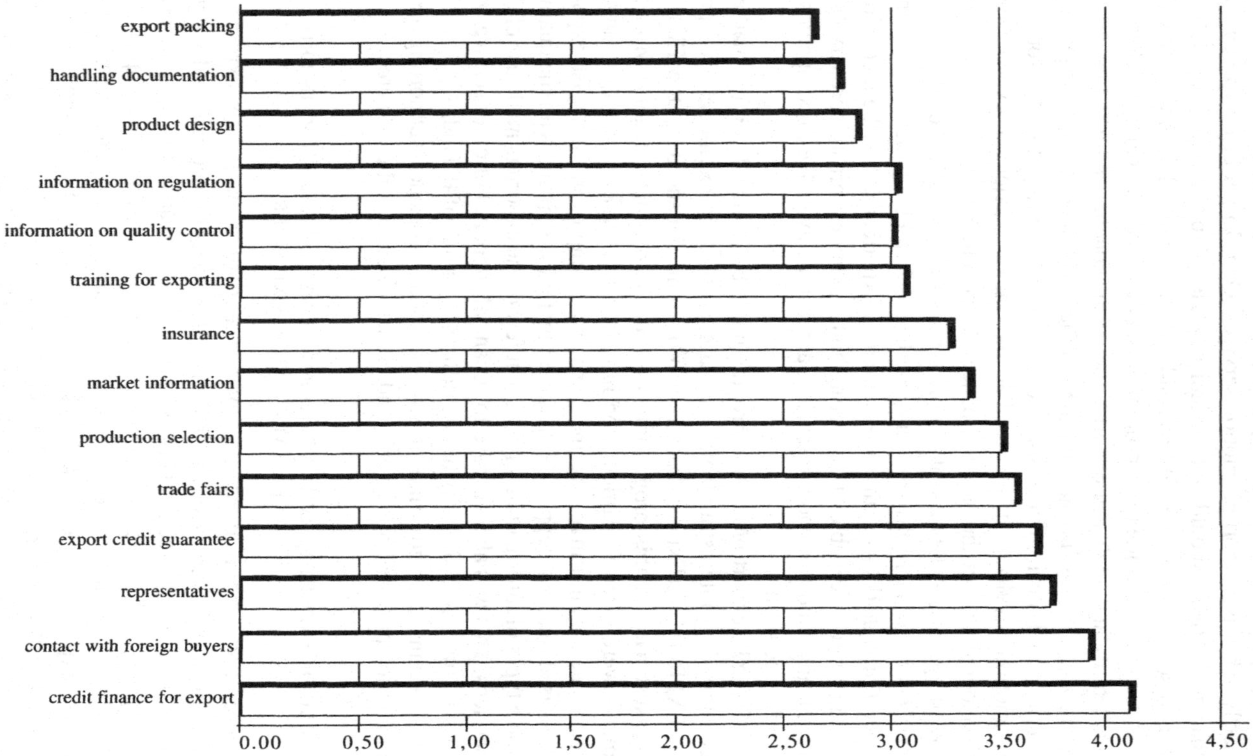

Most, 68 per cent, of the sample of exporters said they were willing to pay for export services. A majority (59 per cent) says that government should partly subsidise export promotion services. Only 15 per cent exporters think that government should not subsidise while 24 per cent of exporters say export services should be fully subsidised by government. If most are willing and ready to pay for export promotion services and the major problem is the availability and quality of export services, the conclusion for the government is simple. It must stimulate and support the development of export promotion services and institutions. Since exporters are willing to pay for export promotion services, it seems that the major barrier to export service development is not the lack of finance. We conclude that the main reason for low usage of most types of export services by exporters looking for new markets is the lack of these services. In most cases, the services given the fewest high marks were those least used by exporters. It may be that there are few institutions capable of delivering high quality export support services. In fact, many export promotion services are just not available to companies that would like them.

Poland's export promotion programme is based mainly on the marketing category. It is interesting that a similar export promotion model was applied in EXPROM 1 (Export Promotion programme financed by the EU). The weakest parts of this programme were in the product category. Most high marks were given to participation in trade fairs, marketing and training, the least – advice on firm management and quality improvement. Polish exporters who used financial support seem quite satisfied with it and with the quality of some types of information services, but few of the exporters made use of these services. This was also the case for financial support. For other services there may be uneven availability across different regions of Poland.

It seems that government support should consider supporting export promotion provided by regional and branch chambers of commerce.

USE OF EXPORT SERVICES AND BARRIERS TO EXPORTING IN PRIVATE AND STATE-OWNED EXPORTERS

Since 1989 the role of state-owned exporters in Polish exports has systematically decreased. In 1990 their share was 95 per cent and six years later only 39 per cent. This is due to the privatisation of state-owned enterprises and an export expansion by newly created private companies.

There is no difference in the scale of expansion between private and state owned exporters on the new foreign markets. Most of our sample of private and state-owned exporter-producers began exporting to the new foreign markets in the last five years. The major directions of both types of enterprises' export activity were to the EU and the former USSR countries.

But there are differences between the two groups of enterprises in their strategy and perception of exporting as a source of new income.

(1) Within our sample more private than state owned exporters had created a base and conditions for exporting. 60 per cent (14 companies out 23) of private exporters had a marketing department for exports. But only 40 per cent (6 companies out 15) state owned and one foreign owned enterprise did. Among private exporter-producers companies 22 per cent provided export training, but only seven percent of state owned did. The private firms' strategy of development was more export oriented than state-owned enterprises. The latter concentrated their activity more on the domestic market.

(2) The share of exports in sales is higher for private exporters than for state owned.

(3) Private firms appear more active in using export services in entering new markets than state owned. Private firms looked for export support mainly to the chambers of commerce. Of private exporters 26 per cent used export services for entering new foreign markets but none of the state owned companies used them. Also the chambers of commerce reported that 74 per cent of their clients were private exporters. SOEs more often than private firms used FTOs and Polish Embassies. The state-owned enterprises seem more tradition bound than private ones.

(4) Both groups value highly the credit and contacts with foreign buyers delivered by export promotion institutions. Private firms emphasise the high quality of information on quality control and on regulations. The state owned exporters stressed the value of product design and credit finance.

(5) In our sample only 26 per cent exporter-producers indicated export services they would like to use but that were not available in Poland. Seven out of 15 state-owned enterprises pointed to such services but only four out of 23 private ones. State-owned exporters seemed to possess better knowledge about potential services that could help exporting.

(6) Most of the firms in the sample were ready to pay for export services. But 47 per cent of state-owned enterprises and 22 per cent of private companies did not intend to use export services if they had to pay for them. This can mean that the demand for export services is greater among the private than the state-owned exporters. The private exporters recognised the importance of services for export development. Differences in the opinion on the government involvement in subsidisation of export services are small. Over 50 per cent of private and state-owned exporters stated that export services should be partly

subsidised. Only 22 per cent private companies and 27 per cent state-owned exporters wanted full subsidisation by government. It partly explains why the share of state-owned enterprises in the chambers of commerce operation was so small. The differences suggest that privatisation stimulates the propensity to export. Progress in privatisation should influence export development.

Conclusions of Survey

We aimed to reveal both weak and strong points of institutional support for exporting in Poland. Our main focus is on the exporters' opinion of the availability and quality of export promotion services in Poland.

(1) The major sources of export services for our sample of firms were the chambers of commerce. But the chambers' potential for export support is limited. They serve mainly small exporters: small trade intermediaries and producers. The export credit insurance corporation – KUKE is important and so is the government, partly by supporting participation in trade fairs.

(2) Only 15 per cent of our sample used export promotion services for entering new markets. They mainly used them for maintaining their position and for increasing exports to markets where the FTOs had previously exported. The firms in the sample display more features of newcomers than of experienced exporters. At the beginning of the 1990s they took over export outlets from the FTOs and have been trying to keep these markets.

(3) More than half of our sample used only about a third of the export services listed in our questionnaires, mainly different kinds of advice on exporting. They used the export promotion organisations mainly for help in getting contacts with foreign buyers, in training for exporting, in using trade fairs and in getting general information about foreign markets. Our sample seldom used product support, export information and financial support. These services are especially important for newcomers in the export sector. They are much needed by exporters at the first stage of entering foreign markets.

(4) The most highly valued instruments were product selection for exporting, contacts with foreign buyers and credit finance for exporting. The least appreciated were information on relevant business practices, export packing and information on quality control.

(5) The biggest deficiency of the Polish export promotion programme was the low availability for exporters of most of the export services we selected for our survey. Most seldom used services were in the category of product support and market development.

(6) There are also discrepancies in the quality and availability of export services and instruments among different institutions and regions in Poland.

(7) Institutional infrastructure for export development is weak in Poland. There are many export promotion institutions but their effort does not meet the exporter-producers' demand for export services. There is an urgent need to change this situation.

CONCLUSION

We have argued that the deep institutional changes in the Polish export sector during transition were the result of Poland's transformation strategy. Direct institutional support for exporting had little effect. Polish export promotion policy differed from that of Hungary and the Czech Republic. The major source of this difference was the high priority of combating inflation. This implied a limited scope for using the exchange rate to support exports and increased the role of other policy measures.

We hypothesised that liberalisation and de-monopolisation, privatisation and the adjustment of domestic prices to world prices had a decisive impact on institutional change in the export sector. During the first three years of transition there was almost no direct institutional support for exporters but their number increased from 2,000 in 1989 to over 30,000 in 1992 (small and medium exporters from some hundreds to over 25,000). The increase in micro exporters to almost 28,000 in 1992 was startling. The surge in exporters was accompanied by a steady contraction of the share of foreign trade organisations – the former monopolists of Polish foreign trade. This means that the development and the restructuring of the Polish export sector was determined by the newcomers' behaviour, which urgently needed the institutional support for exporting. But, as we observed, even though the government announced the introduction of an export promotion policy in 1994, direct institutional support for the exporters was too weak to influence institutional change in the export sector. This hypothesis was confirmed by the answers from our questionnaires, which covered mainly large exporters, the group to which the government policy was particularly directed. According to our survey only 15 per cent of the exporters used direct export support. They seldom used product support, export information and financial support, all of which are especially important for newcomers to exporting.

The largest deficiency of the Polish export promotion programme was the low availability for exporters of most export services. There were also discrepancies in quality and availability of export services and instruments among the different institutions and regions in Poland. The Polish experience confirms that policies to encourage exports are not specific to the export sector. Questions arise whether a more intensified existing export promotion policy or a different model could better speed success.

NOTES

1. In 1989 its share was 14.2 per cent.
2. The share of former Soviet Union in Poland's exports was in 1980 – 31.2 per cent.
3. In 1989 the share of the former USSR in Poland's exports was 64 per cent.
4. In 1985 in Poland the share of exports in GDP accounted for seven per cent and imports – seven per cent while in the Czechoslovakia – 13 per cent and 13 per cent and Hungary – 17 per cent and 16 per cent. Per capita foreign trade turnover accounted for [1985] in Poland $500, the Czechoslovakia – $1,200 and Hungary – $1,400 [*Jasinski, 1995*].
5. The share of tariffs in budget revenues accounted for eight per cent in 1991, 8.5 per cent in 1992, 7.7 per cent in 1994 and – 7.7 per cent and 6.7 per cent in 1995.
6. Partly as a result of tactical consideration, that is, to secure a better negotiating position in talks with the EC and EFTA on trade concessions.
7. In the latter half of 1989 the monthly rate of inflation averaged some 30 per cent
8. In this section we refer to opinion of exporters presented by Foreign Trade Research Institute in its survey of 600 manufacturers-exporters operating in manufacturing industry in 1994–97. See Polska polityka handlu zagranicznego, Warszawa [*1996, 1997*]; Handel zagraniczny Polski, Warszawa [*1997, 1998*].
9. Own calculations based on the Ministry for Foreign Economic Relations ranking, 1994, p.8, Central Statistical Office, 1997, pp.11–12.
10. 'Mocne i slabe strony malych i srednich przedsiebiorstw produkcyjnych w Polsce w 1995 roku oraz konsekwencje dla polityki' ('Strengths and Weaknesses of SHEs in Poland in 1995 and the Consequences for Policy'), report prepared for USAID GEMINI-PEDS Project, Warsaw, Nov. 1996, p.108.
11. It is based on the results of our survey based on questionnaires. These were sent to 150 exporter-producers, 100 chambers of commerce and four foreign trade organisations. We got 46 answers from exporter-producers, seven from chambers of commerce and four from FTOs.
12. 'Strengths and Weaknesses of SHEs in Poland ...', Warsaw, 1996.

REFERENCES

Balcerowicz, L. and A. Gelb , 1995, *Macropolicies in Transition to a Market Economy: A Three-Year Perspective*, Warsaw: CASE, *Studies and Analyses*, No.33.
Bak, H. and E. Kawecka-Wyrzykowska, 1991, 'Transformation of the Foreign Trade System in Poland in 1990–91 (with Special Regard to Poland's Foreign Trade with the European Community)', in H. Bak, S. Góra, E. Kawecka-Wyrzykowska and S. Ladyka, *Re-integration of Poland into Western Europe by Internal and External Liberalisation*, WIRI, Prace i Materialy, No.48.
Beers, C. and G.Biessen, 1995, Trade Potential and Structure of Foreign Trade: The Case of Hungary and Poland, Research Memoranda, 95.02, mimeo.
Bell, J., 1997, 'The Role of Export Promotion Organisations', in B. Fynes and S. Ennis, *Competing from the Periphery. Core Issues in International Business*, Dublin.
Biessen G., 1996, East European Foreign Trade and System Change Tinbergen Institute Research Series, Amsterdam and Rotterdam.
Central Statistical Office, 1995, Warsaw: GUS.
Dabrowski, M., 1997, 'The Financial System in Poland and Trends of its Development', 'Economic Scenarios of Poland', Conference Papers, Warsaw: CASE Reports.
Diamantopoulos A., Schlegelmich, B. and K. Katy Tse, 1996, Understanding the Role of Export Marketing Assistance: Empirical Evidence and Research Needs, *European Journal of Marketing*, Vol.27.

Export Promotion and Institutional Change in Poland

Dichtl, E. and H.-G. Koglmayr, 1987, 'Country Risk Evaluations and Export Market Entry', in P.J. Rosson and S.D. Reid, *Managing Export Entry and Expansion: Concepts and Practice*, New York: Praeger.

Durka, B. and J.Chojna, 1998, 'Udział podmiotow z kapitałem zagranicznym w polskim handlu zagranicznym', in *Inwestycje zagraniczne w Polsce*, Warsaw: IKC HZ.

Handel zagraniczny Polski w 1996, 1997, Warsaw: IKC HZ.

Hoekman, B. and S. Djenkov, 1996, 'Intra-Industry Trade, Foreign Direct Investment, and the Reorientation of Eastern European Exports', Working Paper, Washington, DC: World Bank.

Jasinski, L.J., 1995, 'Kurs walutowy a konkurencyjnosc cenowa polskiego eksportu', in *Ceny towarów w polskim eksporcie do krajów uprzemyslowionych*, Warszawa: IKCHZ, mimeo.

Keesing, D. and A. Singer, 1991, 'Development Assistant Gone Wrong: Failures in Services to Promote and Support Manufactured Exports', in P. Hogan, D. Keesing and A. Singer, *The Role of Support Services in Expanding Manufacturing Exports in Developing Countries*, EDI Seminar Series, Washington, DC: World Bank.

Komitet Integracji Europejskiej, 1996, Ocena umowy przejsciowej dotyczacej handlu i spraw zwiazanych z handlem miedzy Polska a Europejska Wspólnota Gospodarcza i Europejska Wspólnota Wegla i Stali, Biblioteka Europejska, Nr 12.

Kamiński, B., Sept. 1993, 'How the Market Transition Affected Export Performance in the Central European Economies', Working Papers, Washington, DC: World Bank.

Kamiński, B., Wang, Z.K. and L.A. Winters, 1996, *Foreign Trade in the Transition: The International Environment and Domestic Policy*, Washington, DC: World Bank.

Lavigne, M.,1992, 'The Reform of Industrial Enterprises in East European Economies and the Incentives to Export', in C. Frateschi, G. Salvini (eds.), *A Comparative Analysis of Economic Reforms in Central and East Europe*, Aldershot: Dartmouth Publishing.

Macieja, J., 1995, Rozwój przygranicznej wspólpracy gospodarczej w latach 1994–1995, Warszawa: Centrum im. A.Smitha.

Marczewski, K, 1995, 'Evaluation of the Foreign Trade Policy Instruments in 1994 in the Light of the FTRI Survey in Poland's Foreign Trade Policy 1994–1995', Warsaw: FTRI.

OECD, 1997, Report on Poland, Paris: OECD.

Plowiec, U., 1994, 'Polish Export Promotion Policy', in *Economic Policy and Finance for Development*, a report on the Polish–Japanese Joint Seminar on Economy and Finance, Warsaw.

Plowiec, U., 1995, 'Financial instruments of export support', in *Poland's Foreign Trade Policy*.

Pluciński, E., 1997, 'O Integracji inaczej, "Nowe Zycie Gospodarcze', No 17.

Polityka handlu zagranicznego Polski w latach 1995–1996, 1996, Warsaw: IKC HZ.

Poland's Foreign Trade Policy 1994–1996, 1995, Warsaw.

Polish Export Promotion Programme EXPROM, 1996, Polish Chamber of Commerce, EC-Phare Programme, Warsaw.

Program promocji polskiego eksportu, EXPROM, Podsumowanie wyników kwestionariusza, Polish Chamber of Commerce, EC-Phare Programme, 1996, Warsaw.

Rosati, D., 'Foreign Economic Policy and External Balance in Poland in the 1980s, 1989', FTRI, Discussion Papers No.7.

Rutkowski, J., 1997, 'Wspieranie eksportu za pomoca instrumentów finansowych', in *Zagraniczna polityka gospodarcza Polski 1996–1997*.

Seringhaus, F.H. and P. Rosson, 1990, *Government Export Promotion: A Global Perspective*, London: Routledge.

Wolodkiewicz-Donimirski, Z., 1996, 'Export of Small and Medium-Sized Enterprises in Poland', in *Integrating Small and Medium Sized Enterprises in Transformation Countries into European Trade Flows and Co-operation Schemes*, Gdansk: Gdańsk Institute for Market Economics.

Wziatek-Kubiak, A., 1999, 'Aktywnoœæ w zakresie ekspansji miêdzynarodowej', Working Papers INE-PAN, No.11.

Zagraniczna polityka gospodarcza Polski 1996–1997, 1997, IKCHZ, Warsaw.

Zielinski, M.F., 1995, 'Elementy polityki handlowej w Polsce w latach 1990–1992', in M.Dabrowski (ed.) *Polityka gospodarcza okresu transformacji*, Warsaw: PWN, CASE.

171

7

Lessons for Export Promotion

ALASDAIR MacBEAN

The experience of various countries in seeking to increase export earnings reveals a mixture of successes and failures. Creating a stable economy and investing in physical and human capital seem to have been the most powerful contribution governments have made to economic performance, in terms of growth in both national income and exports [*World Bank, 1993; Krugman 1994; Kwon, 1998*]. Consistently following policies of import substituting industrialisation behind high protection has generally proved inconsistent with success in exporting. That has been true of most African and Latin American countries and most of South Asia. But countries like South Korea, Taiwan, Thailand, Malaysia and China did have high levels of protection for many industries in the earlier phases of their development before adopting outward looking policies [*World Bank, 1993; Wade, 1990; Amsden, 1989; Lardy, 1992*]. Some, including Alice Amsden and Robert Wade, argue that this helped their subsequent success as exporters [also *Kwon, 1998*]. But what is certain is that those countries which did adopt export promotion either from the beginning like Singapore and Hong Kong, or after one or two decades of import substituting industrialisation, or used an EP policy combined with selective ISI, did achieve very fast growth in exports [*Kwon, 1998*].

The effects of institutional support for exporting on actual exports are hard to detect. Probably, even with quite sophisticated econometrics and a large number of years in the sample period it would be nearly impossible to detect the stimulus to exports from even an excellent system of support for exporters. The difficulty arises from the greater impact of so many other factors. Protection against imports, a devaluation, a surge in domestic or foreign demand due to different rates of growth, or a change in tastes would all swamp the effects of measures such as export credits and help with export related information and marketing. With most data limited to 1989 to 1996, as is the case for the CEEC and CIS transitional economies, it is clearly impossible. Even for the East Asian countries with a larger sample period, both the level and the effects of institutional support would be hard to measure. The effects of their macroeconomic, educational, commercial, and industrial policies would also have to be considered in a properly specified model. It is therefore hardly surprising that the few studies of export support policies and institutions have tended to give only impressionistic judgements on their success (or failure) in increasing exports. Generally the studies have been highly critical and argued that, at least in the context of developing countries, the institutional support for exports has been largely unsuccessful [*Keesing and Singer, 1991*]. Empirical assessments of export support policies have generally been based on surveys, comparing what advice and support they provide with some ideal or with what exporters say they want. Our own approach has been similar in the studies of the Czech Republic, Hungary and Poland. Examples of both the impressionistic and the empirical approaches are reported in Chapter 2 of this study.

Many industrially developed countries seem to consider it worthwhile to have quite extensive programmes of export support, Germany, Italy, Spain, the UK and USA among them. Of course, to justify such expenditures their governments do not need to show a large impact upon total exports or their rate of increase. All that is necessary is for them to expect that the present value of the gains minus expenditures (properly discounted) on supporting exporters is positive. The expenditures tend to be relatively small, less than one third of one per cent of export revenues for these countries. As most governments continue with these support policies it is evident that they consider that the extra net gains from exports, achieved by such support, do exceed its costs.

What this suggests is that if better policies and methods of export promotion, including institutional support for exporters, can be adopted in the transitional economies they can make positive gains. Our analyses become important as highlighting aspects of the means of increasing exports that seem to have worked and those that have not.

WAYS OF INCREASING EXPORTS

There is a broad consensus on the importance of getting the general macroeconomic and resource allocation policies right. If an economy is out of macroeconomic balance, with an excess of public and private expenditure over output and near full capacity operation of its production it will inevitably run a current account deficit. Goods and services will be sucked in from abroad and products, which might have been exported, will be consumed in the domestic economy. This situation may be tolerable as long as the rest of the world is happy to supply capital at interest rates which are lower than the productivity of the capital in that economy. But it will certainly make exporting difficult and will tend to push up wages and prices. That in turn would cause the real exchange rate to appreciate and reduce the competitiveness of goods and services produced in that economy. Both theory and experience demonstrate that economies, which operate with significant, sustained, budget deficits, tend to produce these circumstances and their export performance suffers. Financing the government deficit by borrowing from the banking system or printing money also tends to produce inflation and again pushes up the real exchange rate making it difficult to export. These are the reasons why most international institutions urge countries to maintain macroeconomic balance, at least, on average over a typical cycle.

By proper policies for resource allocation in market driven economies we mean a judicious mix of liberalisation, proper taxation systems with effective collection, effective legal structures and law enforcement, effective corporate governance, and efficient capital markets. The intended outcome is that decision-makers: directors, managers, financial institutions, investors should have adequate information and sufficient incentives to direct their activities to the most socially profitable uses of resources. This means low tariffs on imports, with controls reserved for such purposes as protecting citizens from harmful imports such as illegal drugs, low standard pharmaceuticals and unsafe toys, or limiting access to weapons and so on. As far as the foreign trade sector is concerned the aim should be to have, on average, neutral incentives as between producing for the home market and the foreign market. That means that taxes, subsidies or controls should not distort most prices.

There are, however, many issues that cannot be dealt with simply by leaving it to markets. The existence of economies of scale or externalities (infant industry arguments), lack of adequate information and markets to handle all types of risk create situations where the incentives embodied in current market prices may be misleading. All of the services that are 'public' or 'merit' goods require government provision or subsidies to private providers. These include the obvious ones of health, education, defence, policing, but may include many others. Government may also have to subsidise, tax or control for external benefits. These include benefits stemming from basic research or from constructing an underground transport system that relieves congestion and lowers costs to non-users as well as users of the system. Taxes may be required to offset costs such as environmental effects of production, or measures to protect common resources, which would be overexploited if left to the market. The income distribution from freely operating markets may not meet the socially acceptable. Thus government tax and expenditure policies are likely to be required to improve the income distribution between rich and poor, in addition to adjusting incentives.

In relation to the external sector there may be various issues that are not dealt with optimally by leaving them to the market. Adequate market mechanisms may not exist for dealing with the various risks involved in exporting. The legacy of central planning and a command economy in many transitional economies leaves special handicaps. Local banks in transitional economies have little experience in providing export credits. As all exports were generally handled by a few large specialised trading organisations, often acting under instructions from ministries, and more or less in accordance with a national plan, most managers have relatively little experience of dealing with foreign customers. The market failures, already recognised in the industrially developed economies of the OECD in their export support programmes are many times more serious in the transitional economies. This situation should justify greater discrimination in favour of exporting than would be correct for a mature, market-directed economy such as most of the OECD countries. The turbulence involved in dealing with the inflationary pressures when controls were loosened and hoarded money was spent, at the start of transition, handicapped exports by high real exchange rates and excess domestic demand. These special factors are, to some extent, recognised in the rules of the WTO. The rules do permit transitional economies to register subsidies and allow them several years to remove them or bring them into line with WTO standards. But transitional economies may require rather more time to adjust than the WTO rules or other, sometimes stricter, trade treaties permit. There is a case for looking again at the relief granted to transitional economies, perhaps most importantly in the EU because of the large volume of their trade with the EU, and to consider whether more time should be allowed for adjusting explicit and implicit export subsidies. But even within the limits permitted by international agreements a lot can be done in the transitional economies, by both direct and indirect measures, to raise exports. Which measures should be emphasised depends on the existing state of development, the composition of exports and markets, and the degree of transition already attained.

THE CEEC CASE

The CEEC have already extensively liberalised their economies. Most industry is now in the private sector, but problems of corporate governance in manufacturing and financial institutions, particularly in the Czech Republic, are holding up progress in improving efficiency [*EBRD, 1997: Ch.5*]. When combined with wage increases which outstrip increases in productivity, inflation and an appreciating real exchange rate raise export prices, or lower the profitability of exporting when prices are determined in the foreign markets. Although inflation is low compared with most transitional economies it is currently high in all three countries at 13 to 16 per cent compared with average rates of inflation in the OECD of under three per cent.

These countries are already far down the transition road. But further reductions in inflation, more open and honest relations between financial institutions and industry, less 'crony capitalism', management made more responsive to shareholder's interests, and better developed and regulated financial markets are all measures which would indirectly assist exporting by making their industries more competitive. The design of taxation so that it causes fewer disincentives to exporters, particularly in Poland, would also be helpful.

THE ROLE OF FOREIGN DIRECT INVESTMENT (FDI)

In most of the countries reviewed in this work foreign owned subsidiaries and joint venture companies have been major contributors to exporting. In Hungary they provided 80 per cent of exports (gross). In Poland their contribution is also becoming large (in 1996 about 38 per cent). In the Czech Republic no official data have been published on the share of foreign invested companies in exports but the view of analysts is that it is substantial, as much as 60 per cent. Growth has been faster in foreign owned firms than in domestic firms and efficiency is higher and growing faster in them. Their output is very export intensive [*Zemplinerova and Benacek, 1997*]. Volkswagen-Skoda has a rapidly rising share of machinery and transport exports which are the largest single category in total exports. In Ireland foreign invested firms contributed substantially to the rapid growth of exports (Chapter 3). Most of the export successes of East Asia have been greatly assisted by the foreign firms and joint ventures there. Direct foreign investment also seems to promote bilateral trade between the supplying and the recipient country [*Lin, 1995*].

Clearly, if a country, particularly a small country with a highly educated workforce, wishes to expand exports fast then there is a strong case for it to adopt an open, liberal and attractive regime for foreign direct investment. Firms attracted to such a country will generally come to use those skilled workers for producing exported goods or services. This does not necessarily require countries to outbid each other in terms of incentives such as special protection, tax waivers, accelerated capital depreciation allowances or other short-term inducements for firms to invest there. Rather, what attracts long term foreign direct investment in manufacturing is stability in the political and economic climate, an open economy, a regulatory and taxation system that does not discriminate against foreign investors, good industrial relations, flexibility in the labour force and high productivity relative to wage levels [*Balasubramanyam and Salisu, 1991*].

Not only does a liberal, open regime attract FDI it also tends to enhance the benefits from it. FDI is shown to be more growth promoting in countries that have export promoting trade regimes [*Bhagwati, 1978; Balasubramanyam et al., 1996*].

176

IMPROVING THE ENVIRONMENT FOR INWARD INVESTMENT

The record of our three CEEC in attracting FDI is already good. Hungary started earlier and has progressed further in the volume of FDI that it has attracted, proportionately a great deal more than the larger country, Poland [*Chapter 1, Table 1.1*]. Their trade regimes meet the required liberal standards. Their taxation systems are moving to conformity with EU norms. But all three have a legacy of anti-market institutional arrangements inherited from the recent past. Areas where they might improve their attractiveness to FDI include better legislation and enforcement of the laws bearing on commercial activities. The Czech Republic's credibility as a stable economy suffered a blow in 1996 when a group of Czech financial institutions went bankrupt. The weaknesses in Czech banking and financial regulation became apparent. Revelations of corruption, fraud and rent-seeking activities in banking, insurance and investment institutions caused a sharp contraction in investments by foreigners. There have been delays in reforming banks and introducing new laws and regulations. The existing laws are complex and 'rife with inconsistencies and loopholes. Enforcement is in its infancy, and it suffers from rent seeking, procrastination and the bureaucracy of an overburdened state judiciary' [*Zemplinerova and Benacek, 1997: 6*]. The process of legal and judicial reform in the commercial sphere needs to be speeded up and given the resources to back enforcement to increase investor confidence.

High marginal tax rates and Czech customs arrangements may also deter foreign companies, particularly non-EU companies, from investing in the Czech Republic. Reforms are in train to allow the tariff free status for imports for export processing to be extended to imports used intensively in production for exporting. Although the literature on FDI suggests that the basic economic environment is the crucial determinant of the relative attractions of one country over another for foreign investors rather than special tax breaks, it may be wise for the Czech Government to match the average incentives given by other European countries.

Because of macroeconomic imbalances that had been built up in the previous years, Hungary faced a Mexico-type crisis at the beginning of 1995. The stabilisation package introduced in March 1995 achieved considerable success, especially by 1997. But compared with its main trading partners the rate of inflation remained relatively high. The more stable economy helped in attracting investments, both domestic and foreign. But, by 1997, the private sector was already producing about 80 per cent of GDP. Privatisation embraced not only manufacturing companies, but also the banking sector, public utilities and other services. As a result much less industry remains to be privatised. Yet it was privatisation which attracted a great deal of the foreign investment in previous years.

The more effective service sector, which FDI has helped to create, however, does tend to boost foreign and domestic investments. Moreover, the liberalisation of the economy has continued. These factors have contributed to a significant change in the commercial and business environment inside Hungary and should prove attractive to investors. But, investors and firms still suffer from the relatively high rate of inflation, corruption, bureaucracy and the instability of the legal system (in terms of quickly changing and non-transparent laws and regulations). Hungary provided generous fiscal and financial incentives to foreign investors in the first years of transition, but has now moved towards a more equal treatment of domestic and foreign investors. The Government has also established a special supplier programme to create linkages with the domestic economy for foreign subsidiaries and joint ventures that were already resident. While the incentives are still generous, they are no longer out of line with other countries in the region. Overall, Hungary may find it more difficult than formerly to maintain the volume of inward foreign investment.

In Poland, unlike Hungary, the influence of FDI on exports was small in the early 1990s. But FDI has been rising rapidly since 1995 (Table 1.1), and its contribution to exports in 1996 was about 38 per cent. Poland's policy towards foreign investors in the earlier reform period was to offer special fiscal incentives. But after several years of relatively generous incentives Poland moved towards a policy of equal treatment as between foreign and domestic investors. Membership of OECD does impose constraints on Poland's treatment of foreign investors, and certainly means that it cannot discriminate against them. Although Poland was not seen as an attractive location for FDI, as compared with say, Hungary, in the first few years of reform, partly because of the tough macroeconomic policies it followed, now it is proving much more attractive. Its share of FDI going to the three economies has grown to 33 per cent, and according to the forecast of the WIIW (Economic Research Institute in Vienna) Poland will account for about half of the total foreign investment going to the Czech Republic, Hungary and Poland in 1998. The Polish case does seem to accord with the general proposition that what attracts FDI is the general economic and political situation rather than specific fiscal incentives for foreigners.

OTHER MEASURES TO PROMOTE EXPORTS

Given that the CEEC have already established a generally good economic environment for exporters what else can they do? In our view they could significantly increase and improve the quality of government and other institutional support provided for exporters.

This should be targeted on those sectors of industry that most need it. These are mainly the small to medium-sized exporters or potential exporters. Many firms need little help to export. These include subsidiaries of foreign firms, joint ventures and firms in export processing of materials supplied by foreign buyers, large firms with the ability to mount their own export sections or with their own trading companies. All these have little need of official help with marketing, or in most cases with meeting quality standards. They usually get help from their foreign owners, partners or close trading partners. Small and medium sized firms are, traditionally, the firms most in need of support for entering, maintaining and expanding export markets. But even among the small and medium, many believe that their requirements are so technically specialised that it is highly unlikely that help would be forthcoming from typical export support systems. Their very specific needs might be satisfied through jointly financed, innovative programmes rather than from the more general and traditional schemes.

In the countries surveyed we found many examples of firms which had little or no need of help for the reasons outlined above. Some medium sized firms had long historic connections with their trading partners who supplied them with detailed engineering drawings, technical assistance and components. These partners usually then bought the finished product or component from them. They had an assured export market. Some even had machinery supplied and finance arranged by their trading partners. Of course, if such firms wish to expand, or earn higher returns by developing market autonomy they may well need assistance through training and marketing help.

Large companies, sometimes supplying turnkey projects or complete power stations to foreign countries found it relatively easy to obtain export credit guarantees and export credits (although in Poland, in particular, the high cost of credit remained a problem even for large companies). Often for these large projects they had clear government support. But many smaller firms, exporting manufactures of various kinds, found existing export services of little or no help.

The need for help is not just a function of size. It includes the type of products sold, the sophistication of the products and technologies used, and the markets aimed at. Given scarce resources some form of rationing has to be applied to the provision of services. If the users pay full market prices for the services the market will deal with that issue. But, if this is an area where buyers are not fully aware of their own needs, are concerned about risks and are unused to paying for such services then they may have to be subsidised and the excess demand produced by subsidies will force some form of selection. This is best done by decentralising decisions to a local level. Organisations like local chambers of commerce or local consultancy firms are much more likely to know which firms are most in need of help and most likely to benefit from it than large central organisations.

Mechanisms for providing subsidies and making payments require to be designed with care. There is a fine balance between the need to avoid waste and fraud on the one hand, and excessive bureaucracy and delay on the other. Incentives to use help efficiently require that the users should pay a real price. This ensures that they do not make frivolous demands. Governments have to judge the appropriate overall level of subsidies for export support. But more decentralised agencies, more in contact with the users are in a better position to judge what users are willing to pay and what should be the appropriate level of subsidy for each type of service. A reimbursement system where users pay and reclaim against invoices may be the easiest to control if many private organisations are involved in providing services. It has the advantage that the user is free to choose the supplier that he or she considers is the best. It gives the user the power to switch to other suppliers if dissatisfied. It forces competition among the suppliers of credit, market information, production advice and so on.

When firms were asked what services they wanted most they generally stressed credit guarantees and export credits. All the countries that we studied already had some systems in place to provide these. The problem was that few firms proved able to make use of these facilities. The total amount of exports receiving such backing tended to be three per cent or less in our three central European examples. More resources, more advertising of the services and more assistance to firms in making applications for insurance against political and commercial risks, and export credit would help. A form of credit, which many desired, was pre-production finance for export orders. The domestic banks were generally unwilling to provide this. But in a country where many exporting firms were short of cash because of past bad debts from the early nineties' trade with former Soviet Union countries, the lack of such finance could frustrate exports or force exporters into a weak bargaining position with their customers. Some foreign banks are starting to indicate their willingness to provide such finance. It is one area where the official export bank should show a greater willingness to consider such loans.

Many of the other wants expressed conflict with international norms regarding subsidies to exports. But requests for contact services, consulting services, advertising services and transfer of know-how are feasible and most countries already try to help with these activities. But to judge by the degree of dissatisfaction expressed by the users they are not supplied effectively. How can they be improved?

Nowadays, finding appropriate contacts abroad or assisting foreign firms to find suppliers or partners is probably best done through electronic data banks and web-sites, which can be accessed through the Internet. Most firms probably have computers and modems that would enable the use of such systems. If they are too small then local economic chambers or chambers of commerce should be provided with adequate computers or terminals, which would facilitate such data searches. Actual introductions are probably best facilitated by commercial staff attached to overseas trade offices or embassies or within the home country by staff of chambers of commerce.

Information on requests to tender for World Bank or EU contracts are also likely to be best handled electronically. Visiting their web-sites will often be the best way, but it may also be a useful back up for one organisation to collect all such information and alert potential suppliers by electronic mail. The Czech Republic appears to have several organisations duplicating this service. The costs of duplication here may outweigh any benefits from competition.

LESSONS FOR OTHER TRANSITIONAL ECONOMIES

The three Central European Countries studied here are among the most advanced of the transitional economies in terms of their history, adjustments they have already carried out and the economic progress they have made. Many of the export promoting policies they have adopted follow examples of the developed market economies and to a lesser extent East Asia. In foreign trade they have all totally abandoned the practices of the centrally planned economies. Much of their success in increasing exports can be attributed to their success in achieving relative political and economic stability as compared with Russia and most of the Commonwealth of Independent States (CIS). They have also gone much further in terms of restructuring their economies and privatising a large part of their industry. So far it seems improbable that the various export support systems that they have adopted have done much to aid exporters. They are currently engaged in trying to improve these systems. What can the CIS countries learn from the experiences of the CEEC in relation to export growth? What would be relevant to them? Can they short circuit the process and avoid some of the time consuming weaknesses that have made a great deal of the efforts of the CEEC in this field largely irrelevant to most exporters?

Many of the CIS have quite different economies from the CEEC. They are much more heavily dependent on agricultural and mineral exports, which are generally bought and sold by large enterprises in international commodity markets, or under long-term contracts. The nature of the goods exported and of the markets is such that they need little of the traditional export support services. Few of the CIS have significant manufacturing sectors that could, as yet, compete in free markets. Countries like Kazakhstan are rich in minerals and have great potential to attract foreign investment into oil and metals, but are still far from free market economies, and in 1996 attracted much less foreign investment than any of our three CEEC. In terms of corporate governance, legal frameworks and enforcement they lag behind the CEEC. Some like Tajikistan remain embroiled in civil disturbance and political conflict, which severely detract from the possibility of attracting foreign investors or developing non-traditional exports. Tajikistan's main export is aluminium, based on an abundant supply of hydroelectricity. Again this is not the kind of export that requires marketing skills.

Probably the most important advice for the countries of the CIS is to get the fundamentals right before worrying overmuch about export support policies. These fundamentals are political and economic stability, reduced regulation, and clearly expressed laws with fair and objective enforcement, effective corporate governance, and increased competition. Once all the remaining biases against exporting have been removed is the time to start seriously considering institutional support for exporters. But, they may learn from the difficulties which have faced the CEEC in devising and creating export support systems which reach the exporters who really need such help: the small to medium sized firms in most manufacturing. No one can provide a country with a recipe for successful institutional support for exporting; too much depends on the type of exports, the markets available, the environment for foreign investors, the budgetary resources available, the limits set by international trade treaties and conventions, and so on. Probably the best that can be done is to supply countries with information on what other countries have tried by way of export promotion, drawing attention to some of the more conspicuous failures and weaknesses, which can be avoided. That is what this study has attempted to do.

REFERENCES

Amsden, A.H., 1989, Asia's *Next Giant: South Korea and Late Industrialisation*, New York: Oxford University Press.
Balasubramanyam, V.N. and M. Salisu, 1991, 'Export Promotion, Import Substitution and Direct Foreign Investment in Less Developed Countries' in A. Koekkoek and L.E.M. Mennes (eds.), *International Trade and Global Development*, London: Routledge.
Balasubramanyam, V.N., Salisu, M. and D. Sapsford, 1996, 'Foreign Direct Investment and Growth, New Hypotheses and Evidence', Discussion Paper EC7/96, Department of Economics, Lancaster University.
Bhagwati, J. 1978, 'Anatomy and Consequences of Exchange Rate Regimes', *Studies in International Economic Relations*, Vol.1, No.10, Washington, DC: National Bureau of Economic Research.
EBRD, European Bank for Reconstruction and Development, 1997, *Transition Report*.
Krugman, P., 1994, 'The Myth of Asia's Miracle', *Foreign Affairs*, Nov.–Dec.
Kwon, J.K., 1998, 'The East Asian Model: an Exploration of Rapid Economic Growth in the Republic of Korea and Taiwan Province of China', Geneva: UNCTAD, Discussion Paper No. 135, May.
Lardy, N.R., 1992, *Foreign Trade and Economic Reform in China 1978–1990*, Cambridge and New York: Cambridge University Press.
Lin, A.L., 1995, 'Trade Effects of Foreign Direct Investment: Evidence for Taiwan with Four Asean Countries', *Weltwirtschaftsliches Archiv*, 131 (3).
Wade, R., 1990, *Governing the Market*, Princeton, NJ: Princeton University Press.
World Bank, 1993, *The East Asian Miracle: Public Policy and Economic Growth*, Oxford: Oxford University Press.
Zemplinerova, A. and V. Benacek, 1997, 'FDI – East and West: The Experience of the Czech Republic', Prague: ACE Project Paper, mimeo, Charles University.

Appendix

Interview Guide Questions for: (1) Ministries, (2) Trade Support Organisations, (3) Users and Potential Users of Export Promotion Support, (4) Trading Companies (Export-Import Companies). Questions used as basis for interviews and questionnaires in each of the three countries studied.

QUESTIONS FOR MINISTRIES:

1. What was the role in foreign trade and trade policy of your Ministry before 1989?

2. How has it changed?

3. What were the reasons (internal/external, most important or influential) for the changes?

4. How were the changes phased?

5. Can you estimate the effect of your changes on exports? In which areas were you most successful?

6. How does the Ministry view your country's export performance in relation to the economy's needs?

7. What are the main barriers to a better export performance: internal (e.g. taxation, lack of facilities to rebate taxes on inputs, lack of credit or credit guaranties, etc.) external (tariffs, non-tariff barriers, in which markets)?

8. What changes and /or new measures do you intend to implement to reduce these barriers (e.g. legal reforms, negotiation with EU, and other trading partners)?

9. Do you consider export (trade?) promotion an important function of your Ministry, or do you think the selection of what to export, by whom, to where should be left to be determined by market forces? Or is there a need for Non

Governmental Organisations (NGOs) to assist exporting? Why?

10. What models of EP do you consider to be most relevant to your country? (East Asian, OECD?)

11. Please indicate the relative importance of the following forms of support for exporters by grading them 5–1 where 5 means most and 1 least important.

- a. export credit guarantee
- b. credit finance for exports
- c. insurance
- d. market information
- e. product selection for exporting
- f. product design
- g. information on quality control
- h. information on regulations (and market access)
- i. handling documentation
- j. information on relevant business practices
- k. export packaging
- l. trade fairs
- m. contacts with foreign buyers
- n. trade representatives abroad
- o. training for exporting
- p.
- q.
- r.

please use blanks for any other services used.

12. Do you consider Export Processing Zones (Special Economic Zones, etc.) to be useful in increasing exports? What is approximate share of EPZs in exports?

TRADE SUPPORT ORGANISATIONS (e.g. a Trade Development Board, Export Guarantee and Insurance Co., Export Bank, etc.)

OBJECTIVES OF QUESTIONS Their aims, facilities provided for exporters, and evaluation of their own performance.

We should know what organisations exist from published sources. We need to find out what they claim to do, what they actually do, and how effective (cost effective) they are. What they claim should be in their constitution, but we may need to verify that.

Proforma for questions for TPOs (trade promotion organisations)

Preliminary information(preferably obtained before interview)

Name of Institution.. Public or private sector
....

When established/privatised.. Funding (source and amount)......................................

Number of employees...

QUESTIONS

What is educational background of staff: Education/training (% graduates, courses directly relevant to export support, etc)?.....................

Number who speak English, German (other main foreign language)?
....

How many other languages covered by how many staff? ....

What overseas representation do you have? ....

1. Please indicate the relative importance of the following forms of support for exporters by grading them 5–1 where 5 means most and 1 least important.

  a. export credit guarantee
  b. credit finance for exports
  c. insurance
  d. market information
  e. product selection for exporting
  f. product design
  g. information on quality control
  h. information on regulations
  i. handling documentation
  j. information on relevant business practices
  k. export packaging
  l. trade fairs
  m. contacts with foreign buyers

n. trade representatives abroad
o. training for exporting
p.
q.
r.

please use blanks for any other services used.

2. How many companies have used your services in the last week?

3. What were their size and which sectors?

4. Which services were most sought after? (list them)

5. Which services were you able to provide ?

6. What percentage,if any, do the users pay of the costs of providing these services?

7. What is your system for following up clients to see whether they made sales as a result of your help?

8. What are the results of your evaluations of your organisation's performance?

9. What do you estimate have been the total sales resulting from your help in the last fiscal year?

10. In which areas did your efforts make the biggest difference in terms of increased exports (which markets, type of products, small or large firms)

USERS and POTENTIAL USERS OF EP SUPPORT

OUR OBJECTIVES:

To find out: Their assessment of their requirements. What use they have made of EPOs, if any. How they assess various types of help and the institutions which have provided help.

Preliminary information (Some obtainable from published data before visiting)

Name.. Main Products.......................................

Number of employees..........

Private or public sector..................When established................If privatised, when?........................

Foreign Partner?..............

Partner's share in total capital...................Value of exports and share in total sales................................

Share of subcontracting and outward processing in export sales ....Share of intra-company trade................

Do you have an export marketing department?

QUESTIONS:
1. Current export markets?

2. Which export markets have you entered during the last five years, with or without assistance?
Did this involve major changes in products?

3. Which export markets would you want to enter?

4. Which export support services have you used and from what agency?

5. Where you have used a particular service please give your asessment of its usefulness to you by giving it 5 for excellent down to 1 for unhelpful (leave blank where not used)

        a. export credit guarantee
        b. credit finance for exports
        c. insurance
        d. market information
        e. product selection for exporting
        f. product design
        g. information on quality control
        h. information on regulations
        i. handling documentation
        j. information on relevant business practices

k. export packaging
l. trade fairs
m. contacts with foreign buyers
n. trade representatives abroad
o. training for exporting
p.
q.
r.

please add any other services used in space provided.

6. Please list any services which you feel should be provided and which are not available in the
Czech (Hungary, Poland) economy.

7. Would you be willing to pay full cost for the kinds of services provided?Why or why not?

8. Do you think such services should be wholly or partly subsidised by the state, or paid for by a small levy on all foreign trade?

9. Please list the organisations which you have contacted for help in exporting. Rank them 5, best, to 1 worst, for the quality of assistance you received.

TRADING COMPANIES (EXPORT-IMPORT COMPANIES)
Objectives of our questions: To find out how State Trading Companies have changed from pre to post transition era. How much trade do they now handle? What proportion of foreign trade goes through foreign trading (export-import) companies? How much is handled directly by the manufacturers themselves? What are the TCs' objectives? Have they diversified their activities, moved into manufacturing, joint ventures, foreign investment, etc? Have they any model in mind in seeking to adapt to a market economy? Are their new entrants to the field of export-import business? Do they specialise purely in international trade or are they involved in internal distribution as well? Do they provide finance to manufacturing companies, or assist them to get credit from banks?

QUESTIONS

Use company reports, etc. and official statistics to obtain background information. before approaching companies.

We should be able to find out numbers of such companies, whether they result from break up of old state trading companies, or are new entrants. Do they specialise in particular types of product, e.g. chemicals,agricultural products, textiles, toys, or are they diversified across product ranges?

1. When was your company established? What size in terms of number of employees and/or turnover?

2. If you were formed from a state trading company how has your business changed? (Previous size, types of products, markets?)

3. How do you find your customers? Do you generally take ownership of the products you sell, or do you buy and sell on commission?

4. Are you specialised or general in the products or services sold?

5. What kind of qualifications and experience do your staff have? Do you have training programmes for staff? Do you have overseas offices?

6. What do you consider are the most serious internal or external obstacles to exporting from your country today?

7. What trade support services of government or private sector origin do you use, if any?

8. If you use them what is your assessment of their value to you?

9. Do you feel there is a need for government or other assistance to exporters? If so, what kinds would you like to see?

10. What model of Trading Company do you consider appropriate to your needs (Japanese, Taiwanese, European?) and how do you see your organisation developing to meet new challenges?

Index

Index

Printed in the United States
by Baker & Taylor Publisher Services